The Words and Music of Carole King

THE PRAEGER SINGER-SONGWRITER COLLECTION

The Words and Music of Carole King

James E. Perone

PRAEGER

Westport, Connecticut
London

Library of Congress Cataloging-in-Publication Data

Perone, James E.
  The words and music of Carole King / James E. Perone.
      p. cm.—(Praeger singer-songwriter collection, ISSN 1553–3484)
  Includes discography, bibliographical references, and index.
  ISBN 0–275–99027–3 (alk. paper)
  1. King, Carole, 1942—Criticism and interpretation.   I. Title.
  ML410.K636P47   2006
  782.42166092—dc22   2006027248

British Library Cataloguing in Publication Data is available.

Library of Congress Catalog Card Number: 2006027248
ISBN: 0–275–99027–3
ISSN: 1553–3484

First published in 2006

Praeger Publishers, 88 Post Road West, Westport, CT 06881
An imprint of Greenwood Publishing Group, Inc.
www.praeger.com

Printed in the United States of America

The paper used in this book complies with the
Permanent Paper Standard issued by the National
Information Standards Organization (Z39.48–1984).

10 9 8 7 6 5 4 3 2 1

Contents

Series Foreword

Although the term, *Singer-Songwriters*, might most frequently be associated with a cadre of musicians of the early 1970s such as Paul Simon, James Taylor, Carly Simon, Joni Mitchell, Cat Stevens, and Carole King, the Praeger Singer-Songwriter Collection defines singer-songwriters more broadly, both in terms of style and in terms of time period. The series includes volumes on musicians who have been active from approximately the 1960s through the present. Musicians who write and record in folk, rock, soul, hip-hop, country, and various hybrids of these styles will be represented. Therefore, some of the early 1970s introspective singer-songwriters named above will be included, but not exclusively.

What do the individuals included in this series have in common? Some have never collaborated as writers. But, while some have done so, all have written and recorded commercially successful and/or historically important music *and* lyrics at some point in their careers.

The authors who contribute to the series also exhibit diversity. Some are scholars who are trained primarily as musicians, while others have such areas of specialization as American studies, history, sociology, popular culture studies, literature, and rhetoric. The authors share a high level of scholarship, accessibility in their writing, and a true insight into the work of the artists they study. The authors are also focused on the output of their subjects and how it relates to the their subject's biography and the society around them; however, biography in and of itself is not a major focus of the books in this series.

Given the diversity of the musicians who are the subject of books in this series, and given the diversity of viewpoint of the authors, volumes in the series will differ from book to book. All, however, will be organized chronologically around the compositions and recorded performances of their subjects. All of the books in the series should also serve as listeners' guides to the music of their subjects, making them companions to the artists' recorded output.

James E. Perone
Series Editor

Acknowledgments

This book could not have been written without the valuable assistance of a number of people. I wish first to thank Karen Perone for offering moral and technical support for this and all of my book projects for Greenwood Press and Praeger Press, and for offering much-needed input at every stage of every project.

Over the course of writing several books, the entire staff of the Greenwood Publishing Group has been most helpful and cooperative. I wish to extend special thanks to Acquisitions Editor Daniel Harmon for his assistance in putting this book together and for his continuing support in the development of the Praeger Singer-Songwriter Collection, and to the entire staff of Apex Publishing for helping me fine tune this book. I also wish to thank Eric Levy and Rob Kirkpatrick for their assistance in getting the Praeger Singer-Songwriter Collection off the ground over the course of the first few years of the twenty-first century.

Before beginning to write this book, and throughout the writing of it, I have been communicating with Sheila Weller, a *Glamour* magazine writer who has been writing a book on Carole King, Joni Mitchell, and Carly Simon. I wish to thank Sheila for the chance to share thoughts and insights about Carole King's songs and their importance.

I also wish to thank my graduate mentor and dissertation advisor, the late John Clough, for initially instilling in me the love of academe and the belief that there is a place for me in the academy. Likewise, I would like to thank my friend and former colleague Kelly F. Lowe, whose obvious love of, and expertise in, rhetoric reaffirmed the lessons in the importance of academic scholarship that Professor Clough taught me years ago.

Finally, I wish to thank the entire staff of Carole King Productions, especially Leah Reid, for their assistance in selecting and obtaining permissions for the photographs of Ms. King that are included in the photo essay. Special thanks goes to Lorna Guess, Carole King's personal manager, for all that she has done to help this project along.

Despite my own best efforts and the assistance of those named here, there are bound to be errors in this book, and these are solely my responsibility.

Introduction

CAROLE KING AS MUSICIAN AND CULTURAL ICON

Born Carole Klein, on February 9, 1942, in Brooklyn, New York, Carole King became one of the most successful songwriters of the rock era. She wrote or co-wrote such hits as "Up on the Roof," "Pleasant Valley Sunday," "Will You Love Me Tomorrow," "You've Got a Friend," "The Loco-Motion," "Hey Girl," "(You Make Me Feel Like) A Natural Woman," "I'm into Something Good," "Go Away, Little Girl," "I Wasn't Born to Follow," "Jazzman," "I Feel the Earth Move," "Now and Forever," "One Fine Day," and "It's Too Late." King had worked as a teenager in the music industry, recording demo songs with fellow high school student Paul Simon, and recording several singles in the late 1950s and early 1960s. Her career a singer/pianist, however, was slow to develop; all of the hit songs King wrote during the decade of the 1960s were popularized by other performers, including the Drifters, the Animals, Steve Lawrence, the Cookies, Little Eva, the Byrds, the Monkees, the Shirelles, Aretha Franklin, and Blood, Sweat and Tears. King was one of the first, if not the first, woman in American popular music history to have a composing, arranging, and conducting credit on a recording—this for the 1962 Little Eva album *The Llllloco-Motion* (Dimension 6000).

After more than a decade as one of the greatest behind-the-scenes musicians in popular music, Carole King made it into the spotlight. Her 1971 solo album *Tapestry* eventually sold more than twenty million copies, stayed in *Billboard*'s Top 200 album charts for 302 consecutive weeks, and was viewed by many as one of the most important feminist statements of the day. The social statement of the album was not found in the words or in the music nearly as much as it was in the fact that King wrote, sang, arranged, played, and controlled her product. In short, *Tapestry* was feminism in action. And *Tapestry* appeared at precisely the same time as other seminal works by some of the performers who, along with Carole King, defined the early 1970s singer-songwriter movement, including James Taylor, Paul Simon, Don McLean, Cat Stevens, Carly Simon, Jim Croce, and Joni Mitchell. Critics credited King's work on *Tapestry* as freeing female pop vocalists from having to affect a diva-esque approach to singing, and her gospel-inspired work as a pianist on the album has been called "the first widely recognized instrumental signature ever developed by a woman in American popular music."[1]

Although *Tapestry* still stands as Carole King's masterpiece—indeed, it is frequently listed as one of the most important record albums of the entire rock era—she recorded other albums from the 1970s through the present, including *Fantasy, Colour of Your Dreams, City Streets, Music, Pearls: The Songs of Goffin and King, Wrap Around Joy, Simple Things, Love Makes the World, Welcome Home,* and *Thoroughbred.* She set *Really Rosie,* by noted children's author Maurice Sendak, to music for a television program that eventually turned into an off-Broadway stage musical. And King has contributed new songs to films such as *One True Thing, You've Got Mail, I'll Do Anything,* and *A League of Their Own.*

Carole King became a spokesperson for the environmental movement in the 1970s and has continued to be socially and politically active for progressive causes into the twenty-first century. Today, King supports the Rockies Prosperity Act, "an ecosystem approach to protecting and restoring the Northern Rockies bioregion,"[2] and the White Cloud Council, an organization devoted to preserving green space and which she cofounded. She has performed benefit concerts for a variety of Democratic political candidates, including George McGovern during his 1972 presidential campaign, Gary Hart during his failed 1984 primary campaign, and John Kerry during his 2004 presidential campaign. She also performs for charitable organizations that support children's and environmental causes. In addition to her benefit appearances, King performs live from time to time in a variety of venues, including a July 15, 2005 concert appearance on NBC's *Today Show* that coincided with the release of her live album, *The Living Room Tour.*

In addition to the recognition she has received from the public (via record sales), Carole King has been officially recognized by her peers in the entertainment industry. The National Academy of Recording Arts and Sciences presented King with the 1971 Grammy Awards for Best Record of the Year ("It's Too Late"), Album of the Year (*Tapestry*), Song of the Year ("You've Got a Friend"), and Best Female Vocal Performance (*Tapestry*). In addition, James Taylor's recording of "You've Got a Friend" earned him a Grammy for Best Male Vocal Performance, thereby making the most widely recognized Grammy categories a sweep for Carole King. King was inducted into the Songwriters Hall of Fame in 1986. In 1988, their peers in the National Academy of Songwriters presented King and her one-time husband and musical collaborator Gerry Goffin with the prestigious Lifetime Achievement Award. For their songwriting contributions, Goffin and King were inducted into the Rock and Roll Hall of Fame as nonperformers in 1990. Both because of her popularity as a singer-songwriter-pianist in the 1970s and her longstanding association with the music publishing establishment, Carole King remains one of if not *the* best represented composer of the rock era in sheet music publications of her songs.

SCOPE AND ORGANIZATION OF THIS BOOK

This book focuses on the music, lyrics, and recordings of Carole King; therefore, the book is arranged chronologically and has biographical information woven into the discussion of King's songs and recordings. I have also devoted a chapter to a discussion of other artists' recordings of the compositions of Carole King during the 1960s when King was one of the best-known members of the Brill Building establishment.

Carole King has more than 500 copyrighted songs, some written in collaboration with others and some solo-written works; thus a detailed analysis of the collected compositions would be impossible. Because of the nature of the Praeger Singer-Songwriter Collection, I have focused on the songs that King herself recorded, although I have also included study of some of the better-known songs that King—usually in collaboration with Gerry Goffin—wrote for other performers. It should be noted that the vast majority of King's pre-1970 songs are collaborative efforts. She often wrote the music while Goffin wrote the lyrics. Even after she became an established solo artist, however, Carole King collaborated with such lyricists as Toni Stern, David Palmer, Rick Evers, and others. My focus is on the lyrics that King has written, but I will also discuss the lyrics of her collaborators to the extent that such discussion relates to King's work as a composer and a singer/vocal interpreter of lyrics.

The bibliography includes many sources for further information on Carole King and her work. I have not included references to concert reviews, with a few notable exceptions (King's 1973 concert in New York's Central Park and several of the major performances on her various comeback tours, for example). For a detailed listing of important concert reviews of King's pre-1999 performances, the reader may wish to consult my book *Carole King: A Bio-Bibliography* (Greenwood Press, 1999). I have included annotations for most, but not all, bibliographic citations.

Note that in the "Discography," I have included information pertaining to the principal medium for each release. Most of King's albums were also issued on 1⅞ ips audio cassette (and several were also issued on 3¾ ips 8-track tape). I have not included information pertaining to these tape releases because tape was not the primary medium through which the music was sold by King's record companies and because cassettes and 8-tracks of Carole King albums of the early 1970s and 1980s are not likely to have survived into the twenty-first century to the extent that vinyl and CDs have. Speaking of compact discs, it should be noted that most, but not all, of King' albums of the 1960s, 1970s, and 1980s that were originally released on vinyl have been reissued on compact disc. King's albums that remain unreleased on CD, those during the late 1970s when she recorded for Capitol Records, can still be found, providing that the listener who wishes to investigate this music can find the original releases in a specialty shop, or perhaps on an online auction Web site such as eBay.

I have included an index of names, places, and song and album titles. Song titles include those written by Carole King and by others; however, the album titles in the index are only those recorded by King. I have included only the most extensive and most important discussions of King's work in the various subheadings of her entry in the index.

Other Voices

The story of the words and music of Carole King does not begin with her own work as an internationally known performer in the 1970s. She first became a well-known figure in the music industry as a composer, specifically, a composer of songs for other performers. Although this book focuses on her work as a singer-songwriter, it is necessary to study the music she wrote before she became a successful singer for two main reasons: (1) her early compositional work helped set the stage for her later famous solo recordings, and (2) her compositional work from the late 1950s through the late 1960s represents one of the most important and most popular bodies of American popular songs of the era.

THE BRILL BUILDING

Scholars and fans alike argue about just when rock and roll music came into being. Certainly, Hank Williams's "Move It on Over" (1947) exhibits elements of what would come to be known as rock and roll, but the song is really more of a country song that is in 12-bar blues form and has a strong beat to it—and, significantly, an electric guitar solo. It also happened to anticipate the melody almost note-by-note and the musical style of "Rock around the Clock" by seven years. Some would argue that Fats Domino's "The Fat Man" (1949) is the first true rock and roll record, but that song is really more of a fairly easy-going New Orleans-style rhythm-and-blues piece that fits pretty squarely into a musical tradition consistent with the city of Domino's birth. Other scholars would argue—more persuasively in my mind—that Jackie Brenston's 1951 recording of "Rocket 88," a composition, arrangement, and performance probably influenced more by the session's producer/writer/arranger/pianist, Ike Turner, than by Brenston himself, signaled the birth of rock and roll. In this piece of rhythm and blues, with its distorted electric guitar, jagged piano licks (played by Turner) and lyrical themes of women, drinking, and cruising in a fast automobile (and its none-too-subtle sexual subtext), we hear something that is missing in the songs by Williams and Domino—a strong teen appeal and an authentic-sounding teen rhetorical "voice." Ultimately the merger of musical styles like rhythm and blues with country, gospel, and jazz, *and* lyrics that speak to, and of, the emerging post-World War II youth culture defines the start of the rock era.

By the second half of the 1950s, corporate America had taken notice of rock and roll, and a new take on the longstanding Tin Pan Alley tradition emerged in the form of the Brill Building publishers, record companies, songwriters, and performers.[1] Like New York City's Tin Pan Alley of the late nineteenth century through the World War II era, this new version of Tin Pan Alley was characterized by a well-defined corporate ladder and was largely dominated by Jewish-American musicians who lived in the immediate New York area: the George and Ira Gershwins, Cole Porters, and Irving Berlins were replaced (as it were) by the Neil Diamonds, Paul Simons, Neil Sedakas, Cynthia Weils, Barry Manns, Gerry Goffins, and Carole Kings. The song pluggers of the first half of the twentieth century were replaced by the teenagers who cut the demo records of the 1950s and early 1960s.

After she formed a group—the Co-sines—while in high school, Carole Klein (who would take the professional moniker King in the late 1950s) cut demo records with a young high school friend, Paul Simon, for $25 apiece. King would provide the piano and drum tracks, while Simon played guitar and bass; both sang. This high school experience set the stage for King's and Simon's later work as record producers—quite independently from one another—by giving them valuable experience in multitrack recording at a time when the technology was still new.

After high school, King attended Queens College, where she met chemistry major and lyricist Gerry Goffin. Goffin and King began collaborating on songs, married, dropped out of college, and began working as staff songwriters at Al Nevins and Don Kirshner's Aldon Music, which was founded in 1958, at 1650 Broadway in New York City, right across the street from the Brill Building. As had been the case during the Tin Pan Alley era, Brill Building songwriters like Goffin and King operated in what has been widely characterized as an assembly line environment, cranking out as many songs as possible, in the hopes that one might become a hit. Since the songwriters typically were paid on a per-song basis, generating large amounts of material was to the songwriter's advantage. Similarly, record companies of the era took a "shotgun" approach, issuing lots of singles and hoping to have at least a few hits along the way (this was well before the album-oriented era). By 1963, more than 200 of Carole King's compositions had been recorded commercially.[2] Despite the quantity of material that

Goffin and King and their colleagues produced, King has said, "I don't think it was an assembly line, because it was still a creative endeavor."[3] Indeed, creativity was in ample evidence, as well as competition between the songwriting teams. Among the more significant features of these Brill Building songwriters was the trend of male-female writing partnerships: Jeff Barry and Ellie Greenwich, Barry Mann and Cynthia Weil, and Gerry Goffin and Carole King. This feature was important because it represented the first time that women made a sizable impact in the American popular music industry as writers—and, especially, as composers.

Gerry Goffin and Carole King excelled in two particular areas among the Brill Building songwriters: (1) they wrote more hit songs than their colleagues, and (2) they truly mastered the art of making top-quality demo records of their songs. In fact, one of their greatest commercial successes, Little Eva's recording of "The Loco-Motion," was not originally intended to be released commercially: it was made as a demo, designed to show the song's potential to the "real" singer for whom the song was intended.[4] Other recordings, like the Monkees's recording of "Sometime in the Morning," simply had Carole King's lead vocals wiped from the Goffin-produced demo track, with those of another lead singer—in this case Micky Dolenz—recorded on top of the work of the studio musicians. The care with which Goffin and King produced their demo records gave musicians a clear vision of the commercial and artistic possibilities of their songs.

All of this work in the Brill Building era of the late 1950s and early 1960s meant that King, from her high school years on, had a knowledge of and experience in commercial popular music. She was both a part of the grand Tin Pan Alley tradition, and a part of the new post-World War II youth culture. King learned just what worked for particular performers for whom she wrote. At the start of her career, she was primarily a composer, setting others' words to music. All of these aspects of Carole King's experience as a young woman would inform, add to, and, at times, detract from her later career as a solo performer.

THE SONGS OF GOFFIN AND KING, 1960–1969

Although Carole King wrote and recorded several songs before she began collaborating with Gerry Goffin, our discussion here focuses on the compositions of the songwriting team—compositions that were meant for other performers.[5] Because Goffin and King wrote so many songs that were commercially recorded and because the most successful of these were covered by dozens of artists, these discussion focus on some of the most notable songs and recordings.

The "Girl Groups," the Drifters, and Other African American Singers

Gerry Goffin and Carole King's first big hit composition was "Will You Love Me Tomorrow," a song popularized in 1960–1961 by the Shirelles.

This was an especially fitting first hit because it transcended musically and lyrically many of the pop songs of the day. Gerry Goffin's lyrics find a woman asking her boyfriend if he will still love her tomorrow if the two make love tonight (in not so many words). She senses his unspoken vow that she will "be the only one" solely through the look in his eyes and wants verbal confirmation of his love before they take the next step in their physical relationship. Goffin treats the subject with sensitivity.

King's music, in a slow ballad style, solidly supports the lyrics. The real highlight of her setting, though, is in the harmonic writing on the line, "Tonight the light of love is in your eyes." This lyrical suggestion, that tonight really might be the night that the couple goes all the way, as it were, is supported by King's unexpected use of the major mediant (III) chord, which acts as a secondary dominant leading to the submediant (vi) in this major-key piece.[6] In a 1950s pop/rock song, this harmonic shift is unusual and, as such, adds emphasis to the text. It is this harmonic emphasis that brings out the seriousness of the young woman's plight, as it highlights just how close she is to making an important decision—a decision that she will be able to make only if and when the young man makes a verbal declaration of his love and commitment.

Although King's use of the major mediant chord as a secondary dominant may be unusual in the context of 1960, it nevertheless illustrates her ties to the great American Tin Pan Alley song tradition of the past: this is the sort of harmonic text painting done by the George Gershwins and Cole Porters of the 1930s and 1940s. Ultimately, the Shirelles's recording of "Will You Love Me Tomorrow" stayed at No. 1 on the *Billboard* pop charts for two weeks, and remained in the magazine's top 100 charts for nearly five months.

Incidentally, the story of the recording of "Will You Love Me Tomorrow" illustrates King's early desire to be in charge of her compositions and the strength of her musical talent. According to writer Fred Bronson, King, "unhappy with one of the musicians, played kettle drums herself."[7] As we shall see later in this chapter, Goffin and King's focus on what they felt was the correct production of their songs would extend to demo records, making their demos just as definitive as the fully realized commercial releases of the day.

Like "Will You Love Me Tomorrow," many of the early 1960s Goffin/King collaborations were written for the so-called girl groups like the Shirelles. Among the duo's hits not recorded by female African American singing groups, a fair number were initially recorded by African American solo singers. An unnamed reporter for *Time* magazine wrote in 1971 that, "though R&B lost some its ethnic honesty" when Goffin and King began having huge chart successes through these African American singers, the style "still had considerable emotional sweep, plus a new sophistication."[8] It should be noted that although many of these recordings made it into the upper reaches of the *Billboard* and *Cash Box* pop charts, they were also widely successful specifically among the African American audience, as measured on the R&B charts.

Some of this success might be attributed to the popularity of the various performers with different demographic groups, but it was also due to the way in which King, in particular, was able to integrate African American pop music styles into her own writing style. Although a thorough analysis falls outside the scope of this study, it should be noted that the relative chart success of the songs produced by Aldon Music (white, predominantly Jewish-American songwriters, arrangers, and producers working with African American performers) forms a truly fascinating counterpoint to the relative chart standings of records produced by Motown. More often than not, the Goffin–King hits performed better on the R&B charts (which measured sales among a predominantly African American audience) than on the pop charts; generally, Motown recordings did a little better on the pop charts (which measured sales among the majority white population) than on the R&B charts. The irony is that Motown was a black-owned business that incorporated mostly African-American performers, writers, and producers. In a way, this might not be as surprising as it might appear at first glance when one considers that Motown's entire focus in the early 1960s was reaching the widest (and, thereby, the whitest) possible audience. In any case, it does suggest the extent to which Goffin and King were able to bridge racial and ethnic gulfs and to write what appears to have been thoroughly convincing R&B material.

In the twenty-first century possibly the best known of Goffin and King's early 1960s compositions is "The Loco-Motion," a 1962 hit for Little Eva. Eva Boyd became a babysitter for the Goffin's daughter Louise. She had come to the attention of Goffin and King through the Cookies, one of the girl groups who had chart success with Goffin/King material. In addition to her skills as a babysitter, however, Eva Boyd had a voice that worked well on the demo records that Goffin and King cut of their compositions. "The Loco-Motion" was a dance song—a form that was quite popular at the time—with (pardon the pun) a twist: it was not written about a currently popular dance. According to various accounts, the dance was either made up to fit the song, or the song may have been inspired by Eva's dancing around the Goffin household. In any case, Boyd sang on the demo record, which was promptly shipped off to and rejected by singer Dee Dee Sharp. Goffin and King's boss, music impresario Don Kirshner, decided that rather than shop the song around to other popular African American singers, he would simply release the demo as a single. For one thing, this suggests the care with which Goffin and King made demo recordings—they wanted to impress prospective recording artists with the full potential of their material—it also points out that Brill Building songwriters really were essentially contract players, even those who had produced some commercially successful hit songs.

The Little Eva recording of "The Loco-Motion" made it to No. 1 on the pop charts, as did a 1974 recording by the band Grand Funk Railroad. Australian singer/actress Kylie Minogue was only slightly less successful when her 1988 recording of the song topped out at No. 3 on the *Billboard* pop charts. This is, in fact, a remarkable badge of success for "The Loco-Motion"; no other song achieved this degree of success on the singles charts in three different decades in the rock era.

King's music for "The Loco-Motion" is notable for the subtlety of its harmonic language. The verses of the song make liberal use of alternations between the tonic chord (I) and its submediant (vi), and then between the subdominant chord (IV) and *its* submediant (ii). At a crucial point just before the end of the verse, however, King turns the normally minor-quality ii chord into a major-quality secondary dominant. A listener need not be versed in the science of music theory in order to understand the effect that this has: the altered chord sounds as though it leads more strongly to what follows than the "standard" chord would. As I wrote in my bio-bibliography of Carole King, "King, of course, did not invent this particular chord progression, but the almost intuitive sound—it sounds as though it simply could not be any other way—helps make for a true popular classic."[9] As had been the case with "Will You Love Me Tomorrow," subtlety of harmony makes the song stand out from the rock and R&B material of the day.

Little Eva's recording of the song is significant for another reason: the album on which it appeared a bit later in 1962, *The Lllloco-Motion* (Dimension 6000), credited Carole King not only as a songwriter but also as arranger and conductor. This appears to be the first time in the American commercial recording industry that a woman was given writing, arranging, and conducting credit on an album.

Without discounting the performance of the Drifters, or the poetry of Gerry Goffin, it is largely the compositional talents of Carole King that accounts for the success of the 1962 song "Up on the Roof." The Drifters, an African American male vocal group, took the song to No. 5 on the *Billboard* pop charts and No. 4 on the magazine's R&B charts. There are certain aspects of the rhythmic style of the group's performance, as well as aspects of the arrangement (including the strings and mallet percussion) that would sound dated even within a few years of this popular recording. Let us, then, examine the song as a more abstract construction without referring specifically to the Drifters' recording of it.

Gerry Goffin's poetry expounds the virtues of the singer's roof, to which the character goes to escape the humdrum realities of daily life. This rooftop perch gives the singer's character a chance to see the beauty of the stars and to breathe air that is (relatively) unpolluted by the city traffic. "Up on the Roof" certainly was not the only song of the era in which the main character describes a particular location in which he (or she) can find solace in the face of a harsh outside world. In fact, Brian Wilson's "In My Room" is an even more intriguing example, especially in light of Wilson's later virtual withdrawal from society and from the outside world in the late 1960s and the 1970s. It is probably just part of human nature to dream of that idyllic spot where one can escape from all of one's cares. As writers Al Kasha and Joel Hirschhorn demonstrate in their 1980 *Songwriter Magazine* article,

"Anatomy of a Hit: 'Up on the Roof,'"[10] however, the real meat of the song comes from King's musical setting.

King's melody stays primarily in the lower register as the song's singer describes the things from which he or she wishes to escape. In particular, the melody descends as the singer concludes that, because of all the things that are getting them down, "people are just too much to take." This creates a feeling of resignation. However, the next line, which finds the singer's cares drifting "up into space," is set to a rising melodic line, which reflects the floating away of those cares. As the singer climbs the proverbial—and literal—steps that lead up to the roof, the melody stays in a higher tessitura. Certain other individual lines in Goffin's lyrics also receive programmatic treatment from composer King. In particular, the line that describes the roof as "peaceful" is relatively static in terms of rhythm and melody, which reflects the sense of peace the singer feels. And Goffin's description of the stars in the nighttime firmament putting on "a show for free" is set in the highest part of the melody's range. King clearly differentiates between Goffin's lines, not only in the melody; she uses somewhat abrupt, unexpected harmonic shifts at the points at which the melodic range shifts to draw the listener's attention even more fully to the mood changes that occur from line to line. This kind of text setting in King's composition owes a debt to the European Romantic period art song settings of such composers as Franz Schubert, Robert Schumann, and Hugo Wolf. It is somewhat outside the usual purview of Tin Pan Alley (or Brill Building) American pop songs. Because of its merits as a mood piece (through King's careful setting of her then-husband's text), "Up on the Roof" was recorded by a large number of performers, with the Cryan' Shames, Laura Nyro,[11] and James Taylor all making the *Billboard* top pop singles charts with the song between 1968 and 1979. Both artistically and commercially, therefore, it remains one of Carole King's greatest compositional achievements.

The female vocal group the Chiffons had a No. 5 pop hit with Goffin and King's "One Fine Day" in 1963. This song has maintained a great deal of its popularity, appearing on the *Billboard* pop singles charts four times for four different acts between 1963 and 1980. The latter performance was a No. 12 effort by Carole King herself. Despite the lasting quality of the song, and the continuing appearance of the original Chiffons reading of the song on oldies radio and in television and film soundtracks, it is not King's most novel song of the 1960s, at least in terms of compositional technique. In fact, it fits squarely into the prevailing girl group style of the day melodically, harmonically, and lyrically. That it is a good example—almost a textbook example—of this style probably explains why it has survived better than much of the girl group material of the pre-Beatles 1960s.

King makes heavy use of the I-vi-IV-V-I chord progression—almost a cliché of the late 1950s-pop sound—in "One Fine Day." Goffin's text is a bow in the direction of gender stereotype, with the lead singer's character almost seeming to look for affirmation of her own worth on that "one fine day" when the man to whom she sings discovers that he wants her to be "his girl." Because of the perhaps unintentional gender stereotyping in the subtext of the lyrics, it is no wonder that none of the four charting single versions of "One Fine Day" were recorded by male artists. What really distinguishes the song is King's blocklike rhythmic and melodic setting of the words "one fine day," whenever they occur in the verse and chorus. This contrasts with the faster setting of the rest of the text, thereby making the hook line stand out. The melody is largely based on a short motive, which again adds to the instantly recognizable nature of the song.

"They Should Have Given You the Oscar"

Although Babe Ruth, in an earlier day, and Mark McGwire more recently hit an amazing number of home runs, they also struck out quite often: such is frequently the case with the so-called power hitters. Such was also the case with songwriters who worked in the Tin Pan Alley structure both in the original Tin Pan Alley era of the 1880s–1940s and in the Brill Building version of Tin Pan Alley in the late 1950s and early 1960s. A listing of the compositions of Goffin and King include numerous memorable hits, but it also includes more than a handful of songs that never enjoyed commercial or artistic success. Although I will not dwell on the lesser efforts of Goffin and King, it is interesting to briefly consider a couple of examples.

James Darren's recording of Goffin and King's song "Her Royal Majesty" rose to No. 6 on the *Billboard* pop charts. Nevertheless, Gerry Goffin's text, which uses the metaphor of a king—for Darren's character—and a queen—for the Royal Majesty of the song's title—is entirely predictable. King's music breaks no new ground, actually closely resembling early twentieth-century, ragtime-era Tin Pan Alley music. Stu Phillips's arrangement and production, with its oom-pah band style brass, adds to the old-time nature of the song in Darren's recording, as well as to the silliness of the proceedings. All this having been said, it should also be noted that "Her Royal Majesty" is not any sillier than the non-Goffin and King song "Goodbye Cruel World," which Darren also took into the top 10. And, there were plenty of these silly efforts around Nevins and Kirshner's Aldon Music and the affiliated Colpix Records, including the Roy Alfred–Wally Gold composition "She Can't Find Her Keys," a minor hit for actor-singer Paul Petersen.

Goffin and King's composition "They Should Have Given You the Oscar" was yet another song recorded by James Darren. Unlike "Her Royal Majesty," however, this song did not even make it into the *Billboard* Top 100 singles. It was somewhat ironic, then, that "They Should Have Given You the Oscar" was reissued on the 1994 compact disc *The Best of James Darren* (Rhino 71664). This is another of those Goffin and King efforts that does not include a whole lot to distinguish it, except for the overly obvious reference to the acting abilities of the woman to whom the song is addressed as she toyed with the character portrayed by Darren.

Ultimately, every artist of note creates some masterpieces and some lesser works. Part of the problem that dogged Carole King later in her solo career was set into motion by her work on songs like "Her Royal Majesty," "They Should Have Given You an Oscar," and "Happy Being Fat" (a somewhat politically incorrect Goffin–King song recorded by the heavyset singer Big Dee Irwin). What songs like this suggest is the placement of commercial possibilities over artistic integrity and the expression of genuine emotion. Of course, the music industry of the first couple of years of the 1960s—outside of the folk revival genre—did not necessarily think of itself as much as an art as it did as part of the entertainment industry, and there *is* a difference between art and entertainment. The other danger of material like these songs is that in an attempt to create something commercial and clever, the writers and performers created something that may have enjoyed some sales success *but* quickly became forgettable. In the pre-British Invasion 1960s, that was not a complete disaster, but in the late 1960s and beyond, in a time in which rock criticism became an important force as the music moved into the realm of a type of art music, it would be more difficult to recover from embarrassments.

The Middle of the Road

Even in the early 1960s, when they were focusing on material for the girl groups and female solo R&B singers, Gerry Goffin and Carole King wrote a number of successful ballads that were successful on the pop charts largely because of their mainstrean appeal. Two of the best known of these songs, "Go Away, Little Girl" and "Hey Girl," deserve special attention because of what they show us about King's approach to melody and thematic development.

The two songs under consideration were both substantial mainstream pop hits: white pop singer Steve Lawrence took his 1962 recording of "Go Away, Little Girl" to No. 1 on the *Billboard* pop charts, and black singer Freddie Scott enjoyed a No. 10 pop and No. 10 R&B hit with "Hey Girl" in 1963. Despite the differences in the demographics of Lawrence and Scott's audiences (the Lawrence single made no impact on the R&B charts), the two compositions, arrangements, and recordings share an awful lot and stand apart from Goffin and King's girl-group R&B material, as well as from their rock-oriented material of the later, post-British Invasion 1960s.

In "Go Away, Little Girl," King uses one short, principal melodic motive as the generator of the entire tune of the verse. The main focal point is on the end of each of the short melodic phrases. In each of these, the tune rapidly descends and then returns. Because each phrase includes this motive, there is a sameness, or (to phrase it differently) a certain general cohesion in the entire melody. In practical terms, this means that King has no room for text painting of the sort that she does in a contemporary song like "Up on the Roof," in which she uses contrasting melodic motives to suggest the singer's ascent up to the roof. It also means that there is not a whole lot of expansion or development of the motive: she simply uses it in every phrase. And these phrases really are quite short: two measures of music in each. Although it is not the sort of direct text painting one might find in a song in which the composer sets a word like "higher" to a relatively high pitch, King's use of somewhat abrupt phrases does paint the general pleading nature of Gerry Goffin's lyrics. Isn't the phrase, "Go away" short enough to begin with? And, the repetitive statements of this plea, coming from a boy who is falling in love but doesn't want to be falling in love, are matched by the repetitive nature of King's melody. In a sense, all of this repetition suggests that the boy is trying as much to convince himself that he does not want to be in a love relationship as he is trying to convince the girl to leave. The song's success has been confirmed not only by the commercial success of the Steve Lawrence single of 1962–1963, but also by a 1966 top 20 pop single version by the Happenings, and Donny Osmond's No. 1 (for three weeks) hit single version of 1971.

In "Hey Girl" King writes in a different manner, both melodically and formally. Here, she again works from a short melodic motive, or kernel of musical material. The major difference is that in "Hey Girl" she expands and contracts the pitch outline of the motive and builds contrasting phrases out of it. Goffin's text again is a plea of sorts, but this time a plea for the girl to recognize the love that the singer feels for her. As the text moves from pleading to explaining to sharing the singer's intimate feelings of emotional need, King's melody moves from range to range and moves from higher degrees of rhythmic activity to more relative stasis. She might not paint any particular directional words musically, but she paints the range and the evolving nature of the singer's emotions—something that might not be quite as obvious, but that is more sophisticated and subtle.

In studying Carole King's approach to melodic writing, it is important to note the degree to which the motivic writing of "Go Away, Little Girl" and "Hey Girl" differs from the girl group R&B compositions of Goffin and King of the same period. Part of the reason behind the success of these songwriters certainly was the easily recognizable and memorable quality of King's music. Her use of distinctive melodic motives helped her to achieve this quality. In the R&B-oriented songs, though, the instantly recognizable melodic turns—or hooks—largely fall within the kind of repetition and development that comes out of the blues and gospel traditions: she fully integrated these African American genres into her own style. Not only do their arrangements, rhythmic feel, and general style owe little or nothing to blues or gospel, the pop songs "Go Away, Little Girl" and "Hey Girl" both exhibit a type of motivic use that is quite different from that of the blues- and gospel-influenced Carole King compositions in the 1960s.

The British Invasion

The story of Goffin and King's role in the British Invasion of 1964 properly begins with a recording of their song "Don't Ever Change" made by the

American group the Crickets back in 1962. Perhaps best remembered for their work in the brief period during which the rockabilly legend Buddy Holly was a member of the group in the 1950s, the Crickets were an important influence on a number of the British bands to emerge in the early 1960s, most notably, the Beatles. The importance of this band in the United Kingdom can be demonstrated by the fact that although their release of "Don't Ever Change" (Liberty 55441) never made the singles charts in America, it reached No. 5 on the British *New Musical Express* charts. The Beatles themselves never recorded the song for commercial release, but did tape it for an August 1963 broadcast of their BBC radio program *Pop Go the Beatles.* The Beatles recording finds singers John Lennon and Paul McCartney copying the vocal harmony parts of the Crickets note for note.

Another somewhat eerie tie between Buddy Holly and the Crickets and songwriters Goffin and King, incidentally, can be found in another 1962 hit, "Take Good Care of My Baby." This song was taken to No. 1 on the *Billboard* pop charts by Bobby Vee. Back in 1959, Vee and his group—the Shadows[12]—had been the band hired to replace Holly's group for the Fargo, North Dakota, concert to which Holly, the Big Bopper, and Ritchie Valens had been traveling when their plane crashed.

The Beatles had also covered the 1962 Little Eva hit "Keep Your Hands off My Baby" for a January 1963 BBC broadcast, but their best-known cover of a Goffin–King song was their take on "Chains," found on their 1962 debut album. Although the Beatles's versions of both "Chains" and "Keep Your Hands off My Baby" owe a great deal to the original girl-group recordings, they also owe a debt of gratitude, at least instrumentally and conceptually, to the work of the Crickets. Incidentally, a full-page 1963 profile of the members of the Beatles in *New Musical Express* finds Paul McCartney listing Goffin and King as his favorite songwriters.[13] And McCartney has been widely quoted as having said that all that he and John Lennon wanted to accomplish as songwriters early in their career was to "be as good as Goffin and King."

It should be noted that songs composed by John Lennon and Paul McCartney also exhibited some of the same compositional and arrangement traits of the Brill Building songwriters' girl-group songs. For example, musicologist Ian Inglis notes that, "The customary vocal arrangement in which members of the girl groups repeated the lead singer's words in close succession—on tracks such as 'Will You Love Me Tomorrow'—was freely employed on songs like 'Hold Me Tight,' 'You Won't See Me,' and 'You're Going to Lose That Girl.'" Inglis also notes that Lennon and McCartney's compositions resembled those of Goffin and King (and other Brill Building songwriters) in "standard reliance on the AABA form, a melodic contrast between the A and B sections, an unusual complexity in chord progressions, and a routine modulation to a different key in the bridges of their songs."[14]

The Beatles were also influenced by the original early twentieth-century Tin Pan Alley songwriters. In fact, the first professional recording the group made with a member of the band handling lead vocals was the 1927 Tin Pan Alley song "Ain't She Sweet." And one of the first published "songs" written by members of the group—John Lennon and George Harrison's instrumental composition "Cry for a Shadow"—uses the Tin Pan Alley standard AABA form. Both of these pieces were recorded back in 1961, perhaps around the time that members of the band were becoming aware of Goffin and King's songs. Hearing the Beatles perform "Ain't She Sweet," "Cry for a Shadow," and the Goffin–King songs they recorded for radio and for commercial release on vinyl makes crystal clear the connections between the Tin Pan Alley of Milton Ager and Jack Yellen (the writers of "Ain't She Sweet"), the lyrical and musical structures of the Brill Building songwriters, and the early songwriting styles of Lennon, McCartney, and Harrison, particularly because of the shared motivic approach to melody in "Ain't She Sweet," "Chains," and "Cry for a Shadow," and because all three compositions modulate to the subdominant in their "B" sections.

The Beatles, however, were not the only British Invasion musicians to turn to the Goffin and King songbook for material. For example Earl-Jean's summer 1964 top 40 pop version of "I'm into Something Good" was covered by Herman's Hermits later that same year. The British band's version, incidentally, fared significantly better in terms of U.S. sales, reaching No. 13 on the *Billboard* charts. Other British acts, too, turned to the Goffin and King songbook, including the Rockin' Berries, who recorded "He's in Town," and Manfred Mann, who covered "Oh No, Not My Baby." Although these groups did not enjoy the benefits of songwriters on par with the likes of John Lennon and Paul McCartney, and so did not naturally soak up the song construction style of Goffin and King, they did, to some extent, use the types of vocal and instrumental arrangements that Goffin and King used in the original versions of the songs.

The radio and recording success that male groups like the Beatles and Herman's Hermits had with girl-group songs like "I'm into Something Good," "Chains," and "Keep Your Hands off My Baby" suggests something important about the material itself. Not only was King's music, with its heavy use of pentatonic-scale melodies and the basic harmonies of rhythm and blues, easily adaptable to the British beat style, Gerry Goffin's lyrics were transferred from the female perspective to the male perspective with no more than a change of pronoun here and there.[15] This would have been impossible, or would have led to less-than-stellar results, had the song texts relied on traditional, stereotypical gender roles. Commentators have remarked about how the Brill Building songwriters in general lent more assertive voices to female singers, a perspective less reliant on some of the stereotypical perspectives of 1940s and 1950s pop songs. Certainly, this is clearest in Goffin–King songs such as "Keep Your Hands off My Baby" (a 1962 No. 12 pop and

No. 6 R&B hit for Little Eva) and "Don't Say Nothin' Bad (About My Baby)" (a 1963 No. 7 pop and No. 3 R&B hit for the Cookies). In these songs the lead singer's character displays an openly aggressive attitude toward anyone who would try to take their love interest away from them ("Keep Your Hands Off My Baby") or anyone who would speak ill of their love interest ("Don't Say Nothin' Bad"). Musical expressions of "attitude" from women were not unheard of before the days of the Brill Building songwriters, but were more commonly associated with the Bessie Smith blues tradition than with Tin Pan Alley. That a group like the Beatles would include girl-group songs like "Chains" and "Baby It's You" (a non-Goffin and King Brill Building song) effectively on their first album in 1962 provides solid evidence of the greater equality of gender roles allowed by Goffin and King ("One Fine Day" and a few of their other hit compositions excepted) and their Brill Building colleagues even in songs that did not rely originally on openly aggressive female characters. It is also worth noting that the Motown covers recorded by groups such as the Beatles that originally came from the male perspective and had been recorded by artists such as Barrett Strong or Smokey Robinson and the Miracles. In the area of breaking down of stereotypical gender roles in song, then, the Brill Building songwriters were one step ahead of Motown, that other important early-1960s R&B force.

Even "I'm into Something Good," which is not necessarily an "attitude" song, features Goffin lyrics that show a female perspective not commonly found in earlier pop material. Here, we find the lead singer (Earl-Jean in the originally release) telling the listener that she could tell that her current lover was not just "a one-night stand." The implication of this is that the couple may indeed have had sex on their first date. By late 1950s and even early 1960s standards, this was a most unusual admission in a pop song. When the song was covered by Herman's Hermits, the lyrics fit in more easily with the stereotype of the young male for whom sexual encounters did not at the time carry the same negative social baggage.

What all of these Goffin–King songs have in common is (1) their easy adaptability to the new mid-1960s rock style and (2) easy-to-remember lyrical and musical hooks. What Goffin and King would need to do, however, to stay current as rock music evolved in 1966 and 1967, would be to write in styles less directly tied to the easygoing R&B of the early 1960s. Their chance to do so would come about first through writing material that incorporated some of the stylistic traits of British rock, and second through writing for a band that was constructed for an American television program.

Both the Pretty Things, a band that seems to have had something of a cult following that never translated into widespread record sales, and the famous, Eric Burdon-led band the Animals recorded the Goffin and King composition "Don't Bring Me Down." This may not be the Animals's best-remembered single, but their 1966 release reached No. 12 on the *Billboard* pop charts in the United States. In this song Goffin and King adopted the new, mid-1960s British rock style. Musically, it is less tied to the 1950s than many of their early 1960s songs. However, this attempt did not quite represent the near-rebirth of Goffin and King as post-Beatles writers the way that their association with the Monkees would.

The Monkees

Because of their longstanding association with Don Kirshner, Gerry Goffin and Carole King became semiregular songwriters for the Monkees. Originally, this group was a pairing of two singing actors—Micky Dolenz and Davy Jones—with two musicians—Peter Tork and Michael Nesmith—constructed for a television program about a fictional rock band: *The Monkees*. At first, Kirshner supervised the recording of backing tracks, usually performed entirely by studio musicians to which vocal tracks by all four Monkees were added. Eventually, however, the four became a real group of sorts, recording both as vocalists and instrumentalists and undertaking concert tours. And significantly, Don Kirshner was fired by the television program's producers after an incident in which he released a "Monkees" single that used none of the Monkees as instrumentalists, although they had been promised that they would be allowed to perform on their next record. Goffin and King, however, apparently were not tainted in the eyes of the Monkees or the television program's producers by their association with Kirshner, as the group continued to record Goffin and King material through the end of the 1960s.

The group's 1966 self-titled debut album, *The Monkees,* included one song co-written by Goffin, King, and Monkees guitarist-singer Michael Nesmith, "Sweet Young Thing." The song is not necessarily the most memorable Carole King composition, nor is it by any means one of the best-remembered tracks on *The Monkees*. The song "Take a Giant Step," however, also appeared on the album and is worthy of note. In the book *Groove Tube: Sixties Television and the Youth Rebellion,* writer Aniko Bodroghkozy described the song as "a somewhat trippy invitation."[16] Indeed, Goffin's lyrics *could* be taken as an invitation to indulge in psychedelic drugs, although the references are so vague—they could be taken as an invitation to just look at the world from a different perspective—that the song did not seem to run into problems with censors. The vagueness of the "message" is one of the most charming parts of these lyrics. In the hands of the Monkees, who were built up as a sort of American answer to the Beatles, Goffin's line, "Come with me, leave yesterday behind," could be taken as a sly invitation for fans of the British quartet (who had enjoyed a major U.S. hit with the song "Yesterday") to change their allegiance. The way in which one "reads" the lyrics, however, is dependent on the context: in Tommy Boyce and Bobby Hart's arrangement of the song for the Monkees, the rockish, other worldly sound (which includes a Middle Eastern-sounding oboe/shawn obligato) would tend to shift the hearing of Goffin's text toward the "trippy" interpretation. In former Monkee Peter Tork's later folkish recording on his 1994 album *Stranger Things Have Happened* (Beachwood Recordings BR-2522), the lyrical message seems to be that of changing one's view of life, probably to enter a new love relationship. The same is true of the early 1966 recording of the song by the folk artist Taj Mahal.

King's music for "Take a Giant Step" is about as far away from the gospel and R&B style she used for her girl-group compositions as the experimental rock music of 1966 was from the music of the Cookies and Little Eva. In this and in some of her other Monkees compositions of the 1966–1968 period, she makes liberal use of what I refer to as polymodal tonality. By this I mean a central tonality (the pitch-class "C," for example) is supported by the melodic use of the C major scale (C, D, E, F, G, A, B, C) *and* the C mixolydian mode (C, D, E, F, G, A, B-flat, C). King also writes harmonies that come from the mixture of these modes; for example, incorporating the B-flat-major chord (B-flat, D, F), as well as chords that contain the pitch-class B-natural, such as the G major chord (G, B, D). From an aural standpoint, all of this means that some melodic and harmonic aspects of the song come out of the classical tradition, while others are distinctly rock in nature. Several of King's R&B-oriented songs use modal mixture, but her earlier writing is more closely related to the natural melodic-harmonic "conflicts" of the blues. Carole King did not invent the type of modal mixture that finds its way into songs like "Take a Giant Step," but she did adapt her writing style to match the time period and genre by adopting techniques that rock bands were using.

The second album by the Monkees—*More of the Monkees*—featured songs that were performed entirely by studio musicians with vocals added by members of the group only after the backing tracks were "in the can." Goffin and King's contribution, which was produced by Gerry Goffin, was "Sometime in the Morning." Here, Micky Dolenz sings to backing tracks that had originally accompanied a guide lead vocal by Carole King. His vocal was substituted for hers. The song itself is pleasant top-40 pop-rock, with the most remarkable featuring being the way in which the finished recording was constructed.

Although the Monkees as a group broke with Don Kirshner (Goffin and King's boss for several years), they returned to the works of Goffin and King for the late-1967 album *Pisces, Aquarius, Capricorn & Jones Ltd*. This collection includes two songs that Goffin and King crafted for the band: "Star Collector" and "Pleasant Valley Sunday." Each is remarkable in its own way, and each demonstrates the extent to which lyricist Gerry Goffin and composer Carole King had evolved since the late 1950s.

Goffin's lyrics for "Star Collector" describe the activities of a "star collector," a rock band groupie. Although the lyrics do not reach the level of specificity about the more sordid activities of groupies and members of rock bands found in the Rolling Stones's 1973 "Star Star" (an album track on the Stones's *Goat's Head Soup*), it is clear enough that the female groupie does more than merely collect autographs. In fact, this is one of the frankest pop songs of the time in terms of the free sex that took place between male rock musicians and groupies, as well as the lack of respect the musicians felt for those who provided them with companionship and sexual entertainment. It should be noted that although the Goffin–King song and the Jagger–Richards song deal with the same basic type of relationship (rock musician and groupie), "Star Collector" goes much further in exposing the unfeeling nature of the musician's treatment of the groupie than does "Star Star"; Mick Jagger and Keith Richards treat the groupie with disdain and fail to entertain the possibility that it may not be entirely acceptable for the male rocker to use women as sexual servants.

Much better known than Goffin and King's "Star Collector" is the big Monkees hit of 1967, "Pleasant Valley Sunday." The overall effect of "Pleasant Valley Sunday" is partially defined by the track's arrangement, including the well-known opening guitar riff, created by producer-bassist Chip Douglas and played on the recording by Monkee Michael Nesmith.[17] Some, such as Chip Douglas, have suggested that perhaps King did not like the guitar riff, as it had not been part of her initial demo record of the song.[18] Be that as it may, the song is also defined by Goffin's lyrics and King's music. The lyrics satirically describe stereotypical upper-middle to upper-class suburban life in America's "status symbol land." Each verse finds Goffin describing some of the scenes of suburban life (based on the couple's life in West Orange, New Jersey[19]), and the chorus lets the listener know just when and where the individual snapshots are occurring, "Another Pleasant Valley Sunday, here in status symbol land." King's writing in the verses is notable for its twice-stated, unresolved melodic rise. The resolution comes only after the chorus, which itself is based on repetition of a distinctive melodic motive. In the song's "middle eight" section, King develops one of the song's earlier melodic motives. In short, the verses propel the listener into the chorus (which bring the individual scenes into their overall context), and the entire melody has an organic wholeness. The combination of lyrics and music—and arrangement—in "Pleasant Valley Sunday" make it one of King's best mid-to-late 1960s songs. Incidentally, in King's performances of "Pleasant Valley Sunday" on her Living Room Tour of the early twenty-first century, her guitarist, Rudy Guess, incorporated a modified version of the Chip Douglas/Michael Nesmith guitar lick. If Douglas was correct in his assessment of King's reaction to the arrangement, King appears to have realized that it does form an important part of the overall gestalt of the song as audiences know and love it.

The Monkees's 1968 feature-length film, *Head*, included the Goffin–King collaboration "The Porpoise Song" as the opening title music, as well as King's collaboration with lyricist Toni Stern, "As We Go Along." Gerry Goffin produced the recording of "The Porpoise Song," which, more than anything else, resembles the Beatles' "I Am the Walrus." The lyrics make veiled references to such things as Monkee Micky Dolenz's work as a child actor in the television program *Circus Boy*. Although it is difficult to separate King's music from Goffin's heavily orchestrated English acid-rock-style production and arrangement (in the manner of the Beatles's "I Am the Walrus" and "Strawberry Fields Forever"), melodically and harmonically, King had fully embraced the prevailing experimental rock style of 1967. By the time the film was released, the rock world had largely left this orchestrated style behind and had moved toward more of a harder-edged, blues-based approach, but as a representative of what had up until that time been seen as one of the most mind-expanded (chemically or otherwise) styles in pop music, "The Porpoise Song" succeeds. However, this is something of a one-off song for Carole King; her other *Head* composition, "As We Go Along" is more representative of what King would be doing as a solo artist in just a couple of years.

"As We Go Along" is an early collaboration with lyricist Toni Stern, who would emerge as the most important writing contributor—save King herself—on *Tapestry*. From the folkish, quintuple meter, riff-based opening onward, the song stands apart from the rest of the material of the *Head* soundtrack. It suggests some of the Back-to-the-Land Movement inspired music of the 1969 Woodstock era. Although Canned Heat's "Going Up the Country" comes to mind, as well as some of the early country-rock of Graham Parsons, the Byrds, Rick Nelson, Bob Dylan, and the Monkees's own Mike Nesmith, "As We Go Along" displays a musical sophistication absent from some of the simpler folk-country-rock music of the era. Stern's lyrics are an appeal to open up one's life to the possibilities of living in the moment, a sort of affirmation of the late-1960s hippie spirit. "As We Go Along," too, would have been a perfect song for King to have included on one of her *Tapestry*-era albums, as it suggests so strongly the reflective musical and lyrical style of the singer-songwriter movement that would emerge in the early 1970s.

Despite the outward appearance of a folklike, acoustic simplicity created by King's harmony and melodic shapings, "As We Go Along" appears to be a carefully crafted composition by a professional songwriter when one considers the less obvious rhythmic shaping. The opening quintuple meter riff establishes a pattern of stasis (represented by the three repeated pitches on quarter-notes), followed by a shorter period of relatively high-level rhythmic and pitch activity (the two sets of dotted-eighth-note/sixteenth-note pairs over the course of the final two beats of the riff). Basically, this creates the feel of a rhythmic stumble at the end of each measure. By and large, this establishes the pattern taken up in the song's melody in nearly all phrases. The real exception is the melodic phrase associated with the key line in the lyrics, "We'll make up the story as we go along." This melodic phrase begins actively and then settles down for the words "as we go along." King's reversal of her well-established rhythmic-melodic pattern sets this text up as the key focal point. Again, like "Pleasant Valley Sunday" and some of King's best solo work to come, the organic wholeness of the musical setting of the lyrics of "As We Go Along" reveals Carole King as a writer who, consciously or unconsciously, operated on a higher level than the archetypical pop song writer.

Aretha Franklin and Other Middle and Late 1960s Notables

One of the strongest confirmations of Gerry Goffin and Carole King's ability to write material that could break through traditional musical boundaries came with the success of Aretha Franklin's recording of "(You Make Me Feel Like) A Natural Woman." There were, however, several other notable non-Monkees-related accomplishments in the middle and late 1960s. Let's consider some of these before tackling the formidable "Natural Woman."

Blue-eyed soul singers, the Righteous Brothers, recorded Goffin and King's "Man Without a Dream" back in 1966. King's music includes memorable vocal and instrumental hooks. Goffin's lyrics resemble some of the more memorable and clever lyrics of Smokey Robinson of the time period, in the way in which basic human emotions are presented in a phrasing that causes them not to sound like the clichés they could become in the hands of a less resourceful writer. The words and music fit within the R&B tradition, but move away from the norms of what Goffin and King were doing in the early 1960s into a more mature, erudite style.

When Carole King formed her short-lived band, the City, and recorded a virtually ignored album with the outfit, she included a number of songs of diverse musical styles. Among these was "Man Without a Dream," which was the only track on the album with lead vocals by someone other than King (Danny Kortchmar sang lead on the song). Another interesting song performed by King's band was "Wasn't Born to Follow," the title of which has also been given as "I Wasn't Born to Follow" on various recordings. Here Goffin and King created a song with a meandering, country-rock influenced melody and arrangement that keeps perfectly in step with lyrics about the roaming, freedom-focused life of a late-1960s hippie. The Byrds included the definitive version of the song on their 1968 album *The Notorious Byrd Brothers*. The Byrds give the song extra poignancy by placing it immediately after the antimilitary draft song "Draft Morning" on the album. When actor/filmmaker Dennis Hopper was working with the Byrds's lead guitarist Roger McGuinn and selecting music for the soundtrack of the counterculture classic *Easy Rider,* he included this recording. Back in 1968, the country-rock style was just in the process of being defined by the Byrds, Gram Parsons, Michael Nesmith, and Rick Nelson, among others. Goffin and King's contribution to the genre, especially in the hands of the Byrds, sounds completely authentic within the spirit of the era.

One of the most memorable and longest staying Goffin and King compositions of the second half of the 1960s, however, is "(You Make Me Feel Like) A Natural Woman." The legendary Atlantic Records producer Jerry Wexler also contributed to the song, which became an important hit for soul singer

Aretha Franklin. Franklin's 1967 recording is significant for several reasons. First, it reached No. 8 on the *Billboard* pop charts, making it a legitimate hit single. More important, however, it illustrates the extent to which Goffin and King were able to write material that would be suitable for an authentic gospel-inflected soul singer. Aretha Franklin was a soul singer of major importance at this point in her career, and her recording of the song serves to legitimatize Goffin and King's move beyond the R&B girl groups, the mainstrean crooners, and the rock bands, to "real" soul music.

"(You Make Me Feel Like) A Natural Woman" is significant even if the Aretha Franklin factor is removed, however. Not that it necessarily would be easy to imagine the song performed by someone other than Franklin, or King herself on *Tapestry,* so definitive were both of their recordings, and so tied is the song to the gospel-soul style with which Franklin was so closely associated, and which would become one of King's best singing styles once her solo career became established. The influence of gospel music can be found in both King's melody and harmony. Regardless of who recorded it, "A Natural Woman" is clearly a feminist statement at least a couple of years before the women's movement "officially" took shape. The lyrics revolve around a woman who is clearly completely comfortable with her sexuality and with sexual expression with her man. Such expressions from female characters in top-40 songs were rare even in the 1967 "Summer of Love." As is the case with so many of Carole King's songs, however, the real impact of the lyrics comes through the way in which they are set to music. Here, the thoroughly gospel-style setting suggests the near religious elevation of romantic and physical love expressed by the character who sings the song. In other words, whatever impact Goffin and Wexler's title line and lyrics might have on their own is heightened by King's convincing musical setting.

The 1960s work of Carole King, mostly writing in collaboration with Gerry Goffin, left a legacy of fine, commercially successful pop songs. These songs cut through stylistic, gender, and racial barriers, and many of them remain staples of oldies radio in the twenty-first century. Goffin and King were the stars of the Brill Building songwriting establishment, in part because of the care they took with their demo records. On many of their demos, King sang, arranged, and/or played piano. The question then arises, "Couldn't someone with that combination of talents establish a solo performing career?"

Before *Tapestry*

THE EARLY SINGLES

The story of Carole King the recording artist began in her teen years, way back in the 1950s, even before she had emerged as a leading Brill Building songwriter. Some of the singles she recorded—"Oh Neil" and "Short Mort," in particular—were highly derivative, in that they were based on currently popular songs. Others just did not seem to have quite what it would take to be commercially successful at the time.

Easily the best known of the early Carole King singles, "It Might As Well Rain Until September" eventually worked its way up to No. 22 on the *Billboard* pop charts in 1962. Lyrically and musically, the song is pretty standard Brill Building, Tin Pan Alley fare, save for some unexpected chromatic harmony from composer King. In retrospect, "It Might As Well Rain Until September" may not have been a career breakout for Carole King because it was a mismatch between material, arrangement, and King's voice. For one thing, Goffin and King originally wrote the song with Bobby Vee in mind. When Vee released it as an album cut instead of featuring it as a single, King released it as a single. The unison multitracked vocal seems a little clumsy, especially the imprecise cutoffs. More important, however, the lyrics, music, and arrangement seem to be aimed squarely at the top-40 pop audience and King did not sing in the kind of voice required for 1962 pop success. Her voice is somewhat bland in the recording. Who knows what might have happened had she sung a song appropriate for the kind of bluesy inflections that would define her best vocal work once her solo career got fully underway in the 1970s.

Carole King's only other pre-1971 chart single was the 1963, No. 94 pop song "He's a Bad Boy." From all appearances, someone at Colpix/Dimension decided that King should not be cast as a pop singer, but rather as a folksinger. This Goffin-King tale of a young woman who is in love with a "bad boy" is not convincing folk, either as a composition or as a performance. On this and other King recordings of the 1960s, there is a curious feeling of a non-Brill Building approach. That is, the Brill Building approach was to tailor songs to particular singers. What "It Might As Well Rain Until September" and "He's a Bad Boy" suggest is an attempt to mold the singer to fit the song. Because King had not yet established a definable "voice" as a singer (from a technical standpoint and from a personality standpoint), perhaps this was understandable as a way to try to establish a niche; however, it was not particularly artistically or commercially successful.

Now That Everything's Been Said

Carole King's marriage to Gerry Goffin ended in 1968; however, the two would often continue to collaborate as songwriters, and King would continue to consider Gerry Goffin a dear friend into the twenty-first century.[1] King, along with her daughters Sherry and Louise, moved to California, specifically to the Laurel Canyon section of Los Angeles, an area that was already quite well populated by rock musicians. She then set about forming a band. As King has been a somewhat reluctant live performer over the years, her band, the City, would have difficulty establishing a following. When their only album, *Now That Everything's Been Said*, was released, they did not tour to support the recording, much to the detriment of sales. The City certainly had sufficiently strong musical credentials. In addition to King—who was already acknowledged as one of the leading songwriters of the rock era—on lead vocals and keyboards was Danny Kortchmar on guitar and vocals and Charles Larkey on bass. Kortchmar, perhaps better known as Danny Kootch, had been a member of the radical New York political band the Fugs, as well as the Original Flying Machine, a band that had also included soon-to-be star James Taylor. Larkey, who would become King's second husband, had performed with the Myddle Class and Jo Mama. The well-established studio drummer Jim Gordon was added to fill out the instrumentation. The band played a number of jam sessions with sometime guest James Taylor, but was essentially a studio band. King interested record producer Lou Adler in the group. They recorded *Now That Everything's Been Said* in 1968; the album was released in 1969.

Now That Everything's Been Said begins with the Goffin and King song "Snow Queen," which had been recorded by the Roger Nichols Trio the year before. The City's version shows off the influence of a fluid jazz style on King the composer and pianist. In fact, the song is a jazz waltz and contains some resemblance to a rock-influenced take on Dave Brubeck's work of the 1950s. This kind of jazz-rock fusion was not all that common in 1968; the really big commercial impact of bands like Chicago and Blood, Sweat and Tears in the music industry would come over the next couple of years. Musically, then, "Snow Queen" is at once somewhat off the beaten path of 1968 pop music and anticipatory of a style that would be in vogue shortly after the release of *Now That Everything's Been Said*. Goffin's lyrics describe a woman who, as a result of her lack of emotional commitment, is known as the Snow Queen.

The album's second song, "I Wasn't Born to Follow,"[2] certainly is better known, but not for this particular recording. The song would be recorded by the Byrds and appeared on the album *The Notorious Byrd Brothers*; it would later find its way into the popular soundtrack to the counterculture film *Easy Rider*. The City's performance includes some gospel-influenced piano work from King. Goffin's text and King's musical setting suggest the hippie life-style of the late 1960s. The text paints the singer as a rugged individualist at one with nature. The music includes just the most basic tonal harmonies and includes much motivic repetition in the melody. In some respects, this comes close to being a quintessential hippie, back-to-nature song of individualism. It should be noted that the version recorded by the Byrds is more compact than the rather long, meandering version recorded by the City.

The King–Toni Stern composition "Now That Everything's Been Said" is a jazzy pop tune that, more than anything else, resembles some of the late-1960s work of songwriter Laura Nyro, the author of popular top-40 hits like "Save the Country," "Stone Soul Picnic," and "Eli's Coming." The tune and harmony—and King's musical arrangement—are catchy, but they are not particularly memorable. Most troubling, however, is that the lyrics fail to make much of an impression. In some respects, they seem to be little more than a series of sounds that accompany a nice tune. Therefore, it is something approaching album filler—the kind of song that illustrates King's ties to the Brill Building assembly line—something listenable, but not a classic.

King collaborated with David Palmer for the song "Paradise Alley." The song's lyrics find the singer—in this case, the multitracked King—wishing for the "days of plenty" to replace the doldrums of her present life. The music and the musical setting represent another typical late 1960s pop style. The chorus hook is one of King's better such efforts, but the entire gestalt of the song does not approach the great hits that Gerry Goffin and King wrote for other artists earlier in the decade; nor does it approach the great songs that were to appear in a few years on King's *Tapestry*.

Goffin and King's 1966 song "A Man without a Dream" had been recorded by blue-eyed soul singers the Righteous Brothers to good effect as an album track and single B-side. The City's take on the song is not as soulful; it is the only track on *Now That Everything's Been Said* on which Danny Kootch takes over lead vocals from King, and it is considerably more sparse than some of the more effective recordings of the song. For example, in the Monkees's 1969 recording on the album *Instant Replay*, singer Davy Jones is backed by Bob Alcivar, Bill Holman, and Bones Howe's fuller, brassy arrangement. The Monkees's version, in fact, tends to resemble what one might have expected to hear at a Las Vegas show by a somewhat soulful mainstrean singer like Sammy Davis, Jr. Strangely enough, though, this Vegas-style approach works. The City's version makes good use of the easily memorable guitar hook that King composed; however, this is more muted than what is heard on other versions of the song. King's music exhibits a clear affinity for mainstrean soul style. The instrumental hook is easy identifiable and memorable, as is the largely pentatonic vocal melody. Incidentally, the turn of some of Goffin's phrases suggests an erudition that is somewhat inconsistent with the nature of the soul style, which tends to emphasize raw human emotion over erudition. This slight stylistic disconnect in part explains both the highly memorable nature of the song and—ironically—the reason that it was a good enough but not a classic Goffin–King hit. As I mentioned earlier, however, although the lyrical style might be somewhat out of character for hard-core soul, it does resemble some of the work of Smokey Robinson as a lyricist.

Although I will not detail all of King's collaborative compositions on *Now That Everything's Been Said,* there is one more that certainly deserves mention. Like "I Wasn't Born to Follow," "That Old Sweet Roll (Hi-De-Ho)" would also became an important hit, but, again, not for the City. With its title transposed to "Hi-De-Ho (That Old Sweet Roll)," this song would become a significant hit in a couple of years for the jazz-rock combo Blood, Sweat and Tears, which issued the song as a single and as a track on their third album.[3] In the gospel-infused music of King and the pseudo-gospel text of Gerry Goffin, one can again hear echoes of their contemporary, Laura Nyro, and especially her song "And When I Die" (which, not coincidentally, Blood, Sweat and Tears had included on their second album). Perhaps more than most of the tracks on *Now That Everything's Been Said,* the City's recording of "That Old Sweet Roll (Hi-De-Ho)" anticipates the stylistic influences (gospel) and texture of the breakthrough *Tapestry* album. To top it off, Carole King is a thoroughly convincing singer when she performs this type of clearly African American-influenced song. King's authentic-sounding approach to the gospel style of the song on this album contrasts with the somewhat cutesy, flippant recording of "That Old Sweet Roll" she would make for her 1980 album, *Pearls: The Songs of Goffin and King.*

"That Old Sweet Roll" is a powerful recording. So why did it go nowhere when released as a single in 1969? For one thing, the fiddle solo seems a little strange for the overall black gospel feel of the song. For another, a single by a virtually invisible band was not as likely to be successful in the late 1960s as one by a band that was making live and televised appearances. Had this record been issued as a Carole King single—especially if the fiddle solo had been replaced with an instrumental break played by someone more closely associated with pop music of the time—it *may* have stood a good chance of becoming King's breakout record.

Ultimately, the real story behind *Now That Everything's Been Said* probably is best expressed by Danny Kortchmar, who in 1999 said, "The seeds of the enduring classic album *Tapestry* were planted here, and I consider myself extremely lucky and proud to have been a part of it all."[4] Kortchmar is right: the City's lone album featured King's compositions in collaboration with lyricists such as Gerry Goffin, David Palmer, and Toni Stern; it featured the gospel, jazz, and rock-influenced instrumental work of King, Kortchmar, and Larkey; it featured Lou Adler's production (which really only hinted at the clarity of sound that he would achieve on *Tapestry*). And although *Now That Everything's Been Said* was not itself a commercial success, it proved that Carole King's songwriting was still evolving stylistically and was still commercially viable. Unfortunately it took covers of two of this album's songs, "I Wasn't Born to Follow" and "That Old Sweet Roll (Hi-De-Ho)" to prove that commercial viability.

Although Carole King's project with the City was a product of 1968 and 1969, and she would release her first official solo album in 1970, she did not focus solely on her own projects in 1969. In fact, she played piano on some of the most important recording sessions of James Taylor's career in December 1969. These sessions produced Taylor's first hits, "Fire and Rain," "Sweet Baby James," and "Country Road." Taylor and King would continue to be loose collaborators over the next couple of years, during which time the two artists—along with Joni Mitchell, Carly Simon, and Paul Simon—would virtually define the new introspective singer-songwriter style.

WRITER

Assisted by her fellow former members of the City, Danny Kortchmar and Charles Larkey, as well as James Taylor on acoustic guitar and backing vocals, Joel O'Brien on drums, Ralph Schuckett on organ, John Fischbach on Moog synthesizer, and Abigail Haness and Delores Hall on backing vocals, Carole King cut her first official solo album, *Writer*, in 1970. As implied by the album's title, all of the songs were written by King—in collaboration with lyricists Gerry Goffin and Toni Stern. The one missing ingredient from this album that could be found in both *Now That Everything's Been Said* and *Tapestry* is producer Lou Adler. Because of other commitments, he was unable to produce *Writer*, leaving those chores to his associate, the aforementioned keyboardist John Fischbach. Another thing missing from *Writer* that would mark several of the more memorable songs of *Tapestry* was the presence of Carole King as a lyricist. Ultimately, *Writer* was a commercial failure, despite its superficial sonic resemblance to the albums that King recorded on either side of it. A number of factors probably contributed to this failure: (1) unlike *Tapestry*, some of the songs here exhibit an emotional detachment or are largely dependent on the instrumental work of King's associates, (2) the production does not emphasize the immediacy of King's voice to the extent that Lou Adler's did (both on *Now That Everything's Been Said* and, to greater extent, on *Tapestry*), (3) the packaging—including the cover art—does not make a strong connection with the audience, and (4) *Writer* does not contain quite the same kind of instant hit material as *Tapestry*. This is not to imply that it is in any respect an artistic failure; it forms a most important part of the Carole King canon, especially as it helped to lay the groundwork for *Tapestry*.

John Fischbach's production and Gerry Goffin's mix represent something of an attempt to make *Writer* a commercially viable, almost archetypical late 1960s/early 1970s pop album. Some of the songs have something approaching the immediacy of the songs of *Tapestry*. Unlike King's only slightly later masterpiece, however, here her voice tends to be covered in the mix, and Danny Kortchmar and guest artist James Taylor's acoustic and electric guitars dominate the instrumental texture. Carole King, the groundbreaking piano player of *Tapestry*, is here a decidedly background session player on her own solo record. This is especially regrettable on a song like "Raspberry Jam," a largely instrumentally based song in which King's piano sounds like it is placed in another room, even during her brief solo passage. Another problem with the overall sound of the album is that the stereo separation of the mix gives the album a real studio feel. Not that there is anything inherently wrong with that. The problem is that in comparison, *Tapestry* sounds like a live studio performance with a few well-placed overdubs.

Gerry Goffin and Toni Stern's lyrics for *Writer* generally are not quite as personal sounding and "me" focused as are Stern and King's lyrics on *Tapestry*. In short, this just is not the archetypical introspective singer-songwriter album that *Tapestry* would be. This can be seen on so many lyrical and musical levels. Consider, for example, King's string arrangements on "Eventually" and "Up on the Roof." Her use of a full string section contrasts with the sparseness and clarity of the string quintet she incorporates into a few songs on *Tapestry*. To top things off, there is far too much of the stereotypical acoustic guitar upper-neighbor-note/lower-neighbor-note turns and suspended fourths that define the early hit recordings of James Taylor from the same period.[5] Every one of these guitar figures and every covered-over piano lick makes *Writer* less of a Carole King solo record and more of a generic example of what was a style that was rapidly growing in popularity. The real problem with the somewhat generic nature of some of the lyrics, arrangements, and mix is that this entire singer-songwriter genre was predicated on personal—and not generic—expression.

Like its predecessor, *Now That Everything's Been Said*, *Writer* is more stylistically far-flung than *Tapestry* would be. King makes foreground references to country, country-rock, jazz, the folkish singer-songwriter style, pop, and (a fairly gentle version of) hard rock. This is completely understandable given the eclectic nature of King's writing, especially when it involved (in typical Brill Building fashion) having to tailor material to a wide range of performers. Although this might show off her ability to write convincingly in a number of current pop styles, it means that *Writer* tends not to be as focused musically as it could be.

Even the cover art of *Writer* is a misread of the times and the entire gestalt of the new singer-songwriter movement. The cover features a less-than-full-size photograph of King standing in front of bare, leafless tree limbs with a painted-in rainbow coming out of her head. The starkness of the image, particularly with the bare tree limbs, contrasts greatly with the hominess of the full-cover photo on *Tapestry,* showing a barefoot, jeans-clad King sitting on a window seat in her home holding a tapestry she stitched by hand. Her out-of-focus, somewhat startled-looking cat adds to the this-is-just-me-at-home feel of the art.[6] *Tapestry*'s cover art is highly personal; in comparison, *Writer*'s seems to miss the point.

Critics generally reacted favorably to *Writer,* although some reviews of the album pointed out its flaws. *Rolling Stone*'s Melissa Mills, for example, described the arrangements as "excellent," but characterized King's voice as "just not very strong."[7] Jon Landau, another writer for *Rolling Stone,* found less fault with King's singing than he did with John Fischbach's "labored and sloppy" production and arrangements that "sounded like they were pieced together in the studio."[8] Landau did note, however, that the album paved the way for *Tapestry. Stereo Review* described the performance as "beautiful," the production as "good," and the arrangements as "stunning."[9]

These comments aside, it is easy for writers to play armchair quarterback on Monday morning, compared with the complexity of composing, arranging, and performing a pop album. The fact is that *Writer* contains some good songs, good recording and mixing, and good performances. The disappointment—and possibly the lack of commercial appeal of the album at the time of its release—comes from the fact that the album clearly is moving in a direction that would firmly put Carole King on the map as a recording artist, but contains what appear to be stylistic misreads of what the singer-songwriter style would be, or too many Brill Building approaches, to be a cohesive artistic and personal statement.

Writer begins with the rock track "Spaceship Races," a most curious love song. In Gerry Goffin's lyrics, King says she is willing to take him to the spaceship races, but will gladly take him home if he doesn't "go in for far off places." The lyrics are abstract enough that "Spaceship Races" is an intriguing track by itself, but it—along with King and Toni Stern's "Raspberry Jam"—tends to stick out as being less direct, less connected with simple human emotions expressed in a straightforward way than the album as a whole. This is about the closest thing that King had ever written to hard rock and is a convincing example of the style, although the brief run out, coda section resembles a slower paced Motown-gospel mix. Ultimately, though, "Spaceship Races" tends to sound like an album track that could have been found on a record by just about any late 1960s rock band. It does little to establish a voice for Carole King as a performer, and it is not her most distinctive composition.

"No Easy Way Down" is a perfect match of music and lyrics and finds King making use of her gift to write and sing convincing-sounding gospel-influenced music. Another effective feature of this recording is King's background brass arrangement. The way in which she voices the instruments is far removed from the then –popular, bright-sounding bands such as Blood, Sweat and Tears and Chicago. In fact, the darker-timbre voicings favored here by King anticipate the scoring that would become instantly recognizable in 1975 as the sound of the *Saturday Night Live* house band. The song itself would have fit nicely on *Tapestry*. Had this been a *Tapestry* track, however, the organ probably would have been more muted, and the piano would have been more thoroughly integrated into the texture rather than being relegated to one of the stereo channels. In fact, one of the most noticeable differences between John Fischbach's production and Gerry Goffin's mix on *Writer* and Lou Adler's work on *Tapestry* is the extent to which *Tapestry* highlights King's (usually nicely multitracked) piano playing compared to the extent to which the instrument is deemphasized on *Writer*. Melodically and harmonically, King's composition is perfectly in keeping with the black gospel style, showing the extent to which she had thoroughly integrated the style into her compositional vocabulary.

Writer's third track, "Child of Mine," also could have easily been included on King's breakthrough album. This is the most personal, autobiographical song on *Writer*. Gerry Goffin's lyrics tell the couple's child—presumably one of the Goffin-King daughters—just how glad the singer is that the young person is "a child of mine." This, despite any differences in direction or outlook that parent and child might have. King's musical setting features a melody with a narrow range and a simple rise and fall, which is entirely appropriate for a tender love song from parent to maturing child. In its simplicity and autobiographical feel, it clearly is a product of the singer-songwriter era and, as such, anticipates King's work on *Tapestry* and on *Rhymes & Reasons*, which would prove to be King's most cohesive introspective singer-songwriter-style album.

Goffin and King's "Goin' Back" is another track that anticipates some of the lyrical and musical style of *Tapestry*. Goffin's lyrics find King singing about her desire to return to the roots of her childhood. The texture is entirely in keeping with music of the singer-songwriter movement of the early 1970s. This sound is enhanced especially by the obvious presence of James Taylor on backing vocals and guitar. For some reason, producer Fischbach and mixer Goffin treat Taylor's backing vocals to significantly more reverberation than King's lead vocals. Unfortunately, this creates the effect that Taylor is somehow caught "off microphone." It is not a particularly polished-sounding approach to production and, as such, is another one of the characteristics of *Writer* that would not carry through (fortunately) to the Lou Adler-produced *Tapestry*. In its guitar-focused arrangement, "Goin' Back" might sound like an archetypal song of the 1970s singer-songwriter style, but because King's playing is deemphasized, the track loses some of the sense of intimacy that might have been more appropriate. One of the things that came to define the mature singer-songwriter style of the time was the singer-songwriter, who is clearly heard on his or her instrument. All of the introspective songs of this type that would appear on *Tapestry, Music,* and *Rhymes & Reasons* would make significantly heavier use of King's piano.

One of the more curious stylistic mixed signals of *Writer* can be found in the instrumentation of "To Love." Somehow, mixing electronic-sounding harpsichord with country guitar picking sounds like a mistake. The synthesized harpsichord of "Child of Mine" sounded a little out of place (mostly because of its "fake" quality), but only a little compared with the sound of the instrument in what is essentially a country song. Although the liner notes credit King with the arrangements, one can only hope that this strange-sounding instrumentation was put in place because of the presence of synthesist John Fischbach. The song also suffers from being so stylistically different from the rest of the album. This diversity/stylistic disconnection tends to call into question the authenticity of the country-rock style voice King adopts in the song. It is a song better suited as an album track by a singer more closely associated with the country-rock style.

"What Have You Got to Lose" includes lyrics from Toni Stern that find the singer's character encouraging someone with whom she is in love, but who is reticent to become involved again after a recent failure in love. King's music of encouragement is upbeat with chords and arrangement that vaguely call to mind some of the popular light jazz of the 1970s on the Creed Taylor International (CTI) record label—specifically music by Bob James, Hubert Laws, George Benson, among others.

Although "Eventually" is not necessarily one of Carole King's best-known compositions, it is important to note that this song was singled out in *Stereo Review*'s review of *Writer* as being structured like "a mini concerto."[10] Although there really is nothing about "Eventually" that technically resembles the form or structure of a concerto (usually a three-movement piece that features a solo instrument accompanied by an orchestra), there is a hint at classical music that can be found in King's string arrangement. What the piece really comes closer to is an anthem for positive social and environmental change. King's music is quite simple, both melodically and harmonically, which is entirely appropriate for a song in which the focus is clearly supposed to be on the lyrics. She accomplishes some nice text painting by placing the melody low in her vocal range. This highlights the sense of resignation that the singer's character feels as she notes that the problems around her are not being solved as quickly as she might like. It is, however, a song of hope; given some effort, all of these challenges will be met "eventually." King's melody has a memorable hook, especially the figure to which she sets the word "eventually." With its social consciousness and musical strengths, it certainly is one of the great "sleepers" of Goffin and King's songwriting partnership.

King and Toni Stern's "Raspberry Jam" is mostly a band jam. The emphasis clearly is not on Stern's lyrics, which use raspberry jam spread on toast at each morning's breakfast as a metaphor for starting life and relationships anew. This is the kind of jazzy piece that might have made for a nice album track for a 1967–1968-era band. Because one of Carole King's main strengths as a vocalist is in communicating messages that sound as if they come straight from the heart, this is not the best song to highlight her talents. And her instrumental talents are not highlighted on the song, which focuses more on the virtuosity of Danny Kootch and organist Ralph Schuckett.

Goffin and King's "Can't You Be Real" sounds as if it could have come from a couple of years before *Writer*. The rock harmonic progression of the song that features primarily the use of the tonic chord (I, or G major), major subtonic chord (VII, or F major), and subdominant (IV, or C major in the case of this song) is nearly a prototypical progression for a whole host of rock writers in the 1967–1969 period. Adding to the effect of being a song more of the previous part of the rock era are Gerry Goffin's lyrics, which are focused on the person being addressed in the song, rather than the introspective me-based lyrics of the burgeoning singer-songwriter movement.

"I Can't Hear You No More," with its blues-based and gospel-based melodic turns, and with its Philadelphia soul-influenced arrangement, would have made a nice album track for a soul singer like Aretha Franklin. The song had, in fact, been around for years, having been recorded in 1964 by R&B singer Betty Everett. Everett's recording had made some impact on both the R&B and pop charts. The song was successful enough as an R&B/soul piece that over the years a number of singers had covered it, including Dusty Springfield, Helen Reddy, Lulu, and Russ Ballard. It works well enough for King, but the style of the song and the arrangement are such that it doesn't have the impact of some of King's later compositions that were designed around her physical and rhetorical voice.

The next track on *Writer*, "Sweet Sweetheart," was also recorded by Bobby Vee in 1970. With its mix of gospel and country-rock styles, it doesn't so much resemble a Bobby Vee song or a Carole King song as much as it sounds like a late 1960s recording by the Band. There is a little bit of "Up on Cripple Creek," "The Weight," and "The Night They Drove Old Dixie Down" all mixed in the song and King's arrangement. Like so many of the tracks on *Writer*, it is a good song, but not one that really clearly defines Carole King as a performer.

The last track, "Up on the Roof," finds King doing what she did particularly effectively on the City's *Now That Everything's Been Said* and on her first several official solo albums: updating old Goffin-King songs that had been hits for various other performers. King's string arrangement here sounds somewhat schmaltzy in the context of the overall sound of *Writer*, but it actually wears better than other recordings of the song. If *Writer* is to be viewed as a representative work of the emerging singer-songwriter style of the period, then King's choice of "Up on the Roof" as the well-known, Goffin and King golden oldie for the album was inspired. Goffin's lyrics are personal, and King's arrangement—strings aside—is sparse enough and relaxed enough to allow her character's voice to bring out the moods of the piece.

In *Writer* Carole King explores eclectic musical styles, almost as though she is still trying to find her voice as a performer. As the album does not include any of King's own lyrics, it is somewhat less personal than her next albums would be. *Writer* does, however, find King moving ever closer to her mature work as a writer for Carole King, the performer. Despite the fits and starts that her career had seen through 1970, she would burst forth on the music scene with a vengeance the next year, when *Tapestry* and the singles it spawned ruled the record sales charts and the top-40 radio airwaves.

Tapestry

The City's *Now That Everything's Been Said* and King's solo album *Writer* featured her as a writer, arranger, and performer for the first time since her early 1960s singles, but they failed to bring Carole King the performer into anything approaching the prominence she enjoyed in the music industry as a composer. The 1971 album *Tapestry* turned Carole King into perhaps pop music's most curious overnight sensation. She was already one of the most prominent figures in American pop music (a musician's musician), the public did not recognize her earlier attempts to develop a career as a performer, and now she was literally at the top of the charts. Adding to the irony, she was working largely with the same writing collaborators, performers, and production team that had joined her for the commercial failures *Now That Everything's Been Said* and *Writer*. All this begs the question, "Why *Tapestry?*"

THE SONGS OF *TAPESTRY*

Tapestry opens with "I Feel the Earth Move," a song for which King wrote both words and music. From the opening piano introduction, it is clear that *Tapestry* is completely different from any previous Carole King recording. The introduction makes it clear that this album is focused entirely on King as a singer, pianist, composer, and (to a somewhat lesser extent) lyricist. "I Feel the Earth Move" may be one of the best examples of the perfect combination of King lyrics and music. Unlike anything she had written up to this point, save for a few, immature late-1950s songs, she had complete control over all aspects of the finished song. She makes the most of this opportunity. In one of the most obvious examples of text painting in any song King has ever written, she sets the line in which she describes the downward tumbling of the sky to a melody with a syncopated rhythm. This rhythm displaced the accent that would normally occur on the beginning of the word "tumbling," which creates the musical equivalent of a tumble.

The strengths of "I Feel the Earth Move," however, go much further than the specific musical setting of specific words. The entire up-tempo feel of the piece matches the rush that King describes feeling from the very presence of her lover. There is a suggestion in the lyrics of a strong sexual desire. Part of the strength of the lyrics, though, is that she suggests the intensity of this sexual tension without being explicit—she forces the listener to read between the lines. King enhances this feeling of sexual tension with the raw expressiveness of her throaty delivery.

The other attribute of "I Feel the Earth Move" that is central to the success of the song is King's piano playing and the way in which record producer Lou Adler treats the piano in the mix. The instrument is multitracked and placed up front. Perhaps even more important, King plays an extended (for a pop song) solo and then trades a couple of licks with electric guitarist Danny Kortchmar. Completely absent are the overused James Taylor-style, singer-songwriter cliché guitar licks of *Writer*. We know instantly that this is a recording by a *piano-playing* singer-songwriter.

Tapestry's second track, "So Far Away," again features both the music and lyrics of King. The lyrics, which can be interpreted as the autobiographical longing of a musician on the road for a lover left back home, sound personal. This personal connection to King is enhanced by the sparseness of the texture, which is dominated by her voice and piano. Russ Kunkel's drums, Charles Larkey's electric bass, James Taylor's acoustic guitar, and Curtis Amy's flute solo at the end of the song are all subservient to King's vocal and instrumental work.

"It's Too Late," a collaboration between King and Toni Stern, was one of the big hits from *Tapestry*. It is a song about the end of a relationship, with the acknowledgment that while both partners were at one time very much in love, they grew apart, with neither party to blame. The texture is closer to that of *Writer* than any of the previous tracks on *Tapestry*, with the solos played by Danny Kootch on electric guitar and Curtis Amy on soprano saxophone. King's piano is merged into the overall texture of the band. Unlike some of the songs on *Writer* that suffered from the feeling of a lack of personal connection, in part because of the emphasis on King's co-performers, such is not the case here. The intensely personal nature of the lyrics are balanced by the expressive instrumental work of King, Kortchmar, and Amy.

"It's Too Late" makes for valuable study in terms of how the song serves as a model for a number of later 1970s compositions by King. This can be seen especially clearly in the melody. In both the verses and the chorus, King uses short rhythmic motives to build her longer range, phrase-length melodies. The organic nature of the way in which she combines, modifies, and expands the short, syncopated motives transcends such obvious techniques as simple motivic melodic sequence, a technique in which the same short melodic fragment occurs several times in a row starting on successively higher or lower pitch levels.

King also uses another melodic technique in "It's Too Late" that is found in her later songs, for example, "Being at War with Each Other" from *Fantasy.* In the chorus of "It's Too Late," she establishes a pitch as the highest melodic limit through repetition and the use of relatively long durations on some of the melodic notes. After establishing this important high pitch, her melody descends back toward the tonic, the first scale step of the key. Here, in "It's Too Late," the use of a clear upper and lower boundary note helps to make the melody easy to remember. This is probably partially why the song became such a huge commercial success.

Another important melodic pitch consideration of "It's Too Late" occurs at the song's conclusion. In tonal music (music that is in a discernible key) in general, and in American pop songs in particular, melodies end on the tonic pitch (scale-step No. 1) most of the time. At the end of "It's Too Late," however, King emphasizes scale-step No. 3. This note is part of the conclusive-sounding tonic chord, but leaves the melody with a somewhat unresolved feeling at the end of the vocal melody. This helps to define King's character's true feelings about the end of her relationship. In Toni Stern's lyrics, the character simply acknowledges the end of the relationship, despite the couple's attempts to keep the flames alive. King's slightly inconclusive melodic cadence suggests that the character has not truly reached a sense of closure—there is still a sense of hurt that needs to be cured.

"Beautiful," yet another song for which Carole King supplied both words and music, is one of the great sleeper tracks of *Tapestry.* King's lyrics speak of the need for high self-esteem, self-love, and a positive outlook on life. She defines beauty not in terms of physical beauty but in terms of feeling—one is as "beautiful as [one] feels." King delivers her message of inner beauty without sounding preachy (either on paper or in the context of the song). She is at her best in "Beautiful" as a composer who uses the musical setting to enhance the mood of the lyrics, which is especially important here, because she is setting her own lyrics. In the verses, in which she describes the disen-chanted people she sees around her, she sets the text to a melody that is rela-tively low in her vocal range. The rhythm is straightforward, emphasizing the beats. In contrast, the chorus, in which the lyrics provide King's recipe for success—high self-esteem and optimism—features a higher pitched melodic line that includes a great deal of rhythmic syncopation. The instrumental background features King playing acoustic piano, electric piano, and synthe-sizer, along with Joel O'Brien's drums, Charles Larkey's electric bass, and Danny Kortchmar's conga drum. The presence of the synthesizer, although well in the background of the texture, is the one part of the instrumentation that does not wear particularly well because the timbre (tone color) of the instrument sounds so, well, synthetic (unlike later synthesizers, which would increasingly match the "realness" of acoustic instruments).

The importance of "Beautiful," however, goes well beyond King's musical text setting or the intricacies of the song's instrumentation. The real importance is in the overall message of inner beauty and the sensitive way in which King delivers it. The message fits in perfectly with the spirit of feminism of the day. Unlike some of these songs that preached, however, King's "Beautiful," with its soft-sell approach, has enjoyed a much longer shelf life. It is as relevant and contemporary today as it was in 1971.

The black gospel style of King's "Way Over Yonder" resembles the earlier Goffin–King song "No Easy Way Down," from *Writer.* The present song, however, is even closer in style and texture to what would be heard in the theme music of NBC's *Saturday Night Live* starting in the mid-1970s. King's lyrics describe a place, "way over yonder," where the sweet life will be found. Her references are vague enough to refer either to the afterlife or an earthly location. The song's style, however, suggests the music of the African American church, which is enhanced by the obligato vocal improvisations of Merry Clayton, so the possible sacred meaning of the text comes through most strongly. The lyrical ambiguity—King never actually mentions heaven, or any specific location—is in keeping with the nineteenth-century African American spiritual tradition, in which some of the lyrics could be understood on several levels. The lyrics here are general enough that "Way Over Yonder" does not seem as immediately personal as most of *Tapestry.* If one considers this to be a statement of religious belief of either King or a character she is portraying as a singer, however, it fits within *Tapestry*'s overall theme of definition of self through one's life experiences. It just does not fit the album's gestalt as easily as the overtly autobiographical-sounding songs. Musically, it sounds like a fit for King, but the lyrics seem more appropriate for another singer.

Ironically, one of the *Tapestry* tracks that was not heard as frequently in 1971 as it is in the early twenty-first century is perhaps Carole King's best-known song: "You've Got a Friend." In 1971, the radio airwaves were filled with James Taylor's Grammy Award-winning recording of the song. King's version is fuller in texture—the Taylor single incorporated two acoustic guitars, bass, drums, percussion, and Taylor and Joni Mitchell on backing vocals—with its string quartet and King's multitracked piano (along with guest artist James Taylor on acoustic guitar), bass, and percussion. Perhaps one of the main reasons that King's recording has survived better than Taylor's rendition is that King's is also slower and more reverent. In fact, although it is not nearly as fully orchestrated, it takes on the anthem-like qualities of Paul Simon's "Bridge Over Troubled Water," the Grammy Award-winning "Song of the Year" of 1970. King's lyrics for "You've Got a Friend" also resemble the platonic-style, sisterly and brotherly love theme of the Paul Simon opus of the previous year, although her lyrics are more direct than those of the man with whom she used to cut demo records when the two were in high school.

The presence of James Taylor on acoustic guitar on "You've Got a Friend," along with several other *Tapestry* tracks, is worth noting, especially in light of comments I have made about some of the clichés of the early 1970s singer-songwriter style associated with him. On *Tapestry*, Taylor fits into King's piano-defined musical textures as an accompanying guitarist. This is especially noticeable when one compares the textures of *Writer* and *Tapestry*. On the earlier album, the acoustic guitars played by Taylor and Kortchmar figure more prominently in the mix, and the two guitarists play more intricate fill figures. On *Tapestry*, Carole King's piano seems to be calling the shots.

At first glance, the Toni Stern-Carole King song "Where You Lead" might not seem to be an appropriate fit for an album that took on major significance in the women's movement. It is all too tempting to hear Stern's lyrics as a reinforcement of the stereotype of the woman who puts career aspirations on hold to become a wife. To hear the lyrics that way, however, would be to ignore the strong feminist subtext. Yes, the singer's character ultimately tells her man that "she will follow where [he] leads." She makes it clear in the verses and the middle eight section of the song, though, that she is doing this of her own free will. She also reinforces the fact that she has made this decision/declaration not because of an adherence to social and sexual mores of a time before the swinging 1960s, but because of the life-changing impact this new relationship has had. In the past she could not "get satisfaction from just one man," suggesting that sexually, at least, she was not adhering to the virginal social-sexual mores of the past. In short, King's character has made an informed and empowered decision. "Where You Lead" is a rich song musically, too. The melody is memorable, especially the chorus hook, and the rhythm contains an abundance of syncopation.

If an album can have two sleeper songs—and who is to say that it cannot—then the final track on *Tapestry*, "(You Make Me Feel Like) A Natural Woman," certainly qualifies. With vocal contributions by King alone (she is multitracked on the backing vocals) and instrumental contributions solely by Charles Larkey (acoustic bass) and King (multitracked pianos), the *Tapestry* version of "(You Make Me Feel Like) A Natural Woman" is considerably more intimate in texture than the famous Aretha Franklin recording of 1967. Listening to these two versions side by side is a valuable lesson in the type of intimacy that was at the heart of the singer-songwriter style in the early 1970s. King's arrangement makes the song, which is personal sounding enough on paper, even more personal. Of all of King's late 1960s "oldies," this song was the perfect choice for resurrection on *Tapestry*: the intimate setting of a song that celebrates with near-religious expression romantic love and sexuality fit into the tenets of freedom of sexual expression that were part of the women's movement. In addition, the gospel style of the song allows King to show off one of her particular stylistic strengths as a pianist.

As is the case with "(You Make Me Feel Like) A Natural Woman," "Will You Love Me Tomorrow?" is an ideal Goffin and King golden oldie for King to cover on this, her breakthrough album. For one thing, "Will You Love Me Tomorrow?" was Goffin and King's first big hit song in the beginning of the 1960s. For another, the song's lyrical theme of a woman contemplating the emotional impact of a first sexual experience within a growing relationship—with its subtext that raises the possibility that her lover might just be after sex and not lasting love—further contributes to *Tapestry*'s overarching theme of presenting a wide range of very real experiences and feelings of women.

Goffin and King's "Smackwater Jack" is the one *Tapestry* song that does not seem to fit the album's overall theme of personal, emotion-based songs. Still, it does not seem entirely out of place. The song, with the dark humor of Goffin's improbable tale of the fictional old West outlaw Smackwater Jack, Big Jim the Chief, and the ever-busy undertaker, and its rollicking shuffle-feel music, feels like the perfect vehicle for King and her fellow players and singers to jam in the studio. This is significant, for it places King, the all-around musician, in a position in the recording studio where few women had been. Although King's piano is not a featured instrumental voice on "Smackwater Jack"—Danny Kortchmar's electric guitar and Ralph Schuckett's electric piano are more prominent—there is not the sense of disappointment that comes from her piano being relegated to an accompanying role throughout *Writer*, because it is the only song on *Tapestry* in which her playing merges into the texture. More than anything else, however, "Smackwater Jack" adds some levity to what is otherwise a fairly emotional album.

Carole King has always been deeply personal figure. Her life is her own; she rarely speaks out in public forums and is rarely interviewed. Because she is so quiet about her work, and because the lyrics of the song are so open to interpretation, it is difficult to determine to what extent "Tapestry" (the song) is autobiographical. It could speak of men from her life, or it could be the poet's creation of fictional men who have been part of the experience of a fictional woman. In any case, the overall metaphor of the song, that everything that one experiences in life and in love becomes part of an elaborate, interwoven tapestry, really sums up the entire album. King sets the text to simple music, melodically and harmonically; and her arrangement includes only piano and electric keyboards (all played by King), which allows the listener to focus squarely on the words themselves.

The other critical feature of the song "Tapestry" is the extent to which it ties the entire album together as a coherent package. *Tapestry* (the album) is largely a collection of individual songs, certainly more than it is a conceived-from-start-to-finish concept album. Part of the reason that *Tapestry* was so incredibly successful after the false starts of *Now That Everything's Been Said* and *Writer* lies in the songs, and part of the reason lies in the clarity of the arrangements and record production. I am convinced, however, that part of the reason for the fully whole feeling of the album comes from the way King is able to tie together the individual songs through the title track. "Tapestry" introduces the idea that life—and, by extension, an album—can be viewed as a whole constructed by means of a series of what may at first appear to be unrelated, individual threads.

Tapestry concludes with Gerry Goffin, Jerry Wexler, and Carole King's "(You Make Me Feel Like) A Natural Woman," a well-known hit for soul singer Aretha Franklin in 1967. Like "Where You Lead," "A Natural Woman" might at first seem to be an unusual song for an album that became one of the great feminist statements of the 1970s, that is, if one is drawn only to the part of the lyrics that suggest that King's character will feel completely fulfilled by simply making her mate happy. As is the case with "Where You Lead," however, there is a sense that the character singing the song is making her decision with a feeling of empowerment. And the sense that the song celebrates—but never luridly—the main character as a sexual being who is fully in control of her own sexuality fits entirely within the spirit of sexual freedom and empowerment of the times.

THE SOCIAL IMPACT OF *TAPESTRY*

Not only was *Tapestry* tremendously successful commercially and critically, it also was an important recording sociologically. It appeared just at the time that the women's movement was kicking into full gear, and it fit in perfectly with the mood and spirit of that sociological phenomenon. A number of overtly feminist songs hit the radio airwaves in early 1970, including Helen Reddy's "I Am Woman." For the most part, though, the songs of *Tapestry* and the album as a whole continue to live on while other songs and albums that are more preachy or more militant have faded from public consciousness. The impact of *Tapestry* and its continued popularity can be attributed to a complex relationship of factors, including the album's songs, its musical arrangements, and its packaging. Before examining these features and their relationships to the women's movement, it would be helpful to review the movement itself to put *Tapestry* into historical context.

The roots of the women's movement of the 1970s can be traced back years and even generations to the movement for women's suffrage and back even further in history. The more immediate roots go back to a move toward female empowerment during the Kennedy Administration at the start of the 1960s and the publication of books such as Betty Friedan's *The Feminine Mystique*.[1] The movement was in full swing in 1967 and 1968, at which time "consciousness-raising" meetings were held in various urban centers around the United States and the Miss America Pageant was picketed. Several influential books published between 1970 and 1972 dealt with women's sexual freedom and the politics of sex, including Shulamith Firestone's *The Dialectic of Sex: The Case for Feminist Revolution*[2] and The Boston Women's Health Book Collective's *Our Bodies, Ourselves: A Book by and for Women*.[3]

By the mid-1970s, these would be joined by other books, including Susan Brownmiller's *Against Our Will: Men, Women, and Rape*,[4] and several magazines that were actively marketed to liberated women, including *Ms.* and *Essence*. For more details on the coalescence of several forces in the 1960s into an active women's movement by the early 1970s, the reader may wish to read Debra Michals's article "From 'Consciousness Expansion' to 'Consciousness Raising': Feminism and the Countercultural Politics of the Self."[5]

In the world of American pop music, the feminism of the times was largely limited to the music and life of Janis Joplin, who had lived a public life of sexual and drug-taking freedom, but had died of a heroin overdose in 1970. In 1971, however, Helen Reddy and Ray Burton's composition "I Am Woman" appeared on Reddy's debut album, *I Don't Know How to Love Him*. The more familiar single version of the song was released in 1972 and was found on Reddy's second album, *I Am Woman*. In addition, singer/guitarist Bonnie Raitt began making noise in the music world in 1971, a rare woman playing blues guitar. John Lennon and Yoko Ono recorded several radical left-wing political songs in 1971 and 1972 that supported the women's movement, including "Power to the People," which took to task men of the counterculture left who continued to treat women as something less than equals, and the unfortunately titled "Woman Is the Nigger of the World." The latter Lennon-Ono song is found on the couple's 1972 album *Sometime in New York City*, as was Ono's pro-feminism song "Sisters, O Sisters." A couple of years later Holly Near, Meg Christian, and Cris Williamson recorded significant albums that combined feminism with a pro-lesbian stance.

Tapestry was released just as the women's movement was emerging in popular literature and popular music. Unlike the work of Reddy, Lennon and Ono, and some of the slightly later work of Near, Christian, and Williamson, however, the songs of *Tapestry* do not sound as much like political manifestoes as pure, personal expressions that reflect (for the most part) the basic tenants of the women's movement.

Some of the tenants reflected in *Tapestry* are the need for self-respect and self-esteem, equality with men, the need to be empowered so as to make one's own decisions, and the freedom to be a sexual being. As discussed earlier in this chapter, these tenants can be found in "Beautiful," "Where You Lead," "(You Make Me Feel Like) A Natural Woman," and "I Feel the Earth Move." Other *Tapestry* songs do not so much reflect these basic tenants as portray the kinds of emotions and desires women (and in some cases men) feel in real life. Specifically, "So Far Away," and "Home Again" express the need for roots and the desire to be back with one's mate; "It's Too Late" deals with the very real situation in which a relationship ends without acrimony, but, rather just because the couple falls out of what they thought was a lasting love; "You've Got a Friend" expresses a universal, sisterly/brotherly, agape-type love of one human being for another, regardless of gender; and "Will You Love Me Tomorrow?" ponders the emotional aftermath of a first sexual encounter within a growing relationship. Incidentally, in "So Far Away" King's character is out on the road, working, and wanting to be back home so that she can welcome her lover to her home. In short, her character is the one with a job, and the one who is fully empowered. The album, with its introspective focus on what real-life women experience and feel is beautifully drawn together with the song "Tapestry," which although somewhat impressionistic in its lyrics, could be interpreted as a metaphorical autobiography of Carole King. That leaves the listener with one song, "Smackwater Jack," that is not reflective of female empowerment or the range of emotions and experiences that a real woman of the early 1970s might have.

The musical arrangements, with just a couple of exceptions, feature King's acoustic and electric piano playing. This is important because it emphasizes King's three-pronged work: as a singer, songwriter, and instrumentalist. This last piece of the puzzle may be the most important piece in securing *Tapestry*'s place as a work of the women's movement. Certainly, it was not unheard of for women to be active as instrumentalists in the American pop music of the rock era. Those who were, however, were usually the anonymous studio musicians whose performances were heard all around the world on recordings, but who were largely unrecognized. For example, Carol Kaye was a first-call bass guitarist as a studio musician in the 1960s and played bass and electric guitar on hundreds of recordings by the Beach Boys, the Monkees, the Righteous Brothers, Ray Charles, Paul Revere and the Raiders, and numerous others, although she was never an official member of any band.[6] And there were performers who came out of the folk revival tradition, such as guitarist-singer Joan Baez and pianist-singer Judy Collins. For the most part, however, the instrumental work of the folk revival performers was subservient to their vocal work. On *Tapestry*, Carole King's piano is usually not only the most distinctive accompanying instrument, but she also plays solo breaks on a number of songs. Critics quickly recognized the importance of King's piano being front and center in the arrangements and of her distinctive, gospel-influenced style. Robert Christgau, for example, wrote that King's piano playing on *Tapestry* was "the first widely recognized instrumental signature ever developed by a woman."[7]

All of this was packaged in such a way as to make it *look* as though *Tapestry*, even before one played the record on the phonograph, was a highly personal album by a woman who was entirely comfortable with who she was. The photograph on the front of Tapestry shows a barefoot Carole King sitting on a wooden window seat stitching the tapestry (which is shown in more detail on the inside of the gatefold album cover). Her somewhat surprised-looking cat is in the foreground giving the photography even more of a homey feel. The room in which King is sitting is dark; light comes in through the window she is sitting next to. Once the listener actually experiences the music on the album, this photograph suggests the songwriter sitting at her window on the world, taking it all in, and writing songs that reflect what she sees in her own life and in the lives of those around her. The hazy photos on the inside of the cover show all of the album's principal singers and instrumentalists, with an emphasis on King herself, and the back cover presents all of the lyrics to the songs. This last feature is also worth noting: it probably is no accident that the first album on which King wrote the lyrics to the majority of the songs (7 of the 12 songs were written by King alone) is the first King album to include printed lyrics. This places added emphasis on the words—those stories of real women's emotions and experiences.

Tapestry had a tremendous commercial and sociological impact on American culture, and the album has been continuously available since its release in 1971. King's peers in the National Academy of Recording Arts and Sciences recognized the importance of the album and its songs. The Academy presented King with the following 1971 Grammy Awards: Record of the Year ("It's Too Late"); Album of the Year (*Tapestry*); Song of the Year ("You've Got a Friend"); and Best Female Vocal Performance (*Tapestry*). In addition, James Taylor's recording of "You've Got a Friend" earned him a Grammy for Best Male Vocal Performance, making the most widely recognized Grammy categories a sweep for Carole King as a composer. In the late 1970s and early 1980s, when a few classic albums of the late 1960s and early 1970s were issued in half-speed mastered, audiophile pressings,[8] *Tapestry* was included (Ode HE 44946, 1980). *Tapestry* was also reissued on compact disc fairly early in the CD era (Ode EK 34946, 1986).

As the 25th anniversary of the release of *Tapestry* approached, tribute albums appeared such as *Tapestry Revisited,* which included performances by the Bee Gees, Celine Dion, Amy Grant, Blessid Union of Souls, Rod Stewart, and other notables (Lava Records 92604-4, 1995), *A Tribute to Carole King* by the Overtures (Master Tone 8026, 1997), and *Tapestry* by saxophonist Bob Belden (Blue Note 57891, 1997). *Tapestry* was also mentioned in the 1990s as one of the albums that had changed people's lives at the time of its original release.[9] And anecdotally, when I presented a National Women's History Month Convocation lecture on the importance of Carole King as a major American composer of the rock era after completing my reference book on her in 1999,[10] I was approached by several of my female Mount Union College faculty colleagues who identified *Tapestry* as one of, if not *the,* most important recordings of their lives. These were women who were college age at the time of *Tapestry*'s release. And the same thing happened after a lecture I presented on *Tapestry* itself at a March 2006 National Women's History Month Convocation at the College. Given the millions of copies of *Tapestry* that have been purchased over the past 35 years and the anecdotal evidence I have seen, its influence clearly continues.

The Established Singer-Songwriter: 1971–1974

With the intensity of the success and societal impact of *Tapestry*, Carole King must have been under tremendous pressure when it came time for a follow-up album. The real problem that confronted her was that there could only be one *Tapestry*. This would not have been as much of a problem had *Tapestry* been the product of a long-established star. Although Carole King may have been a star songwriter—one of the brightest songwriting stars of the 1960s—*Tapestry* was her first commercially successful album. Given her gifts as a songwriter and the esteem in which she was already held, King fortunately did not live in a state of perpetual "how can I top this." She quickly got back on the proverbial horse and returned to what she had been doing professionally for a dozen years; she made music. During her first recordings of this period, King stuck fairly close to the *Tapestry* style, but by the end of the period, she was making stylistic changes and moving more in the direction of using her music and her celebrity to address social issues head on. Increasingly, King redefined herself in terms of musical style, especially in her arrangements, and lyrical focus as she moved from album to album. This made for an interesting collection of pop music styles, but it meant that she showed less logical progression from album to album than many artists of the 1970s. This would end up confounding music critics.

MUSIC

Given the tremendous commercial, critical, and sociological impact of *Tapestry*, especially after several years of indifferent public response to her attempts to launch a performing career, one can only imagine the pressure that must have dogged Carole King when she planned a follow-up album. Certainly, King's 1971 album *Music* bears some musical and lyrical resemblance to *Tapestry*. Notably, however, in several of the songs she painted a future direction that was not necessarily bound up in the Brill Building or in the success of *Tapestry*. In that respect—simultaneously reflecting one of the most important albums of the rock era while telling her audience in no uncertain terms that she would not rest on the laurels of *Tapestry*—*Music* is an admirable follow-up album. It might not contain the number of popular radio hits found on its predecessor, but it remains among the best handful of albums that King has produced in her long career. One of its strengths is that it does not rely as heavily on songs originally intended for other artists as *Tapestry* had done; these are nearly all Carole King songs meant for Carole King, performer. A few of the new songs feel as though they might have been composed in a bit of a hurry and without as much concern with how they might fit together on an album, but they are very workable. King's arrangements are strong and innovative; Lou Adler's production is crystal clear and entirely appropriate for the material and performers; and King and her fellow singers and instrumentalists perform beautifully, especially bassist (and King's second husband) Charles Larkey, perhaps the unsung instrumental hero of the album. Throughout the album, however, there is a sense that somehow the intimacy of *Tapestry* is missing—a sense that at the height of the introspective singer-songwriter era, King was moving toward a more generic pop sound. This is especially noticeable in the album's arrangements, which include a fuller instrumentation than that heard on the intimate *Tapestry*.

Although some of the Goffin–King collaborations of the 1960s displayed a sense of social consciousness, albeit on a muted level compared with folk/protest and some rock songwriters of the era, for the most part King had not addressed social or political issues in her career as a performer before *Music*. The album's opening track, "Brother, Brother," however, can be understood as a statement of support for the black power movement. She sings of how she has seen her "brother" "layin' back" and "hangin' on" for such a long time. She then assures him that he should take action to improve his life. King's lyrics are just vague enough that the "brother" to whom she sings could be a sibling. What really paints "Brother, Brother" as a message song related to the struggle for empowerment for African Americans is King's music and arrangement. King's music fits the easy-going soul style of her early 1970s contemporaries, such as Marvin Gaye and Curtis Mayfield. In particular, this can be heard in the short, syncopated melodic phrases. The arrangement includes congas, gospel-influenced backing vocals—with all the parts sung by King herself—and King playing both electric and acoustic pianos. The backing vocal style, congas, and electric piano timbre, in particular, paint this as a Gaye/Mayfield-inspired song, sort of like "What's Going On" meets "We Got to Have Peace." In addition to "Brother, Brother," King's growing social consciousness can be seen in the album's liner notes, where she writes, "Use the power—Register and vote."[1] It should be noted that King actively campaigned for George McGovern in his bid for the White House in 1972.

Tapestry had boasted several songs that were hit singles and album tracks that received significant radio airplay; *Music* had two: the King–Toni Stern collaborations "It's Going to Take Some Time" and "Sweet Seasons," the second and third tracks on the album. This placement is worth noting because *Tapestry* also had been heavily weighted in the hit song department at its opening. "It's Going to Take Some Time" is a song about recovering from a broken relationship. Stern's arch-shaped text begins and ends each verse with the song's title line. The middle part of each verse, a section that is far longer than the "book ends," describes the singer's recovery. The lyrics, then, deal with the now ("It's going to take some time this time.") and with the future. Carole King's music reflects this, with the bulk of the melodic material being filled with syncopations. The tune at the end of each verse, however, smoothes out to long, unsyncopated rhythms that move into the lower range of King's voice. The effect of this melodic setting is that after a build up of hope for the future, the reality of the now (the resignation, the sadness, and so forth) sets in. It is a sophisticated combination of words and music and is haunting in the way in which the singer's character snaps back to the now after going into so much detail about how she'll recover from her loss.

One indication of the "hip-ness" of *Music,* to coin a phrase, is the entire arrangement and sonic impact of "Sweet Seasons." This recording may not have caught the kind of attention of exactly the same audience that would be attracted to the hip jazzy coolness of Walter Becker and Donald Fagen's band, Steely Dan, but "Sweet Seasons" in some very discernible musical and production ways clearly anticipates the sound of Becker and Fagen's work of 1972 onward. As a sudden, somewhat reluctant singer-songwriter pop star, Carole King was not exactly the epitome of "hip," image wise. Musically she had some ideas at the time that might not have seemed to be cutting edge; it is only in retrospect that they can be fully seen in this light. In fact, if one does a "fast forward" to 1979 and listens to Rickie Lee Jones's horn arrangement on her big hit single "Chuck E.'s in Love," one can detect the texture of King's arrangement on "Sweet Seasons." The downside of the song is that Stern's lyrics do not have the kind of personal, autobiographical sound of her lyrics on *Tapestry;* this is even truer of King's *Tapestry* lyrics. Add to this the fact that King's music for the song is so top-40, pop oriented, and one is left with the feeling that, compared with the deeply personal sound of so many of the songs of *Tapestry,* "Sweet Seasons" is closer to conventional pop music than even the big hits from *Tapestry.* There is, however, one particularly interesting personal, autobiographical line in the song that deserves mention. Near the end of the song, King sings about having some kids, making some plans, and building "a life in the open, a life in the country." Although

Toni Stern was King's co-writer on "Sweet Seasons," this stanza of the song would seem to refer to King's daughters Sherry and Louise, King's split from Gerry Goffin and her subsequent move to California, and her eventual move to Idaho. In this respect, the song presents a stronger image of female independence than songs such as *Tapestry*'s "Where You Lead." In that song, King's character was perfectly willing to give up her own plans for the future for the sake of her mate; here she clearly is willing to make a break with the past and start over. When all is said and done, though, the most important feature of "Sweet Seasons" is that it was an ideal AM radio, top-40 pop song, a major hit song that stands up about as well as any of Carole King's hit compositions.

Although *Music* goes a long way toward Carole King writing songs for Carole King the performer, given that the album contains the highest concentration of brand new songs of any King album up to that time, she does turn her attention to the classic Goffin–King songbook for a "cover" of "Some Kind of Wonderful." This track is somewhat less successful than the classic Goffin–King songs that she recorded on *Tapestry*. For one thing, some of the intimacy that is felt on the earlier album is missing from "Some Kind of Wonderful." The instrumental textures are in keeping with, say, her recording of "Will You Love Me Tomorrow," but the intricacy of King's background vocal arrangement here tends to work against the beautiful simplicity of Goffin's text and King's melody and harmony.

King provided both the words and music for "Surely." This is a tender love song, a good album track, but one with poetry that is general enough so that it is more of a standard pop song than a product of the introspective singer-songwriter movement. Perhaps it is unfair to judge King's non-*Tapestry* songs of the 1970–1972 period against the music of this new movement. For one thing, Carole King was and generally always has been more of a songwriter who performs her own songs, as opposed to a fully integrated, confessional, and autobiographical singer-songwriter descended from the folk revival tradition. But *Tapestry* did place King in the company of the James Taylors and Joni Mitchells as representatives of the new style, and the album was overwhelmingly King's greatest commercial success, so it is curious to see the extent to which she retreated from what looked to be a move toward the singer-songwriter style so soon after the brilliant success of *Tapestry*. It would almost seem that Carole King the songwriter still had not quite defined exactly who Carole King the singer, for whom she was writing, was as a musical personality. Or perhaps what appears to be something of a retreat from the singer-songwriter aesthetic on "Surely" and other songs on *Music* was just a case of Carole King, Brill Building songwriter, doing what she had done so successfully back in the 1960s: exploring diverse musical styles using lyrics of a wide diversity of literary voice. In any case, "Surely" does not fit the *Tapestry* paradigm, but it is a pleasant, memorable pop song.

Some of the sentiments of *Tapestry*'s "You've Got a Friend" can be heard in King's "Carry Your Load." Her lyrics speak either literally or metaphorically of two people traveling down the highway together and asks if, as long as they are traveling together, the other person would like for her to help carry his or her load. The melody's moderately quick pace and snappy dotted rhythms give "Carry Your Load" a much perkier feeling than other recent songs that express similar sentiments, including "You've Got a Friend" and Paul Simon's "Bridge over Troubled Water." In fact, this upbeat style associated with a background seriousness is one of several songs Carole King wrote and recorded that suggests the style popularized in the late 1960s and early 1970s by songwriter Laura Nyro. King's earlier Nyro-like breezy songs like "Now That Everything's Been Said" and "Hi-De-Ho" (both found on the City's *Now That Everything's Been Said*) work well, but this one is less successful. Following so closely on the heels of "You've Got a Friend" and "Bridge over Troubled Water," two songs that are reverent and almost anthem-like in their structure and style, "Carry Your Load" sounds almost trivial; the breezy music is just not as effective a match to the words as the two former songs.

"Raspberry Jam" of the pre-*Tapestry* album, *Writer*, is recalled by the next track, "Music." This time, though, King provides her own lyrics. Curtis Amy's tenor saxophone solo is just outside the chord changes enough not to sound like what one would expect on what is essentially a pop (as opposed to a rock or a jazz) album. As such, it is musically interesting, but something of a mismatch for the overall pop stylistic feel of *Music* and tends to fall under the heading of album filler.

Music continues with "Song of Long Ago," another song for which King wrote both words and music. On the surface, this seems to be a simple piece about old friends being reunited to "sing a song of long ago." Whether King means for this line to be taken literally or metaphorically, it works on a general level that can be appreciated by any listener who has experienced a reunion with old friends. However, when one considers Carole King's career as a 1960s hit pop songwriter, her breakup with Gerry Goffin, and her move to California and the new lover (her second husband Charles Larkey) and new friends (including her stalwart guitarist Danny Kortchmar and James Taylor, who just so happens to make a guest appearance on this song), the images of a woman who has moved on to a different life than she had ever anticipated and who is now reminiscing about old friends and a former lifestyle seem deeply personal. In "Song of Long Ago," King makes the autobiographical aspect of the lyrics vague enough so as not to let the listener know quite everything she is feeling. This gives the listener that chance to imagine and better to put themselves in King's proverbial shoes. The shortest song on *Music*, "Song of Long Ago" is one of the more interesting songs in terms of the balance of autobiography and universality.

"Brighter" is another *Music* song with convincing pop sensibilities: it has a catchy tune with the kind of memorable melodic hook that King wrote so well throughout the 1960s. As had been the case with the previous track, "Song of Long Ago," "Brighter" is quite short, at least compared with the other songs on *Music*. It is not as clearly autobiographical, with lyrics that tend toward the general; basically, she tells her longtime lover that he still makes "my day a little bit brighter in every way."

"Growing Away from Me" is one of the most interesting Carole King songs of the period in terms of compositional structure. The text itself is fairly conventional: she tells her lover that he seems to be becoming ever more distant in their relationship, "growing away from me." The music is what makes the song work. The way in which King's melody meanders and the harmony seems to avoid conventional cadences at the points at which the listener might expect to hear them give the song a through-composed feeling, as opposed to the more standard AABA (verse-verse-chorus-verse) structure. To be sure, there are strong elements of conventional Tin Pan Alley song structure here; it is just that it is masked by the melodic and harmonic avoidance of stereotypical-sounding cadences.

"Too Much Rain" is the least memorable song on *Music*. Toni Stern's lyrics use the metaphor of rain falling on the singer to symbolize bad things that are happening in her life. Just exactly what those things might be, the listener does not discover. The main point is that the singer's character does not want the person to whom she is singing to let on to the singer's friends that she is anything but happy. King's music is not particularly memorable, despite the melodic text painting by means of a descending line on the line "too much rain fallin' down on me." Years later, on her 1993 album *Colour of Your Dreams*, in fact, King would again to turn to the rain/tears-falling-down metaphor in the songs "Standing in the Rain" and "Tears Falling Down on Me": these would be much more powerful and memorable songs lyrically and musically.

"Back to California" finds King expressing her desire to be back in her new home of California. The technique of referring to various locales in a song is an old one: one need only recall Chuck Berry's "Sweet Little Sixteen," or the Beach Boys' "California Girls." But it is not just the lyrics of "Back to California" that sounds derivative; the music—especially the instrumental licks—sound too much like the Beatles's "Get Back," which incidentally finds lead singer Paul McCartney referring to one of the song's characters wanting to "get back" to California.[2] Even the "woooh" that King sings at the end of the first stanza echoes McCartney's performance on "Get Back." Add to this the fact that "Back to California" includes an electric piano solo—played by Ralph Schukett—just like "Get Back" had when the Beatles recorded their song along with American keyboardist Billy Preston back in 1969. Another piece of the familiarity picture on "Back to California," though, comes from an entirely different place: King's adoption of a vocal tone that, although smoother and a little less expressive, is eerily reminiscent of Janis Joplin.

The ultimate story of *Music* may be that it found Carole King moving away from the whole gestalt of *Tapestry* a little prematurely. The overall sense of the album is that it resembles its tremendously successful predecessor closely in texture, somewhat in arrangements, but not particularly closely in the level of intimacy and introspection of the lyrics. At the height of the singer-songwriter movement, it veers toward more of a generic pop sound with an undeveloped hint of social consciousness (found in "Brother, Brother" at the start of the album, but missing from the rest of the collection). Even the lyrics that would seem to be autobiographical—such as her desire to "build me a life in the open, a life in the country" in "Sweet Seasons" or the entire premise of "Back to California"—are rendered less so by means of the nature (top-40 pop in the case of "Sweet Seasons"; a virtual remake of "Get Back" in the case of "Back to California") of the music. *Music* went to No. 1 on the *Billboard* pop charts; however, it was not as well received by the record-buying public as *Tapestry*, which is entirely understandable given the unprecedented success of that album, or its successor, *Rhymes & Reasons*. The album raises this question: Would Carole King continue to distance herself from the singer-songwriter movement, or would she turn around and fully embrace the direction that *Tapestry* had taken her.

RHYMES & REASONS

The 1972 album *Rhymes & Reasons* was Carole King's third consecutive No. 1 album. In fact, on *Billboard*'s pop album charts, it held the No. 1 position for five weeks, two more than *Music*. With King's focus on highly personal-sounding lyrics by herself, Toni Stern, Charles Larkey, and the still-present Gerry Goffin, and the more unified musical style of *Rhymes & Reasons*, it is the Carole King album that best exemplifies the sound of the mature singer-songwriter style. Gone are the somewhat self-conscious clichés of the earlier examples of this style, including the incessant suspended-fourth chords in the acoustic and electric rhythm guitar on *Writer* and a few tracks on *Tapestry*. In its place is a clear emphasis on King on multitracked piano parts. It must be noted, however, that if one defines the early 1970s singer-songwriter style in terms of introspective, me-centered lyrics and believes that to be a weakness of the style, then *Rhymes & Reasons* fits the lyrical stereotype of the style without question. Even more than *Tapestry,* this is an introspective theme—or concept—album. Of interest, despite its musical success, and the fact that it was more commercially successful that any King album except *Tapestry,* King moved away from this style after *Rhymes & Reasons* when she began playing a role as a musical social activist on her next album, *Fantasy*. Does *Rhymes & Reasons* have any flaws? Yes, but they are small flaws, like the occasional melodic lick or harmonic turn that sounds too close for comfort to one of the more memorable songs of *Tapestry* or *Music*. In general, too, the songs are so similar in style that few stand out like the chart toppers and radio-rotation-heavy album cuts of *Tapestry*. In the case of *Rhymes & Reasons*, delivering a unified message with a unified musical style decreases the distinctiveness of the individual songs. This, in fact, was one of the concerns expressed by several reviewers. For example, *Melody Maker* suggested that the album suffered from "blandness of songs."[3] Stephen Holden of *Rolling Stone* wrote that although *Rhymes & Reasons* was King's "most unified, personal album," it was "musically less exciting than most of *Tapestry* and some of *Writer* and *Music*." Holden does acknowledge, however, King's excellent vocal work on the album.[4] Writing for *Crawdaddy*, Ellen Wolff decried the weakness of the lyrics on the album, but acknowledged that King "more than makes up for this with impeccable production, fine instrumentation, and possibly her best vocal work yet."[5]

In the face of some of the criticism of King's *Rhymes & Reasons*, it must be remembered that the lyrically introspective, musically understated style it represents was very much in vogue in 1972. This was the year of, for example, Rick Nelson's "Garden Party," one of the best of the autobiographical, confessional songs of the era—and, incidentally, one of the greatest songs ever written about the strange dynamics of the artist/audience relationship in the pop music genre.

Rhymes & Reasons begins with King and Toni Stern's "Come Down Easy." Right from the start, this song makes the point that *Rhymes & Reasons* will sound quite different from any previous Carole King album. The sound is more thoroughly keyboard based and also features Bobbye Hall's work on percussion. Specifically, on "Come Down Easy" Hall plays conga and bongo drums. In fact, Hall's congas and bongos return on more than a few of the songs on *Rhymes & Reasons* and lend a gentle Latin feel that links this first song to several in the middle of the album to "Been to Canaan," the final track on the album. The backing vocals of "Come Down Easy" also signify a difference from any previous King album: here King sings all the vocal lines. Although she had recorded overdubbed backing vocals on tracks on her previous albums, there was always a track or several tracks on which she would be joined by other vocalists. That she is the only voice heard on *Rhymes & Reasons* gives the backing "ensemble" a more unified sound. This is noticeable particularly on "Come Down Easy." On the song and throughout the album, King proves that she is a capable singer, especially in terms of creating a beautiful choral blend. Few singers in 1970s pop music were doing this sort of thing as effectively; naturally, one's thoughts turn to Stevie Wonder as the greatest master of the one-man-band/one-man-choir approach to album making in the 1970s. On "Come Down Easy" Carole King approaches the high quality of vocal blend Wonder achieved on albums such as *Innervisions* and *Fulfillingness' First Finale*. Most of King's backing vocal arrangements on the album, however, are not as elaborate as that of this first track.

The story of how different a song such as "Come Down Easy" sounds from most of the music of King's previous solo albums does not end with the arrangement, however. It is particularly evident in the melodic writing. King's melody is still tuneful and memorable; however, it is built in longer, more complex phrases than most of her earlier work. She seems to be more willing to use repeated pitches in the opening phrase of each stanza. This is not to say that the tune is in any way entirely focused on one pitch; it is just that King does a bit more in the way of balancing relative stasis with more meandering phrases that in her more clearly Top-40-oriented material. This and the more complex phrase structure give the melody almost a conversational flow.

King and Stern's "My My She Cries" is the closest song the team had written and recorded up to this time that reflects some of the aesthetics of the folk revival songwriters who came to prominence in the early and mid 1960s. In particular, the song resembles several of the sad songs about social misfits of the excellent but largely overlooked 1967 Phil Ochs album *Pleasures of the Harbor*. In particular, the character about whom King sings in "My My She Cries" bears a resemblance to the main character of the title song of the Ochs album. The one criticism that could be leveled at this story of a somewhat tragic young woman and man who just cannot seem to get together is that it is not thoroughly developed. The song weighs in at less than 2½ minutes, which is quite enough to establish the premise and the mood, but not enough for the impressionistic story to develop like the best songs in the Anglo-American folk tradition.

In a decided move away from her top-40 style of writing, King uses a lilting triple-meter waltz feel. Again, this is typical of the introspective songs composed by folk revival musicians such as Phil Ochs, Joan Baez, and Tom Paxton as they moved from political protest songs in the 1963–1965 period to story songs that dealt more with the complexities of life for the characters about whom they wrote later in the 1960s. And once again, the musical materials are clearly in the same general realm as the songs on Ochs's *Pleasures of the Harbor*.

The third song on *Rhymes & Reasons*, "Peace in the Valley," is another collaboration of King and Toni Stern. Stern's lyrics set the structural tone for the lyrics King would write herself for the songs on the second half of the album. In particular, "Peace in the Valley" features internal rhymes within some of the lines of the middle eight section; however, this is balanced by a verse-by-verse rhyme scheme that is more typical of pop songs: ABCB, where the letters represent rhymes. This all makes for a feeling of greater complexity, but ironically also a feeling of a touch of lyrical improvisation in the chorus, almost the kind of thing that one might expect to hear at a poetry slam in the 1990s. The theme is the universal brotherhood and sisterhood of humankind, which is tempered by the realization that so far it seems to be impossible for people to live like they are all brothers and sisters. King's musical setting features a melody that exhibits elements of the through-composed style of nineteenth-century art song composers. What she does is to avoid a strict verse-by-verse melodic setting, so that the effect is that one full section of music includes essentially three four-line stanzas of poetry. This lends a partially through-composed feeling to the music. It is in a completely different style, but the balance of strophic aspects and through-composed aspects to the music bears more than a passing resemblance to what the German composer, Robert Schumann, did in some of his art songs of the mid-nineteenth century. Following the song "My My She Cries" as it does, this song's sophistication confirms that *Rhymes & Reasons* is more closely related to a classical song cycle than to a pop song album.

"Feeling Sad Tonight" does not have quite the same kind of classical structural feel as the two preceding songs; however, the inclusion of classically influenced string writing in the song's arrangement again transcends top-40 pop. In fact, it is the string arrangement by Norman Kurban and David Campbell that takes "Feeling Sad Tonight" out of the realm of a conventional pop song. Structurally and rhythmically this is the most popish song on *Rhymes & Reasons*.

The poetic imagery of "The First Day in August" is captivating and raises the question of why Carole King and Charles Larkey did not collaborate on more songs. King's musical setting is clearly influenced by both folk revival music of the 1960s and classical music. King plays the multitracked piano lines with a sense of *rubato* (subtle speeding up and slowing down for expressive purposes) and rhythmic flow more closely associated with classical music than with pop songs. The texture of the song consists of the piano parts and orchestral strings. King's melody contains clearly defined melodic and rhythmic motives. These are beautifully balanced with the contrasting motives of the instruments. Her harmony generally is straightforward and could fit into the classical, folk, or pop style, but in this song she seems to be especially careful about resolving nonharmonic tones in the traditional classical manner. Kurban and Campbell's string writing supports the classical traits inherent in King's composition. The string arrangers carefully avoid the clichés found in many pop songs with string arrangements, using instead a more classical approach. For example, the strings play some contrapuntal lines using motives that are developed from lines in the vocal part and piano parts. The strings are fully integrated into the texture, rather than sounding as though they are simply layered on top of a conventional rock band.

King wrote both words and music for "Bitter with the Sweet." The influence of this song can be heard in the work of later artists. In particular, several of the tracks on Rickie Lee Jones's self-titled debut album of 1979 resemble the jazz-influenced *parlando* (speaking style) phrasing and inner rhyme schemes of "Bitter with the Sweet," although Jones's vocal influences primarily come more from earlier black jazz, R&B, and jump blues singers than from Carole King per se. The jazziness of the vocal line suggests the work of Joni Mitchell at the time, although "Bitter with the Sweet" finds King singing with less overt technical virtuosity than Mitchell exhibits on songs like

"Help Me" and "Big Yellow Taxi." Still, there is that syncopated jazz feeling that clearly connects the contemporary work of Mitchell and this particular King song. One of more notable features of the song is King's use of repeated pitches in the melody, as well as several phrases that revolve closely around one, central pitch. This is really what gives the song its *parlando* feel, and it contributes to the jazz feel of the piece. The melodic construction, combined with the inner rhymes gives the verses of the song a scat-singing-like improvised feeling. It seems a bit strange that when Ode Records released a single from *Rhymes & Reasons,* "Been to Canaan" was the A-side, while "Bitter with the Sweet," a song that would seem to have had more commercial potential and was even more cutting-edge sounding, was relegated to the B-side. Perhaps this was because of the brevity of "Bitter with the Sweet." The song weighs in at just 2 minutes and 19 seconds: fairly short by the standards of 1972-era singles. It is missing an instrumental solo that probably would have moved it into a temporal range and sonic style more appropriate for the period's top 40. Ironically, "Bitter with the Sweet" is exactly the same length as the album's other overly brief song: "My My She Cries," another *Rhymes & Reasons* track that finds King moving beyond the top-40 pop styles with which she had been most closely associated at this point in her career. Still, "Bitter with the Sweet" remains one of Carole King's best compositions to include overt jazz influences, and, to the extent that the acclaimed late-1970s work of Ricky Lee Jones resembles the song, one of King's more forward-looking songs.

King's horn writing on "Bitter with the Sweet" is nicely understated. In fact, it is notable for how different it sounds from the brass writing on King's earlier albums. As opposed to the "hot" sound of the arrangements mentioned previously as being in the style that would sweep the United States on the progressive television show *Saturday Night Live* in the middle of the 1970s, this is decidedly "cool" brass writing. And it is quite different from the melodically based cool-feeling writing King had done on some other earlier songs—in particular the songs that I have mentioned as anticipating the popular style of Steely Dan—as it is more chordal.

The other aspect of "Bitter with the Sweet" that helps the song to work particularly well is the believable, autobiographical-sounding character of some of the lyrics. This is especially notable because Carole King reveals little about her personal life in interviews or in her songs. Most of King's lyrics typically in this song, in fact, sound general and—like most of her lyrical contributions to *Rhymes & Reasons*—impressionistic. It should be noted that the jazzy inner rhymes of this particular song work especially well, and mark "Bitter with the Sweet" as one of King's best lyrical expressions of the 1970s. Despite the impressionistic, almost abstractly philosophical style of much of the text of "Bitter with the Sweet," however, at one point in the song King refers to a male friend who once told her, "everything good in life you've got to pay for" with the down times. She mentions that this friend "knows all about feelin' down." Although King does not provide enough detail for the listener to conclusively identify her friend, the verse could easily refer to James Taylor, who had been a friend of King's for several years and had certainly experienced some well-documented personal and career highs and lows from about 1967 onward. In fact, King's use of the phrase "feelin' down" suggests her song "You've Got a Friend," which happened to be James Taylor's big hit single of the year before. Even if this verse of "Bitter with the Sweet" does not refer to Taylor, listeners familiar with King's work at the time of this recording, her friendship and musical collaborations with James Taylor, and the psychological roller coaster Taylor had ridden in the late 1960s might reasonably have made the connection. Therefore whether or not the intent is there, this verse tends to sound to the astute listener like an autobiographical statement.

The possible specific reference to King's unnamed friend aside, the rest of the lyrics of "Bitter with the Sweet," especially when combined with King's jazzy, syncopated music, tend to set up this ying-yang, almost-karmic situation of having first to experience the bitter in order to experience the sweet as a theoretical, philosophical construct. This is especially important to note in the context of the entire album. Ultimately, "Bitter with the Sweet" anticipates the final two songs on *Rhymes & Reasons*, "Ferguson Road" and "Been to Canaan," a pair of songs in which the character King portrays moves from the bitterness of having just experienced a particular hard-to-take breakup to the vision and the hope of returning to the metaphorical Promised Land of biblical Canaan. When taken as a suite—or cycle—of songs, then, "Bitter with the Sweet" sets up the theoretical construct; the next several songs deal with various aspects of broken relationships, reaching a high point of intensity with "Ferguson Road," and a healing move in the direction of the "sweet" with "Been to Canaan."

Unfortunately, "Goodbye Don't Mean I'm Gone," the next song on *Rhymes & Reasons*, includes some incongruities with respect to the lyrics: frankly, some of King's thoughts are difficult to follow, and some of her use of the English language seems not to fit the musical style. One gets the feeling that it is deeply personal; however, the complex rhyme structure seems to be somewhat incongruous with the country music stylistic inclinations of the music and arrangement.

In "Stand Behind Me," King writes the same kind of internal rhymes and impressionistic lyrics as "Bitter with the Sweet" and "Goodbye Don't Mean I'm Gone." As one listens to *Rhymes & Reasons*, in fact, this use of internal rhymes becomes one of the features that acts as a double-edged sword. On one hand, it provides the songs with a feeling of stylistic coherence; on the other hand, however, it tends to become somewhat predictable. Part of the problem is that unlike the subtle use of the internal rhyme in the middle eight section of the Toni Stern lyrics to "Peace in the Valley," King includes quite a few of these in her lyrics. The effect becomes one of simply trying too hard.[6]

"Gotta Get through Another Day" is another song for which King supplied both words and music. Unfortunately, some of her lyrics do not work particularly well because of their associations outside the realm of pure emotional expression. In particular, one of the premises of the song is that the day about which she sings is "a strange and moody blues day." With the emphasis King gives this particular phrase, one familiar with top progressive rock groups of the late 1960s and early 1970s (such as this author) can tend to hear the lyrics referring to the British band the Moody Blues, which recorded one of its best-remembered albums (*Seventh Sojourn*) at the time of King's *Rhymes & Reasons.* The other problem with the song's lyrics is that this is the third song in a row on the album that features a somewhat elaborate inner rhyme scheme. The songs for which King wrote lyrics form a sort of suite inside the album at large. Although it is almost like a set of variations on a structural theme, it is just too much of the same lyrical structure style in a row. On a song-by-song basis it tends to sound creative and clever, but as one listens to the second such song moving into the third such song, it does not wear well. The other problem with this style of poetry is that it seems to fit better with some musical styles than others. In particular, it is highly effective in the pseudo-beat poetry, hip jazz style of "Bitter with the Sweet," but is less naturally aligned with a song such as "Gotta Get through Another Day."

"I Think I Can Hear You" includes just as many of the internal rhymes as the previous three songs on *Rhymes & Reasons* and essentially completes the four-song suite of variations on the same poetic style. Stylistically, it resembles some of King's moderate-tempo ballads of the previous years in that it features a somewhat jazz-influenced pop melody. Harmonically, the song is sparse, with oscillations between two primary chords. The interaction between melody and harmony is interesting because of King's use of nonharmonic tones and harmonic extensions beyond conventional three-note triads.

The sole Gerry Goffin and Carole King collaboration on *Rhymes & Reasons,* "Ferguson Road," breaks the lyrical mold of the three previous tracks. Goffin's lyrics use a more conventional ABCB rhyme structure in the verses and an ABAB rhyme scheme in the chorus. The lyrics are a little unusual in that the chorus section contains completely different lyrics each of the two times it occurs. King's character returns to "the old Ferguson Road," which apparently is a place that represents a happy childhood to the character, so that she can try to forget someone with whom she has just broken up. King's music seems like fairly conventional folk-pop material except for the striking deceptive cadences at the end of each verse where she sets the line of poetry that indicates that her character's reason for returning to the metaphorical Ferguson Road is to make sure that she will not "give a damn" about the loss of her former lover. This unexpected cadence on a minor chord highlights the bitterness that the character harbors about the breakup. It is one of the more striking examples of text painting in King's entire compositional canon.

Throughout her career, Carole King has been more highly regarded as a composer of music than as a lyricist, and because of her collaborations throughout the 1960s mostly with Gerry Goffin, she has had far more experience as a composer than as a lyricist. In the final track on *Rhymes & Reasons,* "Been to Canaan," however, King writes some of the best lyrics up to that point of her career. The biblical reference to the ancient land of her ancestors is both vivid and a rare autobiographical nod at the same time. Her musical setting contains enough of a pop hook (especially in the melody of the chorus, which is so important in pop music) to have propelled the song into the top 40 when it was released as a single even though it is a moderate tempo piece—not something that one would dance to and not a slow ballad either—and even though the mood is even keeled and mellow. "Been to Canaan" is a perfect song with which to end *Rhymes & Reasons,* especially because it brings back a sense of optimism to replace the hurt and bitterness of "Ferguson Road." King's character has in the past metaphorically "been to Canaan," the Promised Land of old, but has been experiencing difficulties (perhaps referring back to the broken relationship from which she sang about recovering in "Ferguson Road"). Now she is expressing the desire to return. Unlike her musical setting of Gerry Goffin's lyrics about wanting to return to the innocence and the physical scene of good times in the past in "Ferguson Road," in which King gave the words an ironic, nearly sarcastic twist with her biting minor-chord cadences, here she sets her own text in a more upbeat, optimistic style (accomplished through syncopation in the melodic rhythm, clear cadences on major harmonies, vocal range, and an active accompaniment, particularly in the piano). Her character now has hope for the future, but it is tempered throughout the song by the fact that it has "been so long" since King's character has been to Canaan. Incidentally, King brings out the bittersweet nature of the song in her musical writing in a subtle way. Whether intentional or not, she writes one instrumental figure that bears a strong resemblance in rhythm and melodic contour to the tune to which the words "Ah, look at all the lonely people," is set in the introduction to the Beatles's "Eleanor Rigby."

Overall, however, there is a clear linkage between "Ferguson Road" and "Been to Canaan" in mood progression. They are both songs about longing for a return to the good old days in order to move beyond the hurt of the present. The progression of mood from hurt to optimism and healing is a result of King's contrasting musical settings and Goffin's lyrics in "Ferguson Road," which deal as much with *what* is being escaped as *where* the escape can be found. King's lyrics in "Been to Canaan" dwell much more heavily on the promise of her metaphorical Canaan. This suggests that her character has moved beyond the hurt and is about to enter the healing stage. Like the relative similarity of the musical arrangements throughout the album, the use of King's singing voice for all the lead and background vocals, and the suite of internal-rhyme songs in the second half of the album, this mood progression from "Ferguson Road" to "Been to Canaan," as well as the two songs' thematic reference back to the ying-yang construct of "Bitter with the Sweet," gives *Rhymes & Reasons* a much greater feel of coherence and song-by-song connection than any previous (or just about any future) Carole King album.

From a commercial standpoint, *Rhymes & Reasons* was Carole King's most successful album aside from *Tapestry*. As a representative of the mature singer-songwriter style, with its introspection, seriousness, and ties to the lyrical traditions of the hauntingly sad songs of the Anglo-American folk and American folk revival traditions, this is King's finest album. It is the first Carole King album to sound fully like it was conceived as an album and not a collection of individual, self-standing songs. It is, to be sure, a little thin on development. Even in the precompact disc, vinyl record era, a 12-song collection of less than 36 minutes is fairly short. Critics, it seemed, wanted more *Tapestry*-like flash and more musical diversity, but in retrospect it would seem that some of them did not grasp the significance of *Rhymes & Reasons,* or the reasons why it sounded different than *Tapestry*. For example, the British magazine *Melody Maker* complained about the "blandness of the songs" on *Rhymes & Reasons* and suggested that King would do well to return to working with the musicians with whom she had recorded *Tapestry*.[7] But was a fundamental change in King's choice of backing musicians the reason for the stylistic change? The stalwarts Danny Kortchmar and Charles Larkey were still part of the Carole King team, and King's keyboards were still featured to an even greater extent than they had been on any previous Carole King album. Perhaps it was the presence of Harvey Mason in the drum chair, although it should be remembered that two different drummers played on various tracks on *Tapestry*.

The reason for the sonic difference, which *Melody Maker* heard as a negative, was that *Rhymes & Reasons* was the first King album to be *composed* as an album. The City's *Now That Everything's Been Said* was a collection of old songs and new songs written as part of the Brill Building paradigm—a collection of individual songs in widely diverse styles. *Writer* and *Tapestry* also consisted of oldies and newer songs. Especially in the case of *Tapestry,* the production, performance, packaging, and timing of the album's release all worked together to help it become one of the most significant artistic statements of the second half of the twentieth century, but it was still by and large a collection of individual songs written at different times and originally for different performers. *Music,* too, was a collection of individual songs, and, from all indications, a fairly hastily assembled one. In *Rhymes & Reasons* we have for the first time a Carole King album that exhibits all evidence of being a fully conceived, artistic whole, not only in arrangements, packaging, and production (as had been the case with *Tapestry*), but also from the compositional standpoint and progression, including both lyrics and music. And to top it off, King's vocal work really did outshine everything she had recorded up to that time, and the focus on her keyboard playing made this her most personal instrumental performance ever.

FANTASY

In 1973, Carole King released her most socially conscious album yet: *Fantasy*. Although the style of the album is considerably different, the combination of issues-focused songs (racism, warfare, poverty, drug abuse, and environmental degradation) and relationship (romantic love and platonic love[8]) songs, all presented with numerous direct dissolves and segues, and with a conscious attempt to sound visionary, feels similar to Stevie Wonder's 1973 album *Innervisions*. However, and it is a very big however, this album was nowhere near the critical or commercial success of the Wonder package. It is clear, though, that both Wonder's *Innervisions* and King's *Fantasy* are descendants of Marvin Gaye's 1971 groundbreaking *What's Going On*, although neither is quite as focused on social issues as Gaye's album. After three consecutive No. 1 albums, the public took *Fantasy* only to No. 6 on the *Billboard* pop charts.

The critics hated *Fantasy*, with the more hard-core rock critics, in particular, having almost nothing positive to say about it. For example, Aaron Fuchs wrote in *Crawdaddy* that *Fantasy* "reaffirms King's position as one of the most aggressively contrived artists today."[9] What Fuchs seems to get at in his review is the chameleon nature of King's albums. She seemed to present the façade of a rock singer, a top-40 singer, a member of the singer-songwriter fraternity, a Marvin Gaye-like social critic, but at the core of King's work as a songwriter and singer, Fuchs saw little substance.

Aaron Fuchs was not the only critic to make decidedly less-than-flattering comments about *Fantasy*. *Rolling Stone*'s Stephen Holden wrote that *Fantasy* "adds up to a formalized song cycle in which the Carole King Institution issues its summary social and philosophical expression to date."[10] The almost sarcastic tone of Holden's description suggests that he views King's pronouncements as being overly pompous and patronizing. Of interest, some twenty-first century writers look back at *Fantasy* as a bold, effective forward move for King and for the singer-songwriter style. For example, John Borgmeyer, writing in *The Greenwood Encyclopedia of Rock History*, mentions King's songs of "young streetwalkers and drug addiction" as one of the important signs that the singer-songwriter movement had matured from a style in which the musicians focused "on their own personal lives" to a style that was more socially relevant.[11]

Before considering the songs of *Fantasy*, let's think about the place that the album holds within the career of Carole King. It must be remembered that up to the time of *Fantasy*, King had two distinctive careers: (1) as a singer-pianist who had between 1958 and 1971 never quite made the big time, then took the world by storm almost overnight, and then had to try to define herself as a popular mature artist; and (2) one of the leading composers of the 1960s who earned her living by writing in the widest variety of styles for the widest variety of performers. After the success of *Tapestry*, King the performer seemed to shift focus from album to album. I believe that this may have been due in part to the challenge of reconciling the two prongs of her career in pop music. On one hand, she had years of experience setting lyrics on a wide variety of subjects to disparate musical styles, all the while integrating those styles into her compositional palette. The problem with that experience is that it does not necessarily translate well into writing with a focus on *one* performer with a clearly defined style and audience. Whether by accident or by design, King's post-*Tapestry* albums tend to find King the writer trying to define King the performer in different ways. The writer seems to dictate to the performer, rather than the other way around. Although this would seem to run counter to much of King's Brill Building experience, I believe that it is attributable to the fact that King's career as a writer had been dominant for so long. *Fantasy* would be a major shift and would not necessarily be widely accepted by fans or critics, but it would not be the last redefinition of Carole King, performer. This shift in focus, though, is certainly one of the more curious in King's career given the commercial success of the thoroughly singer-songwriter-style *Rhymes & Reasons* and the fact that *Rhymes & Reasons* sounded so real, so authentic.

When experiencing *Fantasy*, the listener should keep in mind that King wrote all the lyrics for the album. Although King's earliest recordings back in the 1950s had been of songs that she had written entirely by herself, and although she had enjoyed considerable success with some of her solo compositions on *Tapestry*, *Music*, and *Rhymes & Reasons*, it still is important to note that *Fantasy* was the first Carole King album to contain solely King-written lyrics. This fact is crucial to place the album in context because, save for those immature songs of the late 1950s, King had always had a lyricist working in close collaboration with her for every project: she did write some of the songs on *Tapestry*, *Music*, and *Rhymes & Reasons* on her own, but at the same time she was collaborating with lyricists such as Gerry Goffin and Toni Sterns on other songs. Part of the reason behind the success of the Brill Building composition teams such as Goffin and King, Mann and Weil, and others was that the writers had someone off of whom they could bounce ideas. Certainly there were clunkers here and there, but at least there were other people involved directly in the songwriting process that might lend some helpful advice. Here for the first time, King was writing alone for an entire project. Logic would suggest that this would have the potential to be a double-edged sword. On one hand, King would have the power to deliver a fully unified message entirely in her own terms for the first time; on the other hand, working without having a strong lyricist-collaborator around could isolate her from the kind of constructive criticism that was at the heart of her greatest work. To be fair, King does acknowledge the inspiration of Charles Larkey in the liner notes, but King's name is the only one in the actual songwriting credits.

The first track on *Fantasy,* the appropriately, but obviously titled "Fantasy Beginning," sets the stage for what is to come—sort of. King announces that she will be playing a variety of roles throughout the album. For example, she sings that sometimes she will be playing the role of a man, and sometimes the role of a woman; she will sometimes be white and sometimes black. King's announcement presents a problem before she even begins to tackle any social issues, as well as some problems once she gets into dealing with issues over the course of the rest of the album. The most immediate problem is that her declaration can tend to come off as being a tad pompous. She sets herself up as the grand observer of the social scene in early 1970s America. Frankly, some listeners—such as this author—do not hear it that way, but it would seem that the critics quoted earlier did hear King's set up as being pompous or patronizing. This would seem especially to be at the heart of critic Stephen Holden's negative reaction to *Fantasy.*[12] Another problem with King's pronouncement is that at times it is decidedly unclear as to exactly who King the singer is supposed to be portraying.

Perhaps this opening track points out one of the fundamental differences between *Fantasy* and a contemporary album of social consciousness such as Stevie Wonder's wildly successful *Innervisions.* King states from the outset that she will be tackling social issues by playing the role of the unfortunate characters she sees in society, whereas Wonder simply begins by presenting his observations of the same types of characters. Wonder does make the point in the song "Innervisions" that everything about which he is singing are visions in his mind, but he avoids the kind of declaratory setup that King uses. This difference in poetic voice—first person versus third person, or becoming the characters versus observing the characters—really is at the core of the negative reaction to *Fantasy.* For one thing, it immediately raises the question, "How can a rich, successful pop songwriter know what it's like to be on welfare or to have to sell your body to be able to buy enough food to eat?" For another thing, the path that King takes requires a singing actor of considerable emotional range and vocal skill: she has to convincingly portray a diverse array of people. King approaches contemporary social issues as an actor portraying an array of characters because she knows that her audience will understand this approach. This tends to come off as patronizing or even dismissive of her audience's ability to make sense of social issues. The approach that Stevie Wonder takes in *Innervisions,* in contrast, requires that he be Stevie Wonder observing what is going on around him. The great irony of these vastly different approaches is that from the standpoint of sheer vocal technique, Stevie Wonder was in the early 1970s in an entirely different league than Carole King or most anyone else in pop music, yet his approach does not make nearly the expressive demands on the singer.

Once King actually gets into the exploration of the social ills, however, there is another significant problem that arises. The setup in "Fantasy Beginning" proves not to be an entirely accurate explanation of what follows. Some of the songs that follow the opening track could easily be understood as role-playing songs; however, more than just a few are clearly *Innervisions*-type observational songs in which King is the one doing the observing, and not some fictional character. Ultimately, this makes for a lack of consistency of poetic voice and weakens the overall structure of the album in spite of the obvious musical connections between the songs that are made through fades and direct segues.

The music of "Fantasy Beginning" continues the multitracked piano focus of *Rhymes & Reasons,* King's previous album. The melody is based primarily on fairly short syncopated melodic motives, something characteristic of many of the songs King had written for herself. In fact, it seems that King defines just who she is portraying in each song on the album by means of the musical settings. Although the texts are sometimes vague—the question sometimes arises whether King is acting out a role or observing a situation as herself—the music seems to define gender, race, and ethnicity, or at least to clarify the fuzziness of the poetic voice. King does this through the use of different musical styles that were prevalent at the time, including Latin, soul, and elements of the folk-rock-based singer-songwriter style. Because she played all the keyboards; sang all the lead and backing vocal parts; wrote all the woodwind, brass, and string arrangements; and conducted the orchestral players, King had the opportunity to use a wide palette of sounds and rhythmic, melodic, and harmonic styles to accomplish this.

King's use of music to define a character perhaps most clearly emerges in the second song on *Fantasy,* "You've Been Around Too Long." From the start, Bobbye Hall's conga drums, King's soul-influenced vocals, David T. Walker's guitar fills, and Charles Larkey's funk-style electric bass suggest Philadelphia Soul. As the brass and stings enter, the Philly Soul style is confirmed. It is not just the instrumentation or the arrangement itself that suggests the popular African American style, however. The song would not be out of place harmonically and melodically on soul radio stations of the day.

If King's musical setting in "You've Been Around Too Long" suggests pretty clearly that the song deals specifically with the plight of African Americans, then the poetic voices from which her lyrics emerge present something of a challenge to the listener. The first verse seems to be coming from the voice of a white character who is fully supportive of the civil rights or even the more radical black power movement. In fact, this character seems to be calling on whomever is being addressed to take political action to put into action the changes they desire. The second verse, however, seems to come from a representative of the disenfranchised minority who indicates that he/she just want to get his/her "peace of mind," like that enjoyed by the majority. The shift in poetic voice seems a little sudden and dilutes the focus of the song somewhat.

The shift possibly would work better if the entire song came from a consistent voice, or if both characters were more fully developed. King's lyrics, however, are so brief in this song, and really throughout most of the songs of *Fantasy*, that character development is not possible. The brevity of the lyrics is quite interesting, considering the almost raplike flow of the jazz scat-influenced lyrics King wrote for her previous album, *Rhymes & Reasons*.

The ballad style song "Being at War with Each Other" follows. Here, King herself seems to be asking the questions about why it is that people are so intent to be "at war with each other" despite their common humanity, and why there continues to be so much environmental degradation in the world. In fact, by focusing on these two subjects in a song with so few words, there is not the sense of focus that might make "Being at War with Each Other" more effective. To be fully effective, the song either needs to focus on one issue or to be more fully developed with respect to both themes.

King's arrangement, and especially her string writing in "Being at War with Each Other," recalls the work of Barry White at the time. This can be heard especially in the unison string writing, which includes many sustained tones. This style of string writing occurs not only in this song, but especially in the "urban," or obviously soul-influenced songs throughout the album. This consistency may provide an orchestrational link between the songs, but it links too many songs of disparate styles and voices. It probably would have been more effective for King to use this style in the songs that sound as though they are designed to come from the voice of a black character in King's fantasy.

"Being at War with Each Other" is notable for King's use of major-seventh chords and other added-note chords usually associated with jazz music. It lends the song a harmonic richness. In fact, this richness is felt throughout the album as King continues to explore the same sort of harmonic style. It should be noted, however, that King had been drawn to these chords in songs from earlier in her solo career. In the case of the major-seventh chords, for example, they add significantly to the harmonic richness of "It's Too Late," from *Tapestry*, and "Been to Canaan," from *Rhymes & Reasons*, among others. Of interest, "Being at War with Each Other" is the sole *Fantasy* song to be included on King's 2005 *Living Room Tour* live two-CD set.

"Being at War with Each Other" makes a direct segue into "Directions." "Directions" maintains the musical ties to the commercial soul of the early 1970s, including much unison string writing, pleasant added-note chords in the rhythm guitar, and nonobtrusive saxophone and brass backing. The lyrics of "Directions" are somewhat impressionistic and indirect. In fact, "Directions" seems much like a song that at once confirms King's statement that the songs on the album are meant to represent a fantasy, or hazy vision while also standing apart from the directness of most of the material on the *Fantasy*. Here her text deals with the "directions" that various life choices present us, the "rejections" that people feel from others, and the introspective "reflections" that help us to make sense out of life.

Because *Fantasy* is one of the rare Carole King albums on which the singer-songwriter wrote and conducted all of her own orchestrations, it is important to note her style as an arranger/orchestrator. King's work in "Directions" and other songs on the album finds her for the most part treating strings, brass, and saxophones like three separate choirs, with three separate roles to play in the accompanying texture. Her string arrangements throughout the album focus on the violins. The saxes and brass fill in the lower parts of the pitch range, but generally with the two groups having separate material. This technique is quite common in big band jazz arrangements. Throughout *Fantasy*, however, there is a sense that King's assignment of separate roles to the three groups is a personal touch. Although some of the textures resemble some of the more fully orchestrated soul music of the period, the instrumental voicings and three-part counterpoint in the accompanying orchestral instruments tend to sound more like a *Fantasy* trademark sound, rather than derivative of any other arranger. It should be remembered that *Fantasy* certainly was not Carole King's first attempt at working as an arranger/orchestrator and conductor. She handled these chores a decade earlier on Little Eva's album, *The Lllloco-Motion* (Dimension 6000, 1962).

"That's How Things Go Down" comes from the voice of a woman who is pregnant by a lover who, for one undefined reason or another, is no longer present. King's character hopes that her lover will return to see their child born, but seems not to hold out much hope, because "that's how things go down." The song is something of a musical tour de force for King, as her piano and organ playing is impeccable, as is her arrangement and performance of the backing vocals. Given the subject of the song, "That's How Things Go Down" does not necessarily possess much in the way of commercial appeal. It is, however, one of the more interesting and well-constructed topical songs of *Fantasy*. It also ends with one of the most effective short song-to-song transitions on the album.

The next song on the album, "Weekdays," comes from the voice of a woman who has to deal with the day-to-day realities of housework, marketing, and other associated tasks, while her husband is at work and her children are at school. In part, she finds herself living vicariously through characters in daytime drama television programs. King does not probe into the character's psyche in a whole lot of depth. There are a number of ways that she as a songwriter could have gone with this story, particularly with *Fantasy* coming at a particularly active time in the women's movement. In fact, it is a little disappointing that she does not probe as much as she might have. King's character seems to express some disappointment in her situation, which does little to stimulate her mind, but there is nothing even close to radical feminism here. In any case, "Weekdays" does work as another part of her loose collection of fantasies about people in the world of the early 1970s; there certainly seems to be nothing autobiographical in "Weekdays."

King's musical setting of the somewhat mundane tale of the reality of life for a suburban housewife in "Weekdays," however, elevates the song. The song's melody tends to meander and the phrases do not have the same kind of natural, logical shape of King's best, hook-laden melodies. At first listening, this might seem just not to be one of the composer's more memorable tunes; however, King changes directions dramatically as she reaches the end of her lyrical statement. As her character indicates her belief that the couple will work things out so that she is "a person, too," because "I'm your woman and you're my man," the melody stretches upward to a clear-cut cadence on the tonic pitch. This unexpected move exhibits the character's belief that, through the couple's love, she will be able to transcend the drudgery of her day-to-day existence. King's musical setting gives her character's words a greater depth, and clearly highlights the distinction between the reality of the character's mundane life (the meandering melody) and her belief that her love for her husband will help her someday to move beyond the unfulfilled feelings of the present (the melodic motion into higher pitch range at the conclusion of the song). It is a song of dependency, with the lead character clearly being a woman with whom the women's movement did not make a connection.

In "Haywood" King's character addresses a friend who apparently suffers from some sort of drug addiction. The drug in question, however, is never specified. She points out to her friend, Haywood, that his (presumably Haywood is male) other friends, the ones who feed his addiction, really are not friends at all. She reminds him of one of their friends who has died, and of what seems to be Haywood's broken relationship with Vallorie, with whom he had planned a life together. She tells him that there is still a chance to build that life, but only if he is able to "shake it" (the addiction). King's musical setting in "Haywood" is soulful, but too lightweight for the message of the need for Haywood to end his addiction. This is one place in which the consistency of orchestration and rhythmic textures of *Fantasy* acts as a detriment to the individual song. A feeling of sadness pervades the song, and is especially enhanced by the mournful brass writing and the flugelhorn solo. This would seem to suggest that King's character is not altogether convinced that she can get through to Haywood. In any case, she does not send one clear signal in the song.

The album's next piece, "A Quiet Place to Live," comes at an interesting point in King's ongoing fantasy. Although some of the song-to-song connections are entirely musical in nature—the lyrical themes sometimes shift quite abruptly—here there is a logical progression from the exposé of the harsh realities of drug abuse in the urban world to the expression of a desire to find "a quiet place to live." Based on some of the references in the song, King might be portraying a character of retirement age who wants to move away from the city so that she can "enjoy the fruits of [her] labor." Or, her character might be a younger person who has achieved financial success and independence and can now leave the rat race of city life. Her references are not specific enough for the listener to be sure, one way or the other. The soft-rock medium-tempo ballad style does not really help paint the character either.

"Welfare Symphony" is easily the most intriguing song on *Fantasy* musically and structurally. It begins with a somewhat eerie chorale-like organ passage that provides a link between "A Quiet Place to Live" and "Welfare Symphony" proper. King's text describes some of the tribulations of an unmarried mother who is a welfare recipient. It is a fairly short, concise text. King's musical setting of the text itself takes only approximately 2 minutes. The entire song, however, clocks in at 3 minutes 47 seconds. More than 1 minute is devoted to an instrumental coda section that includes a dramatic brass and saxophone fanfare that establishes a slower tempo. This fanfare section includes a false ending, followed by an unexpected repeat. It is striking.

"You Light Up My Life," not to be confused with the song of the same title popularized by Debby Boone, follows. This is a simple, lyrically straightforward song of love. Musically, it is in a mainstrean ballad style. This is confirmed by King's orchestration, which resembles that heard in some of the great Burt Bacharach and Hal David top-40 songs of the late 1960s and early 1970s. "You Light Up My Life" is not one of Carole King's most memorable songs, but would certainly make for a workable album track for a wide range of pop vocalists. The problem is that it seems not to fit the album's theme of looking at social issues from a variety of eyes. Certainly, this kind of pure, honest, simple expression of love is a part of life. If the primary motivation behind *Fantasy* is to show many sides of life, then the inclusion of "You Light Up My Life" makes more sense, but the focus seems to be so much more specifically on issues.

Although critics expressed suspicions about the sincerity of King's motives for this concept album, particularly harsh words were expressed about "Corazón," which *Rolling Stone*'s Stephen Holden called "an unintentional travesty of Latin music."[13] To be sure, King's lyrics represent the most rudimentary Spanish. Like a number of King compositions going back to her album with the City in the late 1960s, though, the emphasis is not on the text per se in "Corazón." The words become a vehicle for King's voice to be used as a melodic instrument. It should be noted that King does not use the formalized *canto* and *montuno* sections of much twentieth-century Afro-Cuban dance music.[14] She does, however, adopt the general feel and rhythmic materials of Latin-American pop music. As King does not use the traditional form of Latin pop music, using instead a form more akin to American pop song, her use of a general Latin feel and Latin-style rhythmic materials could seem superficial. Perhaps adding to the negative critical reaction to the song is that her text is exceptionally minimal and rudimentary. If the song is not judged against "real" Latin-American pop music of the time and simply as a vehicle for King's assembled musicians—much like the earlier songs "Raspberry Jam" and "Music"—to jam, it is successful. In fact, when one takes away the lyrics, it is a workable jazz-Latin rock piece. As evidence, it should be noted that, of all of Carole King's compositions of the 1970s, this is the one that has enjoyed the widest success in the jazz world. This success is based largely on Bill Stapleton's arrangement for Woody Herman's big band. The Stapleton arrangement is heard on the Herman band's album *Thundering Herd* (Fantasy Records F-9452, 1974) and is widely available and performed by high school, university, and professional jazz bands. This popular Stapleton arrangement includes some contrapuntal lines and improvised solos that are not found in Carole King's original recording of "Corazón"; however, much of the structure of the Stapleton arrangement and many of the accompaniment brass figures Stapleton includes come directly from King's brass scoring of the song on *Fantasy*.

What is the conceptual role of "Corazón," which seems on the surface to be a simple Spanish-language love song? Given the focus on issues throughout *Fantasy*, it seems like the song is supposed to somehow show Hispanics as another underrepresented minority group. Or perhaps King's fantasy here is simply a vision of street life in a Hispanic section of town, a dance piece filtering out from someone's apartment or from a jukebox in a bar. In any case, the song seems not to fit the issues focus of most of the album.

One of the great ironies of the negative critical reaction generated by "Corazón" is that not only did the song prove to be great instrumental jazz piece, but it was also one of the catchiest pieces of music on *Fantasy*. The song that follows, "Believe in Humanity," however, happens to be another of the stronger tracks on the album. This piece is a funky soul-inspired workout. Compared with authentic topical African American funk of Sly Stone, Stevie Wonder, or James Brown, however, "Believe in Humanity" is more akin to "soul lite," to coin an expression. If one were to pick one "real" soul artist whose output was closest to the King song (at least in terms of lyrics), Stevie Wonder's songs of the time would be the best choice. Like several Wonder songs of the 1970s (and songs as recent as those on Wonder's 2005 album *A Time to Love*), "Believe in Humanity" is an expression of a belief in the basic goodness of humankind. It is a fitting wrap up to *Fantasy*, completely consistent compositionally and orchestrationally with the rest of the songs, but with a message that suggests that all the problems King has been documenting (or at least fantasizing about) can be overcome through love.

Ultimately, *Fantasy* was a disappointment. Critics had few positive words to say about it at the time of the album's release; it sold far fewer copies than *Tapestry, Music, Rhymes & Reasons*, and the album that followed it, *Wrap Around Joy*; and it gave the unfortunate appearance of being a piece of social commentary meant to cash in on a trend. In retrospect, however, Carole King did not receive nearly the credit she deserved for taking chances, for trying to make a difference in the world. Despite the suspicions that profit motives may have been behind King's adoption of social causes, she really had been writing songs with her collaborators that made social commentary and that dealt with controversial issues. It's just that in the past she and her lyricists had used more of a subtle, soft-sell approach to making points and had avoided making the kind of grand pronouncement found in "Fantasy Beginning." And surely, someone with King's years of experience in the record industry must have known that the easiest way to sell a bunch of albums would have been to try to re-create the formula (if there is one) of *Tapestry*. It appears that King was sincere in her concern about social ills and her willingness to try to address them head on. Perhaps, though, *Fantasy* was not the most effective approach to doing so.

Musically, too, *Fantasy* is better than some of the critical reaction of the time would suggest. The key relationships and brief linking passages between some of the songs help to provide for a smooth transition from song to song. And the string, brass, and woodwind orchestrations that King wrote for all of the songs exhibit her skill in incorporating a full palette of sounds, without falling into the trap of using orchestral instruments in a way that seems overly schmaltzy. It is not the only song to suggest this, but "Welfare Symphony" suggests particularly strongly that Carole King had a lot more compositional tricks up her sleeve than the conventional two- to three-minute, Brill Building-descendant pop song.

Another highlight of 1973, and one that is relevant in terms of King's social consciousness, was King's free performance in New York's Central Park. Approximately 65,000 people attended. This performance represented a real turning point in King's career—the one-time reluctant live performer, who was not entirely at home during her 1971 Carnegie Hall concert, was now willing to perform for a significantly larger audience. King's Central Park concert quickly became famous for a reason other than her music. When King realized that her fans had generated a significant amount of trash, she asked them to clean up the park. They complied. King and her fans received commendation from the New York Parks Department Deputy Commissioner.[15] King and her fans' social consciousness had not been forgotten over a quarter century later. After the debacle of Woodstock 1999, *Billboard* magazine's Timothy White contrasted the 1969 Woodstock Music and Art Fair and Carole King's 1973 Central Park concert with Woodstock 1999 and the 1999 Lilith Fair concerts. According to White, the original Woodstock festival and Carole King's Central Park concert were events of great humanity and peace, especially when compared with the meanness of Woodstock 1999.[16]

WRAP AROUND JOY

Perhaps King took the harsh critical reaction to her lyrics on *Fantasy* to heart (*Rhymes & Reasons,* too, had found critics already pointing out what they perceived as a growing gulf between the quality of the music, arrangements, performance, and production versus that of the lyrics), and/or perhaps she noticed the degree to which the public failed to respond positively to the album compared with *Tapestry, Music,* and *Rhymes & Reasons;* but whether in response to these factors or not, she turned in an entirely new direction for her 1974 album *Wrap Around Joy*. Here she would collaborate on every track with co-writer David Palmer. This in and of itself was a huge jump; on *Fantasy* she had written words and music for every song. *Wrap Around Joy* contains some of the social consciousness of *Fantasy*, but in much muted form. This muting reflects back to the subtle background feminism of *Tapestry*, and the effective soft-sell social commentary of some of the songs of *Music* and *Rhymes & Reasons,* not to mention a few 1960s Goffin–King songs such as "Pleasant Valley Sunday." The arrangements, too, are more in line with the conventional top-40 pop music of the day than those of either *Rhymes & Reasons* or *Fantasy*. With its emphasis on mainstream pop, *Wrap Around Joy* reflects back to the work that had been Carole King's bread and butter back in the 1960s. If *Rhymes & Reasons* was King's quintessential singer-songwriter style album, and *Fantasy* was her quintessential (although not hugely successful) soulful concept album of social commentary, then *Wrap Around Joy* remains King's quintessential mainstream pop album. The entire focus is on this type of material and with making connections with the widest possible audience. As a collection of songs written for a Carole King album, it easily outshines any of her previous albums as an album of listenable mainstream pop, for the great *Tapestry* simply was not a collection of songs for King: it was an eclectic mix of old and new that was not *composed* as an album.

Wrap Around Joy begins with "Nightingale," a song that sends a clear signal that this album will be nothing like King's previous two collections. For one thing, it is more fully arranged and produced than any song on *Fantasy* or *Rhymes & Reasons,* especially with the full backing vocals (provided by King and her daughters Louise and Sherry Goffin) and numerous little woodwind, brass, and synthesizer pieces of filigree. The song features an energetic pop rhythmic feel that steps beyond the most upbeat songs of the previous two albums. David Palmer's lyrics praise the "Nightingale" who brings solace and happiness to a man whose hope is waning, which is something unlike the social issues songs of *Fantasy* or the more personal—and therefore less universal—lyrics of *Rhymes & Reasons*. Most striking, however, is King's solid return to easily remembered melodic and harmonic hooks reminiscent of the best of the pop songs she had composed both for herself earlier in the 1970s and for other performers back in the 1960s. Perhaps most notable is the melodic construction. Each verse features two principal styles of melodic phrases: the first phrases stay low in King's vocal range, with the last two phrases reaching hopefully upward. The chorus then moves higher, with another memorable contrasting motive.

"Change in Mind, Change of Heart" continues the full production and arrangement of "Nightingale." In fact, the full backing vocals and the lushness of the string arrangement contrast even more sharply with the predominance of unison string writing on *Fantasy*. This is accomplished without the sound becoming overly sentimental or schmaltzy, however. "Change in Mind, Change of Heart" is a slow ballad with a catchy enough tune to make it an ideal album cut. It might not be King's best-remembered song from the 1970s, but there is nothing about it that even remotely suggests "filler." And, this is one significant feature of *Wrap Around Joy*. Despite the fact that the album is longer than *Fantasy* by two minutes and longer than *Rhymes & Reasons* by six minutes, all of the songs are listenable pop music that ranks with the best of the genre of era. The album's next song, moreover, is one of King's strongest classic pop songs ever.

For my money, "Jazzman" was one of Carole King's best singles. Of course, a single does not make an album, but this collaboration of King and lyricist David Palmer and this performance is King's best work of the mid-1970s, and adds significantly to the overall pop impact of *Wrap Around Joy*. With Palmer's lyrics focusing on the power of the jazz instrumentalist, attributing to him powers of rhetorical and emotional communication, not to mention near-religious enlightenment, it would be tempting to focus too much on the extent to which the power of the song comes from the tenor saxophone work of Tom Scott. Yes, Scott plays perfectly as he portrays the "jazzman" of the song's lyrics; there is no other word for his melodic and rhythmic feel. His playing is not all that far removed from what he was doing on his solo recordings or on the scores of studio appearances he was doing at the time. This performance, more than his spontaneous soprano sax work on Paul McCartney's "Listen to What the Man Said," or anything else Scott ever recorded on a top-40 record in the 1970s (and he performed on more than a few), however, is the perfect match of soloist and material.

In addition to the essential contributions of Tom Scott to the whole gestalt of "Jazzman," the recording is also a remarkable performance by Carole King. In addition to her lead vocals, King sings all the background vocal lines, exhibiting a beautiful vocal blend and nice range. Her keyboards, which include acoustic piano and synthesizers, are prominent throughout the song and perfecting in tune (metaphorically) with the song's feel. In the twenty-first century, "Jazzman" continues to be one of the few 1970s Carole King performances likely to be heard on oldies radio or piped-in oldies in restaurants, standing up strongly in the company of "I Feel the Earth Move," "You've Got a Friend," and "It's Too Late."

"You Go Your Way, I'll Go Mine" is perhaps the closest thing to a *Tapestry*-like song that King had recorded since her famed 1971 album. First, David Palmer's lyrics, in which King's character acknowledges that the relationship she has had with a man who is now building emotional walls now has to end, reach the personal level associated with the singer-songwriter school. King's arrangement confirms this reference back to 1971 and 1972 with the melodic figures she has her guitarists play in answer to her voice: fills straight out of the James Taylor stylebook. Like *Tapestry*'s great breakup song, "It's Too Late," "You Go Your Way, I'll Go Mine" is strong melodically. And like

"It's Too Late" and virtually everything on *Tapestry* and *Rhymes & Reasons*, it is strongly piano based. It is a slower song than "It's Too Late," reflecting Palmer's lyrics, which acknowledge that King's character is still in need of healing after the end of the relationship. And at the risk of appearing redundant, "You Go Your Way, I'll Go Mine" is more lushly arranged and performed than what was typical on previous Carole King solo albums.

The other feature of "You Go Your Way, I'll Go Mine" that deserves special mention is the effectiveness of King's multitracked background vocals. The backing vocals are performed well, are well balanced in the recording's mix, and are creatively arranged. Although this may be most apparent on "You Go Your Way, I'll Go Mine," the consistently high quality of King's backing vocal arrangements and performance really go quite a long way in marking *Wrap Around Joy* as arguably Carole King's best pure pop album.

When read as a poem in the liner notes of *Wrap Around Joy*, each verse of David Palmer's lyrics for the song "You're Something New" seems to be in a fairly conventional ABAB rhyme scheme. King's musical setting, however, plays with this structure by truncating the third line. This in effect gives each verse the feel of the kind of internal rhymes associated with King's *Rhymes & Reasons* album.

One of the disappointments of *Wrap Around Joy*, especially when compared with Carole King's piano-heavy *Rhymes & Reasons*, is that some of King's multi-tracked keyboard parts—especially, though, some of the multitracked piano lines—do not have the same kind of balance and organic wholeness of her previous albums. This is not necessarily true of the song "You Go Your Way, I'll Go Mine," but it does become an issue in the opening of "We Are All in This Together," in which the melody of the solo piano is so fully separated from the accompanying piano. This had been a small issue throughout *Tapestry*. Why the more balanced piano parts of *Rhymes & Reasons* disappear here is a mystery; it seems to be something of a backwards step.

"We Are All in This Together," however, is one of King's better nods at the gospel style. Palmer's lyrics extol the importance of unconditional brotherly and sisterly love for all humankind. The gospel-infused musical setting, which includes a spirited backing chorus arrangement that includes not only the multitracked King, but also the powerful Eddie Kendricks Singers, a group that adds significantly to the effectiveness of the recording.

"Wrap Around Joy," with its bubbling lyrics and gospel-influenced late-1950s/early-1960s style rock and roll, finds King nodding in the direction of nostalgia. This was the kind of thing that other artists who grew up either listening to or performing early rock and roll were doing from the mid-1970s through the mid-1980s. I think specifically of songs such as Paul McCartney's "Name and Address" (from Wings' *London Town* album), John Lennon's "(Just Like) Starting Over," and (probably the best-known example) Billy Joel's "The Longest Time." In the same vein, but more obviously nostalgic was the Carpenters' "Yesterday Once More." Surely, David Palmer's lyrics about "mom" and "dad" and "boys" reflect the kind of thing Carole King might have been singing a dozen to 15 years before this, had her solo career taken off at that time. It certainly was the kind of thing Gerry Goffin and King were writing for the likes of Earl-Jean and the Cookies way back in the early days of their career. This is the kind of top-40 pop style on which Carole King cut her professional teeth, at least for the most part. The brilliance of the song comes from the fact that King does not write an entirely straightforward period piece. Instead, she treats the listener of "Wrap Around Joy" to a few choice unexpected harmonic twists. Ultimately, this serves several important purposes. For one thing, it shows King's growth as a composer from the early 1960s: the chromatic harmonic shifts are perfectly smooth, but beyond the scope of her straight-ahead rock and roll writing of the beginning of her career. The other important thing that the chromatic harmonic twists do is to paint "Wrap Around Joy" not so much as pure, syrupy nostalgia for the past, but as a fun, vital tribute to the values, lyrical themes, and musical styles of a bygone era—it is part nostalgia, part tribute, and part humorous parody. King sounds as though she really is having fun singing the song, which enhances helps the song move beyond mere nostalgia. In addition to its relationship to the songs named previously, "Wrap Around Joy" also fits in nicely with the late 1950s/early 1960s revival that was taking place in American television in the mid-1970s, with popular programs such as *Happy Days, Laverne and Shirley,* and the frequent appearances of the group Sha-Na-Na.

Wrap Around Joy's next track, "You Gentle Me," continues the nod in the direction of 1960s pop. The backing vocal arrangement and the rhythm guitar part suggest girl group material as well as Micky & Sylvia's "Love Is Strange." Some of the synthesizer timbres let the listener know that this is a mid-1970s track, but the innocence of David Palmer's lyrics of love and King's straightforward Brill Building melody, harmony, and vocal arrangement recall the earliest work of King and Gerry Goffin.

King's harmonic and melodic writing in "My Lovin' Eyes" is more complicated and sophisticated pop than the previous two songs. The instrumental and vocal arrangements make superb use of King's added-note chords, and the entire song has an energetic top-40 sensibility to it. It is a song that is perhaps a bit too adventurous harmonically for top-40 radio of the day, but shows that Carole King's commercial, universally likeable style of the 1960s clearly fed into her work on *Wrap Around Joy.*

Although Carole King had lived in California for years at this point in her career, she had written few obviously Los Angeles-oriented songs. Sure, songs such as "So Far Away" and "It's Too Late" were products of her life in the city's Laurel Canyon community, which in the early 1970s included a number of her fellow singer-songwriters. Still, the occasional "Back to California" aside, lyrical references that were obviously specific to her new home were rare. David Palmer's lyrics for "Sweet Adonis," however, find King welcoming her "Sweet Adonis" back from his work trying to find fame while waiting tables. Her "friend" could be an out-of-work actor trying to build a career in New York theater, but some of Palmer's references suggest even more strongly the movie industry of Hollywood. King's music is tuneful and suggestive of the style of several of her *Tapestry*-era melodies, but the best parts of the track are King's lead and backing vocal work and, especially, her instrumental arrangement. Melodically and harmonically the song captures the exuberance of King's character's welcome, but doesn't acknowledge Adonis's struggle as described in the individual verses of Palmer's text.

The social consciousness of *Fantasy* comes rushing back with "A Night This Side of Dying." Palmer's text finds King's character recounting several people she has seen who were suffering from serious drug problems. Palmer's lyrics, King's piano writing and performance, and her melodic and harmonic writing all have a touch of sincere-sounding poignancy. In fact, the song pulls together the best aspects of the singer-songwriter-styled *Rhymes & Reasons* and the social consciousness of *Fantasy*. The musical setting—and especially the arrangement—seem more appropriate for this tale of the tragedy of drug abuse than the Philly soul style of the songs of *Fantasy*. The only thing that seems a little strange is the presence of this song on what is otherwise a thoroughly easygoing pop album. It stands in stark relief to the cheery early 1960s style material that precede it.

The final track on *Wrap Around Joy*, "The Best Is Yet to Come," is David Palmer's expression of optimism in the face of hard times. Some of the images are considerably more closely aligned with clichés than most of his work on the album. King's music is pleasant pop that recalls some of her more upbeat compositions of the past couple of years such as "Sweet Seasons" and "Corazón." It is not as memorable as either of those two songs, though, and tends more than any other track on the album to sound like filler.

Carole King's post-*Tapestry* period found her redefining herself from album to album, moving in the direction of pop on *Music*, returning with a vengeance to the mature, introspective singer-songwriter genre on *Rhymes & Reasons*, moving into social commentary on *Fantasy*, and returning to a top-40 pop focus on *Wrap Around Joy*. This shift from style to style had brought King commercial and critical success and failure. She demonstrated that she still had the ability to write memorable, smash-hit songs, just like she had done for other artists in the 1960s. The biggest question raised by her thematic shifts from album to album would be, just what would she do next? The answer probably would surprise both music critics and fans alike.

Of Children, Relationships, and Social Issues: 1975–1980

From 1975 to 1980 Carole King continued to explore various lyrical focuses and different musical styles. She would surprise many with her 1975 project *Really Rosie*, an album aimed as much at children as at those of her own generation who had children. King issued one more album in 1975, *Thoroughbred*, before moving from Lou Adler's Ode Records to Capitol Records. She would then work with her third husband, Rick Evers, and the band Navarro and explore environmentalism and other lyrical and musical themes associated with King's new home in the American West, before losing Evers to a drug overdose. This late 1970s work generally would not be particularly well received by critics or by fans. At the end of the 1975–1980 period, however, King would achieve a commercial and critical reemergence with *Pearls: The Songs of Goffin and King*, which celebrated and updated the songs that had made her one of the leading composers of the 1960s.

REALLY ROSIE

The hit 1971 album *Tapestry* had finally gotten Carole King's performing career off the ground after the fits and starts that had lasted more than a decade. It had been an important part of the early 1970s women's movement and played a pivotal role in the lives of many young women of the time. King's subsequent albums had been hits and misses and had found her shifting thematic and lyrical focuses. *Really Rosie* represents an even wilder shift. Here, she set the work of noted children's writer Maurice Sendak to music for an animated television special. The album, along with a stage version, followed. While the album might not have been nearly the commercial success of her hit albums of the early 1970s, it garnered positive reviews for King as a composer and performer.

The 1975 cartoon television special *Really Rosie* put Maurice Sendak's 1960s poems about Rosie, a young Jewish girl living in New York City, and the characters around her neighborhood into a new medium. The focus of the television program is on the poems, as set to music by Carole King. The 26-minute show's storyline, that Rosie and her friends are singing songs as audition and rehearsal pieces for Rosie's upcoming film, is a thin structure that simply serves to link the somewhat disparate musical settings of the poems. In this regard, *Really Rosie* hearkens back to the revues that were popular in American musical theater before the development of the mature Broadway musical. The revues of the 1910s and 1920s also had individual songs as their feature: whatever "plot" existed typically was thin and simply provided a segue from song to song. King provides the spoken and sung voice of Rosie in the television program and she captures the spirit of Rosie perfectly, especially since she had at one time been a young Jewish girl growing up in New York City.

King's musical settings are tuneful and listenable, with minimal arrangements (only King, bassist Charles Larkey, drummer Andy Newmark, and guest background vocalists Sherry and Louise Goffin perform on the musical numbers). They are not, however, the most easily memorable compositions of her career. But, this is not King's fault; it is due to the nature of Maurice Sendak's poems, none of which is in a traditional structure associated with pop or classical song. King uses a variety of techniques in setting the sometimes rambling poems, including fitting Sendak's words with strophic form music where it more or less fits the structure of the poem, and writing in a melodic style that is considerably more through-composed in structure than any of her previous compositions in other *Really Rosie* settings. In fact, some of the poems—notably "Pierre"—are so atypical of song lyrics that it is a wonder that they can be set to music that resembles light pop song to the extent that they do.

The *Really Rosie* project did not end, however, with the television special. King released an album that included all the songs from the cartoon, plus a few additional settings of Sendak writings. When the recording was issued on compact disc, the popular press heaped praise on it.[1] Eventually, a stage version of *Really Rosie* emerged and has enjoyed some success. The Sendak–King project has also been the subject of study with regard to gender definition (Rosie is clearly the leader of her gang) and Jewish-American identities.[2]

THOROUGHBRED

Just as she had done so many times in the past, Carole King refused to duplicate the successes of her most recent work when time came for her 1975 album *Thoroughbred*. Save for one significant song, gone were the lyrics of David Palmer, King's collaborator on *Wrap Around Joy*. Instead, King turned to her own lyrics and a healthy dose of the lyrics of Gerry Goffin. Most important, however, was the overall lyrical focus of *Thoroughbred*. To a much greater extent than any of her previous albums, *Thoroughbred* was King's one-on-one relationship album. The album was also a musical stretch of sorts. The songs stylistically fit in the category of pop, but many of them use slightly unconventional structures. This lends a curious feel to the album, for although the lyrics and easygoing style would seem to make for a high degree of accessibility, the sometimes unusual phrase structure of the music forces listeners to stretch their ears beyond what is usually required by top-40 pop. King's supporting personnel represent an interesting mix of well-known Los Angeles session musicians such as saxophonist Tom Scott, bassist Leland Sklar, guitarist Waddy Wachtel, and drummer Russell Kunkel, with some of King's old singer-songwriter friends, including James Taylor, David Crosby, and Graham Nash.

The album begins with "So Many Ways," one of the songs for which King provided both words and music. Her text deals with the ways in which wordless expressions of love can be made. The simplicity of the piano-based accompaniment and King's generally stepwise melody suggest the emotionally focused songs of the singer-songwriter movement. The song is striking because of its unusual form. Most pop songs of Tin Pan Alley used AABA form, which became known as "song form." Even many songs—so long as they were not based on blues models—of the rock era are written in AABA form, or a slight modification, oftentimes incorporating a short "C" section, known as the middle eight. "So Many Ways," however, is in ABABA form, with each section, whether verse (A) or chorus (B), having different words. This form, as well as King's piano part, suggest an approach closer to classical music than to conventional American pop song.

Unfortunately, "So Many Ways" is not one of Carole King's best vocal performances. There is more strain in her voice than the text demands. In fact, it sounds like she was not in particularly good voice on the day she recorded the lead vocal. Significantly, producer Lou Adler treats her voice to more reverberation than had been customary on King's previous solo albums, and more than is used on other *Thoroughbred* songs. Because the album revolves so fully around the theme of relationships and ways in which emotions can be expressed, "So Many Ways" is an effective leadoff, although it would have benefited from more immediacy in the lead vocal.

Thoroughbred's second song, "Daughter of Light," is a Goffin–King collaboration. It is not the most memorable song the team ever wrote, but it has a pleasant melody and some tasty harmonic changes. One of the more subtle attributes of the song, though, is the reference to King's daughter as "beautiful," a lyrical reference to the phrase, "you're beautiful," in "So Many Ways." In fact, this is just of the first of several lyrical connections that tie the songs of *Thoroughbred* together. And the reference to beauty also hearkens back to the *Tapestry* "Beautiful," the song that had glorified inner beauty. The album's next song, "High out of Time," however, contains few musical or lyrical connections to the rest of the songs on *Thoroughbred* or other early Carole King albums. What it does feature is an entirely different vocal texture than that of the first two songs on *Thoroughbred*; Graham Nash, David Crosby, and James Taylor provide backing vocals that are clearly reminiscent of the work of Crosby, Stills, and Nash in the early 1970s. In fact, the song fits their characteristic style so well that it sounds like King could have written it for them. King's vocal arrangement also makes use of the unique texture of James Taylor's voice in his harmonies to King's lead vocals.

The fourth track on *Thoroughbred*, "Only Love Is Real," features both words and lyrics by King and continues the lyrical connections of the album's first two songs. Here, King refers to her "son and daughters," recalling the daughter reference in "Daughter of Light." Basically, though, the song is an ode in praise of love. King writes, "nothing is new under the sun," and there really is not much new in terms of her sentiments. The music is more *ostinato* (a short, frequently repeated figure) riff-based than the vast majority of her compositions. The opening, in fact, resembles the ostinato chord changes of Latin-influenced late 1960s rock songs by Dennis Yost and the Classics IV: the song "Spooky" immediately comes to mind. The song does not exhibit the same degree of immediacy as most of the earlier songs on the album, owing to producer Lou Adler's use of extra reverberation on King's lead vocal.

King's "There's a Space Between Us" includes an abundance of autobiographical-sounding references in the lyrics. Her references to an old friend to whom she needs to return from time to time suggests the public perception of the relationship between King and Gerry Goffin, who, although they divorced in 1968, continued to maintain an ongoing songwriting partnership over the intervening years. The presence of James Taylor on his prominent backing vocals suggests that he could be the old friend with whom King's character in the song wants to reestablish contact. There is a bit of gospel inflection in the song and a little of double-time vocal feel of several of the songs on *Rhymes & Reasons*, perhaps best experienced in "Bitter with the Sweet." Unfortunately, as on the first song on *Thoroughbred*, King's pitch is a little unsteady when she changes volume, and there is more raspiness when she reaches higher volumes than is usually heard in her singing in her earlier recordings.

"I'd Like to Know You Better," the second song to feature the vocal work of the trio of Crosby, Taylor, and Nash, is a far more memorable tune than the first, "High out of Time." In fact, the vocal arrangement, in which King's all-star backup singers are nicely blended into her lead vocal, and the simple lyrical sentiments of innocent romantic interest would not have been out of place on the Crosby, Stills, and Nash album *Déja Vu*. It exhibits something of the innocent elegance of Graham Nash's "Our House." King so fully integrates the lead and backing vocals and captures the spirit of Crosby, Stills, and Nash's groundbreaking album that "I'd Like to Know You Better" sounds for all the world like it was written around the idea of working with an ersatz Crosby, Stills, and Nash on *Thoroughbred*. To the extent that this was King's aim, this represents a return to the kind of writing she did as part of the Brill Building establishment: writing authentic-sounding songs for particular performers.

Goffin and King's "We All Have to Be Alone" deals with the conflict of the need to be cared for in moments of sorrow and the need "to be alone." This is one of Carole King's more complex song structures, as it defies traditional pop song structure. There is something of a repeated chorus, but the song feels much more through-composed than is customary in pop songs. Ultimately, this meandering, unpredictable structure adds significance to Goffin's text: the lyrical sentiments seem more profound and considerably eerier than they would have been had they been set to a conventional AABA musical form. The instrumental introduction, which is based on the song's chorus, is one of the most distinctive introductions Carole King ever composed. Because of the song's structure, it does not have the instant commercial appeal of King's best-known work, but it is a song that deserves to be better known to King's fans, if only for that beautiful introduction/chorus figure.

David Palmer had supplied all the lyrics for King's *Wrap Around Joy* album, including the highly successful song "Jazzman," but his contribution to *Thoroughbred* was limited to "Ambrosia." Palmer's lyrics recount the "fields of sweet Ambrosia" that have replenished the soul of the King's character in the past. King states that she needs to be replenished once again. King's music is suitably optimistic, which makes it a perfect match for the promise the "Ambrosia" holds for the character she portrays. Adding significantly to the quality of the song are the backing vocal contributions of the multi-tracked Carole King and the solo backing vocals of J. D. Souther. Souther is one of those figures who made a significantly more important contribution to American pop music of the late 1960s and 1970s than his rather modest name recognition would suggest. He is, in fact, one of those singer-songwriters who, for one reason or another, is much better known for the songs he composed than for his own performances. In that sense, he is something of a Jimmy Webb or Laura Nyro-type figure, although Souther was considerably more active as a guest vocalist than either Webb or Nyro. The timbre of his voice is much sweeter and blends with King's better than James Taylor's rather more distinctive voice, so King did well to include Souther on this particular track, given the nature of David Palmer's lyrics.

Gerry Goffin provided the lyrics for *Thoroughbred*'s next cut, "Still Here Thinking of You." Of all the album's songs, this one is closest to the lyrical and musical aesthetics of the *Tapestry*-era singer-songwriter movement. In part, this is due to the presence of James Taylor on acoustic guitar. Taylor plays some of those archetypal singer-songwriter guitar figures, including the suspended fourths that resolve to chord tones, but it goes well beyond the mere presence of or even the performance of Taylor. King's musical setting is perfectly in keeping with the *Tapestry*-style combination of soft rock and gospel. "Still Here Thinking of You" is tuneful, based on easily remembered motives like the songs that put Carole King on the map as a solo artist in the early 1970s. Adding to the 1971-style sound of the song are Gerry Goffin's lyrics of introspective dealing with a broken relationship.

Thoroughbred concludes with King's "It's Gonna Work out Fine." Each time I listen to this particular song, I am drawn to the stark contrast between King's use of saxophonist Tom Scott here and on *Wrap Around Joy*'s "Jazzman." The reed player in me regrets how little Scott is called on to do on this *Thoroughbred* track, as well as on "Only Love Is Real," on which Scott's contribution is very limited. This personal bias aside, "It's Gonna Work out Fine" is an optimistic song about a love relationship, set to distinctive music. Much of the song is built on a fairly conventional gospel-oriented rock framework. The ingenious part of King's composition is that she makes an entirely unexpected and unconventional key change as she sets her line, "It's gonna work out fine." This upward modulation conveys the optimism her lyrics contain and serves to drive the point home with dramatic emphasis.

Moving beyond conventional blues and pop song forms, in several of the songs of *Thoroughbred*, Carole King added compositional range to her already remarkable musical achievements. It is an album with a clear focus on relationships and a few direct lyrical and musical connections between songs. It is also, however, an album that wanders a bit in its musical styles and arrangement textures. When all these aspects are added together, *Thoroughbred* emerges as a strong album, but not King's most commercially successful and not her most unified artistic achievement. Although *Thoroughbred* did not include a truly "killer" commercial single, the album reached the *Billboard* top 10 pop album chart, and it remains one of King's albums that deserves to be better remembered today.

SIMPLE THINGS

Carole King's life and work underwent many changes in the mid-1970s. Professionally, she left Lou Adler's Ode label for Capitol. Personally, she fell in love with and married Rick Evers. King, Evers, and the band Navarro collaborated for the 1977 album *Simple Things*, King's first album on Capitol. Despite the album's title, this collection deals with some pretty weighty subjects such as political and economic power plays, alienation, overpopulation, and humanity's apparent inability to get along. Lyricists King and Evers sound a note of optimism about each of these social, political, and personal problems, however, suggesting in just about every case that through simple love and caring, the problems can be solved.

The artwork contained in the gatefold cover of *Simple Things* suggests Carole King's new direction away from Los Angeles and toward the rural American West. Although there were clear hints of this direction contained in the horseback picture of King on the 1975 album *Thoroughbred*, here it is much clearer. The drawings of horses and the photographs of King and Rick Evers paint King not as the sophisticated New York, Tin Pan Alley songwriter of the 1960s, nor as the Laurel Canyon, Los Angeles, star of the singer-songwriter era, as much as they suggest a close tie with the wide open spaces of the West and a tie to the principles of living in oneness with nature and the back-to-the-land movement. King would continue to develop along this line in her presentation and in her music on her 1978 and 1979 albums, *Welcome Home* and *Touch the Sky*.

Critical reaction to *Simple Things* was decidedly mixed. Much of the negative criticism concerned the lyrics. For example, Dave Marsh of *Rolling Stone* wrote that the album "completely lacks the halting dark misery and the striking imagery and metaphor of [King's] best work."[3] An unnamed reviewer in the British magazine *Melody Maker* found the music formulaic and thought that many of the lyrics could not be taken seriously.[4] Writing in *Creem*, Richard Walls described the lyrics as not being as good as the music.[5] However, *Crawdaddy*'s Robert Spitz also found fault with King's music, asking the rather pointed question, "How is it possible for such a gifted writer to release an album with not one—NOT ONE—hummable tune on it?"[6] In contrast, Don Heckman, of *High Fidelity/Musical America*, gave the album a generally favorable review, noting King's craftsmanship.[7]

In a sense, all of the critics were correct in their assessment of *Simple Things*. It certainly was different in sound from any previous Carole King album. Part of this was due to the style of Navarro. Unlike the friends and session players that assisted with King's previous albums, this band gave the album more of a guitar-based sound. Even the saxophone and flute solos by Navarro's Richard Handy are different in basic tone color and style than those by the likes of Tom Scott, Curtis Amy, and other woodwind players on previous King albums. Certainly, the overall sound of the words and music of *Simple Things* has something of an anonymous quality to it, especially when compared with King's earlier solo albums. There are some melodic and accompaniment licks that sound reminiscent of the work of other artists, including more than just a touch of early 1970s favorites as disparate as Elton John and Lynyrd Skynyrd. There are some well-written melodies and interesting song structures, but little that is as instantly singable by the listener as the well-known hits King had written in the 1960s and early 1970s.

The song "Simple Things" begins the album. Rick Evers provided the text, which celebrates the simple things of childhood, such as horses running free, living in freedom, and seeing flowers grow wild. Evers concludes that, "The secret of living is life." Perhaps these are not the most profound sentiments ever put into verse form, but the text does capture the innocence of simply experiencing life as a child would. King sets the lyrics to cheery music. The melody is tuneful, although more complex than the sort of tune that a listener would remember and sing in the shower.

Whereas "Simple Things" hints at country-rock style, "Hold On," another King–Evers collaboration moves a little closer to the genre. The Evers text is impressionistic and more than a little vague. The basic gist of the text is that if one is able to "Hold On" (the song's title) long enough, all of the evil forces that cause life's problems will disappear. King's musical setting includes some dramatic statements by the instruments. Even more than "Simple Things," this song's melody is strong but certainly more complex than most pop songs, and certainly more complex than the great pop hits King had composed in the past. In stretching out as a composer on a song such as "Hold On," King was sacrificing accessibility for art. This is probably the kind of song that created such division among the reviewers of *Simple Things. High Fidelity/Musical America*'s Don Heckman praised King for her craftsmanship on the album, but *Crawdaddy*'s Robert Stephen Spitz bemoaned the album's lack of accessible melodies.[8] "Hold On" clearly is one of the songs that support the assessment of both critics.

In the three remaining songs on side one of *Simple Things,* "In the Name of Love," "Labyrinth," and "You're the One Who Knows," King is her own lyricist. She carries on much of the impressionism of the two Rick Evers texts, but is a bit more direct in her expressions of the philosophy that love of one's fellow humans conquers all obstacles. The three songs, however, find King exploring a wide spectrum of musical styles.

"In the Name of Love" is a slow ballad that celebrates the ultimate importance of love in overcoming every obstacle. King affirms her belief that love governs, or should govern, every aspect of every human being's life, from birth to death. King's musical setting contains beautiful melody and harmony. More than just about anything she had written since *Rhymes & Reasons* (1973), it encapsulates the intense personal expression of the classic singer-songwriter era, as well as the straightforward beauty and simplicity of that earlier era's best musical settings. More than any other song Carole King has ever written, "In the Name of Love" exudes a vibrant sense of spirituality. It deserves to be better known.

"Labyrinth" has a feel of modern Broadway-like theatricality to it, and I certainly do not mean that in any sort of disparaging way. It is just that the song's structure is fairly complex by conventional pop song standards. And the piano lick that introduces several of the song's sections would sound entirely at home in the popular Broadway musicals of the 1970s and 1980s. King's lyrics deal with the labyrinth of "mind games and power plays" that traps not only individuals but also the entire human race. She concludes that if people allow love for their fellow human beings to flow through their lives, they can escape the labyrinth.

Musically, "You're the One Who Knows" is the first of the *Simple Things* songs to suggest a curious muted combination of Elton John's "Honky Cat" (1972) and Lynyrd Skynyrd's "Free Bird" (1973), although here the references to the style of the Lynyrd Skynyrd southern rock classic are strongest. King's lyrics are impressionistic and filled with vague images that revolve around the general theme that the one who helped her find her way out of "Babylon" is now gone. To the extent that her lyrics could be understood as possibly having been inspired by Rick Evers, they took on eerie significance when Evers died of a drug overdose in early 1978. Although these clearly are "how I feel" lyrics, they are hazy enough that the personal immediacy of King's best work of the early 1970s is lost. Musically, the double lead guitar solos and Southern rock feel—in the manner of Lynyrd Skynyrd or the Charlie Daniels Band—take some getting used to for the longtime Carole King fan. They sound nothing like what she had previously recorded. And like most of the material that precedes it on *Simple Things,* the melody is strong, but not hook laden like the most commercial of King's earlier songs. Here, working with Navarro gives King the ability to move into new compositional directions, but it also causes her to lose some of what helped to make her successful as a solo artist—the focus on using her gospel-inspired piano playing to support generally clear lyrics that deal with personal relationships. The song sounds as if it could have made a strong album cut for a band more closely identified with the musical style. I could even imagine it in the hands of a non-Southern rock act like Fleetwood Mac; the melody line is ideally suited for a singer such as Stevie Nicks.

The second half of *Simple Things* leads off with "Hard Rock Café," a song in which King calls to mind the rhythmic spirit, accompaniment style, and chord progression of Ritchie Valens's famous late-1950s arrangement and recording of the Mexican folk tune "La Bamba." She celebrates the escapism that can be found at the neighborhood roadhouse. She includes one brief slower tempo section that reflects the gospel influence that pervades some of her best work of the early 1970s. In one sense, the party-like atmosphere of the song seems out of character for the album. For one thing, the references to Chicano music are unique among the *Simple Things* tracks. For another, most of the songs are somewhat to considerably more serious in nature; none of the others could be construed as escapist. To her credit, however, King as singer and co-producer gives her voice a sense of emotional detachment. By doing so, she becomes more of an observer than a participant in the festivals. She does not reach the level of cool detachment of a performer such as Paul Simon, but she moves in that direction on this track, and it is a better song for it.

In "Time Alone," a very short song, King writes some of the internal rhymes that pervaded *Rhymes & Reasons.* She exploits the double meaning of the title phrase in what is a fairly straightforward love ballad. Her simple, mostly stepwise melody allows the words to speak for themselves.

King's "God Only Knows," not to be confused with the famous mid-1960s Brian Wilson composition of the same name, is another of the album's rock songs. Like "You're the One Who Knows," there is a touch of southern rock here, but also more than just a hint of the Elton John of "Honky Cat" and other tracks on his album *Honky Chateau,* as well as John's well-known "Saturday Night's Alright for Fighting." King's piano thumping plays a fairly prominent role in the beginning of the song, but the extended boogie-on-out instrumental ending is guitar based. This section illustrates just how far King had moved from the sound of the almost exclusively piano-based albums such as *Tapestry* and *Rhymes & Reasons.* King's text is not particularly to the point, but deals generally with the questions of survival and recovery from broken relationships her character has experienced. Whether or not her character will recover, "God only knows." The music and the lyrical sentiments make somewhat odd bedfellows in the song.

Rick Evers and King collaborated on the song "To Know That I Love You," a simple, tender expression of love. The thinner accompaniment texture, as well as the straightforward lyrics, suggests the sound of classic early 1970s King. In contrast to her earlier hits, however, the melody is not as instantly recognizable and memorable.

The final cut on *Simple Things,* "One," is one of Carole King's most elaborate songs, both from the standpoint of her lyrics and her musical setting. The theme of King's lyrics is the universal connection of humankind. To a greater extent than any of King's previous recordings, "One" takes on grand anthem-like qualities, because of its strong secular humanistic message of spirituality through love and King's full vocal and orchestral arrangements. King uses dynamic (volume) extremes and extremes of texture to lead the listener through her message. For example, at the point at which her lyrics are dealing with the concept of "one" meaning one person (herself), the musical setting includes a minimum of accompanying instruments and King's solo voice, but when she uses the word to refer to the oneness of humanity, she is joined by a backing choir and a rich palette of orchestral instruments. She also sets the different lyrical sections to highly contrasting melodic and harmonic materials. Of particular interest is the plaintive melody she uses to set the question about what she, as one person, can do to bring about positive change in the world. It is strong, socially conscious writing, with excellent musical support for the lyrics and remains one Carole King song that deserves to be better known. Unfortunately, though, little of King's work from the brief time period during which she recorded for Capitol has been reissued. *Simple Things,* for example, seems be available only in its original vinyl release, assuming that the interested fan can find a used copy, perhaps from an on-line auction site. And even if she were to include a song such as "One" on one of her small-scale "Living Room" tours, the song would be missing the vital ingredients provided by the rich vocal and instrumental arrangement on *Simple Things.*

One of the most interesting things about *Simple Things* was the extent to which it proved that Carole King was very much her own artist. She showed herself to be totally unaffected by most of the prevailing musical styles of the day, including punk rock and disco. Unfortunately, however, there are signs that she was becoming a musical follower rather than a musical innovator, given the oblique musical references to artists and songs popular approximately five years earlier. King and Evers's love-conquers-all social, political, and personal problems lyrics were not particularly mainstream in the late 1970s. The lyrical sentiments were, in fact, closer to the kinds of things that might have been more commonplace in songs of the late 1960s, and in the early 1970s era of John Lennon's "Imagine" and Cat Stevens's "Peace Train." Little of King's output from the late 1960s and early 1970s clearly presents a sort of hippie or back-to-the-land philosophy and musical style. Here, curiously, that gentle side of the spirit of the counterculture era is alive and well. King would continue to explore similar themes on her next album.

WELCOME HOME

Although King again collaborated with Rick Evers for some of the songs on the 1978 album *Welcome Home,* and despite the scenes of domestic bliss in King's rural home depicted in the album's elaborate artwork, the production of this album ended on a tragic note. Evers succumbed to a drug overdose and died on March 21, 1978, between the time the album was recorded and the time it was released. As much as anything else, *Welcome Home* serves as Carole King's tribute to the spirit of Evers. The album once again features the instrumental work of the band Navarro, which had backed King on *Simple Things.*

The album kicks off in a rocking mood with King's solo composition "Main Street Saturday Night." This song continues the boogie rock style of "You're the One Who Knows" and "God Only Knows," both from *Simple Things.* King describes young people out cruising and looking for dates on a "Main Street Saturday night" in virtually any American town of any size. The rock style fits the lyrics, but is somewhat anonymous, being too close in sound to King's own "Back to California," the Beatles's "Get Back," and a host of other similar late 1960s and early 1970s songs, to sound particularly distinctive as a pop song. Where it succeeds is as a showcase for Navarro as a band; however, this is a double-edged sword on a Carole King album. In "Main Street Saturday Night," the band is at its best, but King herself ends up playing a decidedly supporting role as an instrumentalist. One of the main attractions about King as a performer that contributed to the success of her early 1970s albums and the work she would do after the Navarro years was her dual role as singer and prominent pianist. Fortunately, not of all of *Welcome Home*'s tracks find her so much in the background.

"Sunbird," with its impressionistic short poem of rhyming couplets by Rick Evers and its thinner, more-piano-based texture, would not have sounded out of place on King's best pure singer-songwriter album, *Rhymes & Reasons.*

Even Miguel Rivera's conga playing calls to mind the percussion work that Bobbye Hall did on *Rhymes & Reasons*. King's music is based largely on a short, distinctive melodic motive. As she had done with many of her motivically based compositions of the past, King incorporates the figure into both her vocal melody and the accompaniment. Because of the brevity of the Evers poem, King does not write in a conventional AABA song form.[9] Instead, her music follows an ABA structure, something more closely associated with the instrumental character pieces and the art songs of the nineteenth-century German composer Robert Schumann and other European composers of the Romantic era.

As Carole King acknowledges in the *Welcome Home* liner notes, "Venusian Diamond" is unabashedly based on the musical style of the Beatles.[10] From the opening drone of the tambura, an instrument associated with the music of the Indian subcontinent, and the electronic processing of King's lead vocals, the specific Beatles reference seems to be to the music of George Harrison and John Lennon in the late-1966 through 1967 period. Navarro guitarists Robert McEntee and Mark Hallman even adopt the electric guitar timbre used by Harrison on some of his post-Beatles solo recordings. Some of the more popish aspects of the latter part of the song reflect the influence of the compositions of Paul McCartney. The lyrics, which King's liner notes acknowledge as coming primarily from Rick Evers, with additions from herself and members of Navarro,[11] are impressionistic in the manner of British psychedelic music of 1967, particularly that of John Lennon. This is totally different in style than anything else that Carole King had written and recorded as a solo artist; in fact, it differs from anything she would record in the nearly 30 years that have passed since she recorded *Welcome Home*. Her musical references to Hindustani *raga* (scalar melodic patterns used in Indian music) and the highly impressionistic lyrics, however, have a precedent in her music. One would have to look back into the 1967–1968 era, however, to find a few psychedelic-style compositions of King and Gerry Goffin, such as "The Porpoise Song," which was the theme song for the Monkees's movie *Head*. "Take a Giant Step," from a couple of years earlier than "The Porpoise Song," also includes elements of early psychedelia. "Venusian Diamond" is actually a fun period piece, although its distinctive musical and production style points out one of the unique challenges of *Welcome Home*: the album shifts stylistically from song to song more abruptly and to greater extremes than any other Carole King album. This is not necessarily a bad thing: Stevie Wonder made a huge impact on the R&B and pop album charts in the 1972–1974 period by mixing pop, funk, jazz ballad, and other styles, some of which might seem to be mutually exclusive. This song and this album show King's range as a songwriter, but also tend to have a less focused feel than most of her more commercially successful work.

As an example of the abrupt juxtaposition of stylistic extremes on *Welcome Home*, the next track, "Changes," moves back to the introspective singer-songwriter style. Although the song is brief, less than 2½ minutes, it is one of the most personal songs on the album. In fact, King indicates in her liner notes that the song was written in direct response to the hurt she incurred at the hands of a friend.[12] Her lyrics include internal rhymes that had characterized her writing on *Rhymes & Reasons,* and they are much more to the point than the Rick Evers lyrics of *Welcome Home.* The melody of the song's verse is based on a simple ABAB[1] phrase structure. The overall structure of the song is verse-chorus-verse, with no other repeated sections. As is the case, then, with "Sunbird," the overall form is more in keeping with Romantic period character pieces and art songs (ABA) than with conventional American pop song form. The instrumental accompaniment to King's solo vocal includes acoustic guitar and a sprinkling of electric keyboard. Therefore even though this song structurally and stylistically bears some resemblance to the King–Evers composition "Sunbird," the instrumental texture is quite different than King's singer-songwriter-school material of 1971–1973.

"Morning Sun," with words and music by King, resembles some of the very pleasant, very listenable album cuts written by Goffin and King back in the 1960s. "Sometime in the Morning," an album cut for the Monkees, for example, immediately comes to mind. Perhaps the most interesting thing about the song, aside from the wonderful arrangement that makes great use of the softer side of Navarro, are the autobiographical-sounding references in the lyrics. King writes, for example, that, "like the shoreline that divides the sea and the sand," she is "a surface ever changing." Although Carole King has been perhaps one of the most private stars of pop music throughout her career, these words ring true if one simply considers her musical output. Few pop musicians of the 1970s redefined themselves musically to the extent that King did on her post-*Tapestry* albums. Her words ring especially true as the listener experiences *Welcome Home,* which finds King presenting perhaps the widest range of musical and lyrical styles on any of her albums before or since. Ultimately, though, the main purpose of "Morning Sun" seems to be not so much to define Carole King as to celebrate the new possibilities each new day presents.

Side Two of *Welcome Home* kicks off with "Disco Tech," a composition credited to King and Navarro. The song raises the unlikely image of Carole King as disco diva. King's liner notes explain the reason for what might seem like a strange combination of generally down-to-earth singer-songwriter and boogie-on-out dance music. She writes of the track in the album's liner notes, "Secret Fantasy Department Part 2: could I be a Rhythm and Blues group?"[13] Taken in the spirit of a fantasy-like experiment—and a fun-sounding one for King, Navarro, and the studio horn section—"Disco Tech" is a complete success: it's actually credible disco music with a typically silly lyrical "message." If the song had been meant to chart a new course for King, not only would it have been a few years too late to have been commercially viable (the pop music world was moving from disco to new wave by this point), but it also represents a genre that almost completely obliterates the personal artist-audience connection on which King and her breed of singer-songwriters thrived. "Disco Tech" remains one song that few newer, post-vinyl-era fans of Carole King have heard. *Welcome Home* (like the rest of her Capitol Records catalog) seems to be hard to come by these days, but it is one that is worth the search, if only to prove that King is capable of making just about any contemporary popular music style her own.

"Wings of Love," a collaboration of King and Rick Evers, features an intimate instrumental texture. Here, King's arpeggiated piano chords suggest what would soon emerge as new age, or light jazz, music. Evers's poem is not in conventional pop song verse structure. King allows the Evers text to steer her as a composer; she paints the literal meaning of several of the lines—singing a rising melody as the lyrics speak of soaring, and breaking into vocal harmony on the word "harmony." Some of her text painting is more subtle, though. And because the poem is not written in a conventional, repeating rhyme scheme, King is not constrained to follow a set, formal structure. Her musical setting combines elements of strophic form with some through-composed material. She meets the compositional challenges, turning "Wings of Love" into something more closely related to a contemporary art song than a pop tune. Given the text's focus on the free wonder of love and King's heartfelt setting, "Wings of Love" becomes especially poignant with the death of Rick Evers just a couple of months after the recording of *Welcome Home*.

King's "Ride the Music" combines a music hall feel, accomplished largely by means of King's piano playing and the clarinet work of Navarro's Richard Hardy. "Ride the Music" is a peppy, pretty song, but is one of the more trivial pieces on *Welcome Home*. In the context of what might appear to be the musical theme of the album—diversity of musical styles—"Ride the Music" adds one more element, but not an essential one.

Like its immediate predecessor on *Welcome Home,* "Everybody's Got the Spirit" finds Carole King, as a lyricist, praising the art of music. She incorporates a shuffle style that is positioned somewhere between the Boz Scaggs song "Lido Shuffle" and the mainstream pop, snappy, pseudo-gospel songs of Laura Nyro recorded by the 5th Dimension back in the early 1970s; Nyro's "Save the Country" immediately comes to mind.

"Welcome Home" is a much more substantial song than either of its two predecessors, despite its brevity. Here King's lyrics describe having found a new life and a new home. The implication is that while this place may not be the home of her birth or childhood, she has been moving in this direction her entire life. Her references to the "clear reflection" in the water and the "harmony of season" that she sees in nature would seem to suggest her actual rural home: the home she shared with Rick Evers that is depicted in the album's artwork. King confirms this in the liner notes.[14] Musically, "Welcome Home" reflects King's longtime integration of African American gospel into her style. There is also a melodic resemblance to her *Tapestry* songs, most notably "Beautiful." The combination of lyrics and music sounds believable in King's arrangement and performance and confirms that her journey from New York City to the West Coast had been an important in her life and a long-term move. She certainly makes a stronger case for her love of the western United States than she did in her 1971 *Music* track "Back to California," because this music sounds more honest.

Carole King's *Welcome Home* includes a wide range of musical and lyrical styles. Although this allows King, Rick Evers, and the musicians of Navarro to show off their talents, it tends to make *Welcome Home* disjointed as a package. Taken as individual songs, though, some stand among the more interesting—if largely unknown and critically unrecognized—purely musical accomplishments of Carole King as a composer in the second half of the 1970s.

TOUCH THE SKY

In Carole King's third album on the Capitol label, *Touch the Sky,* she embraces environmentalism and images drawn from her life in the American West. Gone, for the most part, were the musicians of Navarro; only guitarist and vocalist Mark Hallman and percussionist Miguel Rivera remained from the performers on *Welcome Home.* The Norm Kinney and Carole King production team of *Simple Things* and *Welcome Home* was no more; King co-produced *Touch the Sky* with Mark Hallman. Both lyrically and musically, *Touch the Sky* was a much more unified statement than either of her previous two albums. That does not mean, however, that critical reaction was universally favorable toward the album. Tom Smucker of the *Village Voice* acknowledged that the album contained "good melodies and structures," and that it found King singing with a rejuvenated voice. Smucker praised King for turning away from some of the overly personal and "spacy" songs that had—in his view—marred her songwriting after *Tapestry.*[15] On the other hand, Susan Hill wrote in her *Melody Maker* review, that although King was to be commended for taking on worthy environmental concerns, "these laments from Tin Pan Alley hipsters are not instantly affecting." Hill did, however, comment favorably on King's singing and her arrangements.[16]

The album's first song, "Time Gone By," establishes the lyrical theme of the album. King's text emphasizes the idea of balance, equating good environmental stewardship with a balanced, loving relationship between two people, and between different nations and other groups of people. In particular, the song seems to be a response to the extent to which the 1960s values of peace, love, and understanding had fallen away by the late 1970s. The music recalls some of Carole King's best-remembered compositions of the 1960s and the early 1970s. The melody of each verse is simple and based on a short, easily recognizable motive; this part of the tune is in the lower part of King's voice. The chorus, in which she recalls the "time gone by" when the values of peace, love, and understanding ruled the lives of many people, moves into the upper part of her vocal range and exudes the hope of which her text speaks. She accomplishes this not only through the use of register but also with snappier rhythms and by using a tune with a different shape than the melody of the more resigned-sounding verses.

"Move Lightly" features some of Carole King's most passionate, bluesy rock singing. At times she approaches the raw expression of a Janis Joplin. One of the curious things about this song that also carries through the bulk of the album is that even though King does relatively little instrumental work on *Touch the Sky*—she plays piano on 4 of the 10 cuts and acoustic guitar on 2 other songs—there is little feeling of that being a missing ingredient. "Move Lightly" and most of the other songs on the album feature King's newfound blues-country-rock vocal stylings to such an extent that they succeed as almost entirely vocally focused songs.[17] It also helps that most of the songs are serious in tone and really require the listener to focus on the message.

"Dreamlike I Wander" intensifies the country leanings of *Touch the Sky*. This triple-meter song finds King addressing a former lover whom she misses a great deal. Although her lyrics do not speak of death, those familiar with her relationship with Rick Evers and his death the year before are tempted to hear this as a reflection of the difficulty she may have been having dealing with Evers's untimely passing. Whether or not that was King's intent, hearing the song as an autobiographical expression of the experiences of 1978 and 1979 elevates the importance of "Dreamlike I Wander" on the album. The one quibble I have with the piece from a musical standpoint is that it too closely resembles other country style songs by other rock musicians. In particular, the melody, harmony, style, metrical feel, and arrangement suggest the influence, or at least the style, of George Harrison's 1970 song "Behind That Locked Door," which was included on Harrison's first post-Beatles solo album, *All Things Must Pass*.

The album's next track, "Walk with Me (I'll Be Your Companion)," also bears the stamp of country influence, although this is most noticeable here because of the instrumental arrangement and the music of the chorus. The verses incorporate elements of major tonality and the mixolydian mode (a major scale with a lowered seventh scale step), something that King did in some of her rock songs of the mid-1960s, notably "Take a Giant Step."

The final track on side one of *Touch the Sky*, "Good Mountain People," is a more successful and more substantial song than "Walk with Me." With its country rock sound, King's music is a perfect match for her lyrics, which speak of the "good mountain people" of the American West. She highlights the freedom that she feels in the West and the way in which her neighbors— "rednecks" and "hippies," who would have been on opposite sides of the proverbial political fence several years earlier—all manage to live and work together and help "each other out in time of need." King sounds convincing in this spirit of cooperation, environmentalism, and oneness with nature and with people of widely diverse political stripes. And "Good Mountain People" is a strong enough representative of the southern rock/country rock style in music and lyrics that it could have been successfully included as an album cut by a number of groups at the time.

The second side of *Touch the Sky* begins with a somewhat curious song, "You Still Want Her." King seems to be addressing someone who is in love with a woman who has caused him (presumably) considerable pain in the past. Ultimately, King is warning him that this time will not be any different. This country-rock song works well enough on its own and would not sound out of place on an early 1970s album by, say, the Eagles; but it does not seem to fit the overarching theme of *Touch the Sky*, at least to the extent that environmentalism and the importance of people getting along with one another form a connection that runs through most of the album's songs.

"Passing of the Days" is a sort of benediction, or blessing, with a touch of the influence of the musical influence of A. P. Carter's "Will the Circle Be Unbroken" and the Eagles' recording of songwriter Jack Tempchin's "Peaceful Easy Feeling" thrown in for good measure. Although the music is not particularly groundbreaking, it fits the text perfectly. King's lyrics wish the recipient of her blessing well in the face of all the problems of the world. The references she makes to these problems are just metaphorical, and just vague enough that they are pretty easy to decipher, yet do not make the mistake of hitting the listener in the face. For King to have made the descriptions of the social ills (environmental degradation, overemphasis on corporate profits, consumerism, escapism) too specific or too pointed would have taken away from the song's emphasis on the positive message of the blessing itself, which forms the song's chorus.

The song "Crazy" is an indictment of the "chrome American dream," a life of conspicuous consumption. Like the album's second song, "Move Lightly," King's singing here exhibits full-throated passion. She sounds a fully believable country-rock-blues singer. As well as "Crazy" works, however, this kind of material sounds as if it could have been written and recorded by any of a number of singers or groups associated with the genre. Ultimately, because of their adherence to a genre not particularly known for innovative harmonic or melodic structures, the faster *Touch the Sky* country-rock songs—"Crazy" being one of them—take on a more generic sound than her more idiosyncratic and instantly recognizable work of the earlier part of the decade.

It is possible to give a metaphorical reading to King's song "Eagle." The eagle that "wants to fly again," despite having "been shot down," could represent a person, a disenfranchised minority group, women, or a concept such as freedom. Or, the eagle of the song could simply be the grand raptor that someone living in the American West might see flying silently overhead. That is what makes the song so effective: listeners have the freedom to read into King's lyrics what they will. The music is not as memorable as some of the songs on *Touch the Sky*, but King does incorporate some nice gospel-influenced vocal licks.

Touch the Sky concludes with another song, "Red," in which King makes her sociopolitical points in a metaphorical way so that she avoids hitting her listeners over the head. The song supports the cause of Native Americans and is in a slow tempo. King sings with passion, which causes her voice to exhibit some of the expressive edge of folk/protest/blues singers. "Red" is a mood piece and succeeds as such in painting the sad plight of a once-proud, but now conquered people. Its placement at the conclusion of *Touch the Sky* lends a serious tone to the end of the album, which throughout teeters between sadness caused by various social ills and hope that the future will be brighter.

Touch the Sky was in many respects the culmination of the work that King had begun with *Simple Things* and continued with *Welcome Home*. Aspects of boogie rock, and particularly country-rock, little by little became part of her repertoire. With each of these projects, King more fully integrated back-to-the-land, back-to-a-simpler-life lyrics, in addition to the musical manifestations of her new rural life. And she did so with increasing confidence and believability as a singer of this genre. Had Carole King continued on this path, she might have developed a crossover following, picking up country fans. That is exactly the kind of missed opportunity for further development that makes *Touch the Sky* so maddening. As soon as she approached perfection as a writer and performer in a new style, King turned in another direction.

PEARLS: THE SONGS OF GOFFIN AND KING

In organizing this study of the words, music, and recordings of Carole King, I tried to arrange the chapter boundaries based on 5- and 10-year segments. It is fortuitous that *Pearls: The Songs of Goffin and King* was recorded and released in 1980, at the end of one of those segments, as the album marks an important turning point in King's career. After several years of declining public and critical acceptance of her work, King returned to (mostly) well-known songs on which she and Gerry Goffin had collaborated over the years. In part because of wide-ranging success these songs had enjoyed the first time (and sometimes the second and third times), *Pearls* was Carole King's most successful recording in years on several levels. The other crucial factor in the album's success, however, was King's powerful performance and the thoroughly contemporary nature of the arrangements. At the time of the album's release, however, critics duly noted that, King's focus on her older compositions may have been her tacit acknowledgment that her recent songs just were not establishing nearly the kind of connection with audiences (or critics, for that matter) that her pre-mid-1970s material had.[18]

Pearls begins with "Dancin' with Tears in My Eyes," a new Goffin and King collaboration. With Goffin's lyrical references to the glitter ball and strobe lights of the 1970s disco era, and King's disco-oriented music and arrangement, the piece is squarely a song of the times. At least it is a song that represents the pop style of the 1970s. Several reviewers have mentioned "Dancin' with Tears in My Eyes" as one of the highlights of *Pearls.*[19] Using thoroughly contemporary sounding music, King sets Goffin's story of a woman who goes out disco dancing to forget her lost love, but always finds herself dancing with tears in her eyes. Her melody for the verses, but especially for the chorus, is easily memorable, the kind of hook-laden music that defined her songs up through the *Tapestry* era. Curiously, compared with some of the extended mixes that were commonplace in actual, "real" disco music, "Dancin' with Tears in My Eyes" is somewhat short on development. This is typical of just about all the songs on *Pearls:* the 2½-minute songs of the 1960s generally become late-1970s styled 2½-minute songs, even though the pop aesthetics of the 1970s found many prominent artists breaking free of the 2½-to-3-minute limits of the past on a regular basis on singles. King, though, sings the track with a passion that is accentuated by the raw edge in her voice. During the height of her popularity as a singer—nearly a decade before *Pearls*—the vocal edge had been muted somewhat by Lou Adler's production. On *Pearls,* King and co-producer Mark Hallman allow the upper partials of the harmonic spectrum to come forward. This helps King sound like a completely relevant singer of the post-punk phase of the pop era. Perhaps this is not as pretty presentation of her voice as many of her other albums, but it suits the times.

The album's next two tracks, "The Loco-Motion" and "One Fine Day," remain faithful to the original versions of the early 1960s, but include a few instrumental touches (the drumming and the electric guitar timbre) that suggest the late 1970s. By and large, though, these songs are so matter-of-fact in their arrangements and presentation as to suggest a reading of some of the artist's oldies at a concert. King's version of "The Loco-Motion" suffers a bit in comparison with the famous versions recorded in the 1960s by Little Eva and in the 1980s by Kylie Minogue. In particular, her intonation drifts too much in the upper register. When issued as a single, "One Fine Day" reached No. 12 on the *Billboard* pop charts for King, her best-performing single in years. She sings the song convincingly (it is a much better performance than "The Loco-Motion"), and her piano playing drives the recording in a way that hearkens back to some of her best piano work on *Tapestry.*

Because of the nature of Gerry Goffin's lyrics, the album's next track, "Hey Girl," requires something of a suspension of belief, as it was originally a man-to-woman song recorded by Freddie Scott. In the last two decades of the twentieth century, a number of singers have turned to the Brill Building songbook for concerts and recordings. In particular, the classically oriented duo of singer Joan Morris and her husband, pianist William Bolcom, concertized extensively with the Jerry Leiber and Mike Stoller songbook, treating the music of those Brill Building greats with the respect usually afforded classical literature. A versatile, technically gifted singer such as a Joan Morris is capable of making a highly effective musical statement regardless of the text, or any requirements placed on the singer of a suspension of belief. In other words, a musician on the level of Morris can sell the song through her musicality and acting ability. What King does to sell the song is to render an entirely straightforward version, allowing the music to take precedence over Goffin's text. She does not add emotion in an attempt to sound convincing as a character. Someone other than the composer who would sing the song in this way might be accused of missing the emotional content and failing to make the gender transference effectively; however, King's performance works because she is the composer. It might have been better to have omitted this song and included in its place something that would have presented a more mainstream poetic voice or allowed King to present a greater degree of emotion. The problem with *not* including the song is that "Hey Girl" is such an exceptional ballad among Carole King's famous 1960s collaborations with Gerry Goffin. Melodically and harmonically it is more sophisticated and complex than just about any of the "girl group" ballads they wrote during the period.

The next track on *Pearls*, "Snow Queen," suffers from a lack of energy. The slight *ritardandi* (a gradual slowing down) in the instrumental breaks cause this reading of the song to sound tired in comparison to King's performance with the City on the album *Now That Everything's Been Said*. Another former *Now That Everything's Been Said* track, "Hi-De-Ho," succeeds much better here than "Snow Queen." For one thing, a bluesy song like "Hi-De-Ho" is ideally suited for King's vocal style. "Hi-De-Ho," however, is also not without its faults. The tempo on King's *Now That Everything's Been Said* recording of the song seems to work better than the current version, and here on *Pearls* she gets a little too cutesy in her presentation of one of the verses (the one that begins, "Once I met the devil"). The performance style comes off as too flippant, particularly compared with her rendition of the song with the City.

King's recent rural life since her move to Idaho (by way of California) and her temporary move to Texas to record this album paid off handsomely on the recording of "Chains." This is one of those early 1960s Goffin and King songs on which the original arrangement of The Cookies's recording was at least in part responsible for defining the song. At the time it might have been seen as being partially responsible for the record's (and therefore the song's) considerable commercial success. In fact, when the Beatles recorded "Chains" on their first album, they copied the original arrangement nearly note by note, with John Lennon and George Harrison's electric guitars playing the horn licks. On *Pearls*, however, King breaks free of the 1962 recording, putting together a western swing/Texas swing rendition entirely appropriate for the Austin recording studio and for her life in the American

West for the past several years. It works well, suggesting just how universal this Goffin and King song can be. The novelty of the arrangement also makes this one of the most interesting tracks on *Pearls*.

Another *Pearls* track that benefits from the nod in direction to the country music of Austin, Texas, is "Wasn't Born to Follow." The arrangement countrifies the song to a much greater extent than even the well-known version by the Byrds, and also to a greater extent than King's even earlier version with the City. King's multitracked harmony vocals are particularly effective on this song and on the album's final track, "Goin' Back." Although her recorded work as her own best backup vocal ensemble does not receive much acknowledgment, for my money Carole King's best multitracked vocal harmony work ranks with that of some of the best pop recording artists who have done a similar sort of thing, including Stevie Wonder, who is perhaps the best-known one-person band and vocal ensemble of the rock era.

All in all, then, *Pearls: The Songs of Goffin and King* was a mixed blessing for Carole King as an artist. The recording succeeds and King is in fine form as an arranger, singer, and pianist; however, that the album is oldies based really does—as the reviewers suggested—appear to be a tacit admission that her compositional skills were something of a question mark after the declining sales and negative critical reaction to her recordings of the second half of the 1970s. The album's commercial and critical success proved that Carole King still had a substantial following and was poised to return to prominence and relevance. The 1980s would see her explore new, then-current styles and combine these with her innate writing abilities to deliver both good pop music and socially conscious messages that would connect both with her old fans and with newer ones.

6

Reemergence: 1981–1990

In the early 1970s, Carole King was one of a handful of pop musicians who truly captured and exemplified the spirit of introspection and musical clarity that was defined as the singer-songwriter style. At the end of the decade, King's musical settings became more elaborate as she explored a wider range of styles. Unfortunately, this made her end-of-1970s albums (perhaps with the exception of *Touch the Sky*) sound less–than fully integrated as artistic statements. And with her widening range as a composer, she gave up some of the easy accessibility of her earlier work. Whether by accident or by design, her 1980 album, *Pearls: The Songs of Goffin & King,* helped to reconnect King with her public. Carole King, however, had been a musician who was apt to change direction fairly abruptly from project to project. The question for the 1980s would be whether or not she would find renewed success by looking to her past glories or by moving in new directions. Ultimately, King slowed down her recording career rather dramatically, but generally she made more fully integrated artistic statements than she sometimes had made when she had produced a new album each year. During this decade she also contributed songs to film soundtracks, something that she continued to do successfully into the 1990s.

ONE TO ONE

Although King's previous album, *Pearls: The Songs of Goffin and King,* received generally favorable reviews from critics,[1] she did not make a complete break from her work of the 1974–1979 era with *One to One.* In fact, the general critical reaction to the album is summed up by Stephen Holden of *Rolling Stone,* who wrote that *One to One* represents nothing new, as it is cut from "the same cookie cutter" as King's work going back to 1974.[2] What such an assessment fails to acknowledge is that the music is instantly more accessible than that of the albums King recorded after her 1974 hit *Wrap Around Joy* and before *Pearls.* Adding to the mix of *One to One* is a focus on social issues—environmentalism, tensions created between individuals by the need for financial achievement, and child-rearing techniques—balanced by other, more conventional, lyrics about interpersonal relationships. In one respect, however, critic Stephen Holden is on to one aspect of *One to One:* it is something of a compendium of musical genres that Carole King had pursued in the past, updated in foreground style to sound like early 1980s music. King's references to the past, however, do not stop at 1974: there are elements of the *Tapestry* era, as well as some of the Goffin and King pop songs of the 1960s.

The song "One to One" leads off the album. Stylistically, the song closely resembles King's work on *Rhymes & Reasons,* her quintessential singer-songwriter-style album, with clear elements of late 1950s pop (notably the chord relationships). Her former Aldon Music colleague Cynthia Weil (who had co-written numerous hits with Barry Mann in the 1960s) provided the lyrics. King's vocal performance is somewhat more raucous than what she typically recorded during the time of her greatest commercial success, 1971–1974. This continues a trend that started with the added edge that started to be heard in her voice on the late 1970s albums *Welcome Home* and *Touch the Sky.* It is also a sound that could be heard on *Pearls: The Songs of Goffin and King,* and it pervades the entire *One to One* album. The strain evident in King's voice gives the recording a feeling of raw emotional expression, but it also gives her vocal instrument a less commercially accessible sound. There is a fine line between a natural sound and a strained sound, and King crosses the line on *One to One* to an extent never heard on any of her previous recordings. In the late 1980s and early 1990s, King turned increasingly to a slightly harder rock style, a genre that would provide a better match between musical style and the increased edge that her voice developed in the early 1980s.

"It's a War" signals an even stronger sense of return to the style of the jazzy songs with strong rhymes of *Rhymes & Reasons.* King's lyrics speak of the need to "keep your guard up" because of the people's tendency to try to "steal your dreams away." This stands in sharp contrast to the philosophy of love conquers all obstacles that had been such an important part of King's albums of the late 1970s. King does acknowledge that she dreams of a day when she will not have to be so on guard and suspicious, but states that the reality of interpersonal relationships "today" is that of "a war."

"Lookin' Out for Number One," another song that features lyrics by Carole King, also expresses suspicions. In this case, she tells the person to whom the song is addressed that she does not trust her/him because she/he is just "looking out for number one." Between this song and "It's a War," the early part of *One to One* stands in sharp contrast to the optimism and expressions of unconditional brotherly and sisterly love that pervade so much of King's lyrical output. King does give the person she is addressing some constructive advice at the end of the song, writing that by giving in and being more flexible she/he will truly be "looking out for number one." The overall feel, however, is accusatory and negative. Her music is funky to an extent not often heard in her songs, suggesting perhaps more the early 1980s work of a soul musician than "typical" Carole King product. Ultimately, the musical style wears reasonably well; however, the negativity does not.

The fourth song on *One to One* truly is a rarity on a Carole King album: she played no role in the songwriting process. "Life without Love" is credited to Gerry Goffin, Louise Goffin (King's daughter), and Warren Pash. Like the previous songs on the album, this is a song about interpersonal relationships. The most interesting thing about the song, however, is what it tells the listener about Carole King as a songwriter. King's solo performing career had been highly erratic before her 1971 *Tapestry* album. In the nearly dozen years since *Tapestry*, King had proven again and again just how adept she was at writing music that suited the voice of Carole King, the singer. This non-King-penned song does not suit her voice nearly as well as her own compositions normally do.

King's "Golden Man" is a metaphor-laden song in which she describes oneness between people and between humankind and the earth. It is a song of considerably more optimism for the future than "It's a War" and "Lookin' Out for Number One," and as such, is a welcome addition to *One to One*. A fairly long song, "Golden Man" provides solo opportunities for guitarists Robert McEntee and Eric Johnson, as well as keyboardist Reese Wynans.

"Read Between the Lines," another solo composition by King, is a more memorable and catchier song than "Golden Man." In this song she incorporates some of the country-rock style of *Welcome Home* and *Touch the Sky*. The arrangement is made especially interesting by the backing vocals of Mark Hallman (who, with King, co-produced the album) and King's daughters, Sherry and Louise Goffin. There are clear musical connections with the song "One to One," especially in the tonic-submediant (I-vi) harmonic motion. Not that this is necessarily entirely new for Carole King: the verses of "The Loco-Motion" are built on the juxtaposition of a major chord and the minor chord whose root is a third lower. For the most part, King had not made much use of this harmonic motion since the 1960s. In fact, it is something of a marker that suggests the late 1950s and early 1960s. Its presence in a couple of songs spaced throughout this album not only ties together the music of the album but also connects King with the period of her early, monumental success as a pop song composer.

Although "(Love Is Like a) Boomerang," does not exhibit connections to King's work of the 1960s as does some of *One to One*'s material, it is notable for its inclusion of an instrumental lick at the end of each verse that is drawn from King's *Tapestry* hit "It's Too Late." Her lyrics are something of a kinder, gentler version of what she says in a significantly more in-your-face manner in "Lookin' Out for Number One." The message is that if people want to receive love, they must send out their love "like a boomerang." Musically, this song is conventional pop material, and in keeping with King's album material of her pre-Navarro hits. In particular, the song would have fit in nicely on *Rhymes & Reasons*, although King's lyrics here are not so filled with internal rhymes that pervade the earlier album. Curiously, and possibly not by accident, saxophonist Richard Hardy incorporates a lick from Tom Scott's solo on King's 1974 hit single "Jazzman" in his solo at the end of "(Love Is Like a) Boomerang."

Because "Read Between the Lines" and "(Love Is Like a) Boomerang" bubble with optimism, they form an important counterbalance to the negativism of "It's a War" and "Lookin' Out for Number One." In fact, King's placement of the four songs gives *One to One* a feeling of mood progression toward the optimism that usually pervades her songs. This mood change, however, does not necessarily carry through to the end of the album, but it does tend to give the listener a feeling of some emotional closure so that *One to One*'s last three songs tend to stand as three separate vignettes.

King's statement against the government policy of eminent domain, "Goat Annie," follows "(Love Is Like a) Boomerang." The song contains musical and lyrical connections to the Goffin–King narrative "Smackwater Jack," from *Tapestry*. Here, King tells the story of an elderly woman who herds her goats on land that the government eventually decides to take over. She scares the government officials off by leveling and firing her 12-gauge shotgun. Despite the lyrical and musical connections to "Smackwater Jack," this is a song that reflects the fierce independence associated with the rural American West, which was now Carole King's world. In fact, King would find herself in something of a battle between property owners' rights versus federal government rights two years after the release of *One to One* when she decided to close an undocumented public access road that ran through her property in Idaho.[3]

The melody and rhythm to which King sets the words "Goat Annie" at the end of the chorus sound eerily like the way in which the word, "barracuda" is set at the end of the chorus of the 1977 Heart song "Barracuda." King sings this song in a way that conveys glee for the heroine of her story who stands up for her rights. If the musical reference to the song "Barracuda" is intentional, then, it would seem unlikely that Goat Annie herself would be the barracuda, but rather that the government is the barracuda. Even if King did not quote the Heart song intentionally, it is still easy for the listener who is familiar with both songs to read the government-as-barracuda implication into "Goat Annie." "Goat Annie" might not feature King's most effortless-sounding rhymes, but it is a song that works well in delivering political commentary, and it is perhaps the song on *One to One* that best features King's voice.

One to One is not necessarily a fully integrated Goffin–King family album, but Louise Goffin does return to sing the second lead vocal in "Someone You Never Met Before," a song written by her parents. In Gerry Goffin's lyrics, King addresses a friend who apparently has been living a lonely life. She tells the person that a lover may knock on the door when he/she least expects it. King's musical setting is in a gentle triple meter and includes jazzy sounding added-note chords. The melody is memorable in the way that King's best pop melodies have always been, and the entire musical feel fits perfectly the mood of hope for a future relationship for King's friend. This is the kind of easily accessible pop song that one could imagine hearing on, say, a Dionne Warwick album.

One to One concludes with King's solo composition "Little Prince." In this song, she addresses issues of childrearing somewhat metaphorically. The Little Prince to whom she is singing has been "brought up royally." Although or perhaps because he has been raised in the lap of luxury, the Little Prince has not been able to discover just who he really is inside, once all the trappings are taken away. Although King does not address childrearing per se, the implication of her depiction of the Little Prince character is that he has been denied self-knowledge by having been given everything. She sets the verses to a childlike tune, which reinforces the identity of the Little Prince character as a young person. Maybe that was not King's intent—maybe the Prince is older—but the music certainly supports this reading of the song. In the realm of the overall relationship theme of *One to One*, then, "Little Prince" plays an important role: an individual's self-knowledge is one important type of relationship that needs to be explored.

Despite the reaction of critics who did not seem to view *One to One* as a significant step forward for Carole King, I believe it was an important step toward reconciling the three Kings of the past: (1) the Tin Pan Alley pop songwriter virtually without peer, (2) the relationship-oriented singer-songwriter, and (3) the socially conscious artist. Because of the diversity of subjects, some lyrics that don't flow as naturally as the best lyrics King set to music, and a fairly broad range of musical styles, *One to One* does not have the strength or focus of King's best albums; however, it does put her back into the pop mainstream more deeply than she had been since her 1974 album *Wrap Around Joy*. King achieves this by revisiting lyrical themes and musical styles that had served her well in the 1960s and 1970s. There is something of a lyrical progression from near-despair to optimism on the album, as well as some musical connections between songs, but *One to One* is not as fully integrated as King's best albums. Unfortunately, she crosses the line between a natural vocal sound and an almost painful, strained sound on this album. In her next album she would step firmly into the world of 1980s-style pop, finally completely redefining what was becoming a somewhat old style, and sounding more in shape as a vocalist. As for *One to One*, for a fair chunk of the digital era it looked as though this album, like King's Capitol albums, would be unavailable on compact disc. Finally, in 2005, *One to One* was reissued on CD by Wounded Bird Records (WOU 9344). Although it is in many ways a transitional album, and not one of Carole King's top vocal performances, it is an album that deserved to be available once again.

SPEEDING TIME

In retrospect, Carole King's 1983 album *Speeding Time* represents something of a curiosity in her career. On one hand, the album received little critical reaction, although considering some of the reaction to her Navarro-era recordings of the 1970s, that might not have been such a bad thing. On the other hand, however, *Speeding Time* really does represent a discernible break with King's not-so-well-received work of the mid and late 1970s. In fact, from the standpoint of musical styles, it also represents a discernible break with *One to One*, a product of the previous year. The album also finds King surrounded by some leading studio musicians and popular jazz figures of the time, including guitarist Lee Ritenour, drummer Russ Kunkel, and percussionist Bobbye Hall. *Speeding Time* also marks the return of producer Lou Adler, who had produced King's best-known work back in the early 1970s. Despite the presence of Adler, however, this album represents a significant break with King's work of the past. Even the cover art depicts King in a light that stands in sharp contrast to her "Earth Mother" image of the late 1970s. Here she appears positively new wave and techno, at least compared with the way in which she was presented just a few years earlier.

In the first track on *Speeding Time,* Goffin and King's "Computer Eyes," King is backed by synthesizers and sequencers to a greater extent than in any of her previous recordings. The synthesizers seem somewhat at odds with the message of Goffin's lyrics, in which King tells her lover, a character named Computer Eyes, that she needs someone more in keeping with nature. Ironically, "Computer Eyes" is perhaps the one song on the album that does not benefit significantly from the au courant sound of early 1980s dance music. King's music is pleasant enough, but not memorable and tuneful in the way her best compositions are.

King's "One Small Voice," with its tuneful music and message of how "one small voice" can change the world by exposing dishonesty in political leaders, works well. The synthesized string arrangement is also effective. This track, as well as many of the more emotional songs on *Speeding Time,* suffers somewhat from Lou Adler's production, which—in the then-popular early 1980s style—bathes King's voice in too much artificial reverberation. The immediacy of her voice, which helped an early 1970s album such as *Tapestry* and would help her 1993 album *Colour of Your Dreams* make strong connections with listeners, is lost. Emotions that might have come through vocal nuance are masked, making *Speeding Time* sound too much like a product of its time. A number of other prominent artists from the 1960s and 1970s would also fall into the same trap in the 1980s, among them such well-known singer-songwriters as Stevie Wonder and Paul McCartney. The making of anonymous-sounding dance tracks had never been Carole King's forte as a performer, and *Speeding Time* leans too much in that direction to be fully successful as a major comeback album.

The production and King's vocal style on "One Small Voice" can be heard, however, as a positive. In particular, the relative lack of overt emotion matches the bittersweet sound of the minor chords in the piece. And the understated vocals and use of so many minor chords in a major-key piece continue a trend King began with some of the songs on her previous album. Even more interesting, this suggests the approach taken so successfully by Paul Simon, particularly in his solo albums of the 1970s and 1980s. "One Small Voice" is not the only song on *Speeding Time* that features the mix of production and understated vocal; this style defines the album.

Aside from the issues raised by the recording's production, however, "One Small Voice" is a wonderful song. The text uses the familiar story of "The Emperor's New Clothes" combined with the positive impact that "one small voice" can make by pointing out the emperor's blindness to reality. Harmonically and melodically, "One Small Voice" owes a debt of gratitude to late 1950s- early 1960s-pop music. The musical arrangement and rhythmic emphasis, however, clearly suggest the dance music of the early 1980s. It is an intriguing combination of styles that works particularly well on "One Small Voice" and other songs on *Speeding Time*. This kind of stylistic juxtaposition recalls King's *Pearls: The Songs of Goffin & King;* however, this is not an updated oldie, but a new song that sounds as if it could have been composed back in Goffin and King's heyday. The lyrical sentiments, however, are certainly more reflective of gentle political commentary on the 1980s Reagan era.

King's inclusion of her 1962 collaboration with Howard Greenfield "Crying in the Rain" continues the trend that she had established as early as her work in the late 1960s with the City: reworking old songs she had co-written that had been hits for other performers. Stylistically, this take on "Crying in the Rain" follows the basic sound of the tracks on the album *Pearls;* however, this recording is noticeably more synthesizer driven. In fact, the production style, and the use of a minor-chord deceptive cadence in what is essentially a major-chord-based song, makes it sound like the kind of tune that was on the radio in the early 1980s. It might not exactly be a product of Annie Lennox of Eurythmics, but it is a nod in the direction of that brand of 1980s dance/ new wave music. It also "gains" some of that anonymous quality I mentioned before because of the lack of immediacy of the lead vocals. "Crying in the Rain" does include a nice tenor saxophone solo by Plas Johnson, who is probably best remembered for his recording of the *Pink Panther* theme with Henry Mancini back in the 1960s. This solo brings up one of the more interesting attributes of *Speeding Time*—the extent to which the principal instrumentalists are underused. It seems unfortunate that three tracks into the album, King's acoustic piano really hasn't been heard (and her work on piano is much better than her work on synthesizer, primarily because of her ability to use dynamics and phrasing for expressive purposes on the piano) and Lee Ritenour's guitar has played an entirely accompanying role. Although "Crying in the Rain" exhibits some of the anonymity of 1980s pop (due in part to the deemphasis of instrumental soloists), it has the distinction of sounding both contemporary and reminiscent of the past. The arrangement is substantially different from that of the 1962 hit version by the Everly Brothers, but it remains true at least to the basic haunting spirit of that recording, in fact, emphasizing the haunting aspects of the lyrics and music. King's version, too, feels much more substantial than the Everly Brothers recording, which had weighed in at less than two minutes.

"Sacred Heart of Stone," a Goffin–King collaboration, follows "Crying in the Rain." Goffin's lyrics are introspective; King does battle with her "sacred heart of stone." The coldness of her heart has caused her not to find love in the past, and now she has grown to hate it. The somewhat detached nature of King's music, which features short descending melodic motives in a narrow pitch range, and the song's arrangement stand in sharp relief to the deeply personal, inner-conflict of the lyrics. The character seems at once deeply angry at her inner nature and also without hope—thoroughly resigned to the reality of just who she is and what she will always be. Because of this, "Sacred Heart of Stone" is eerie—and effective. Goffin and King's "Speeding Time" is another introspective song that, lyrically at least, would not be out of place on an album by King or any of the other singer-songwriters of the early 1970s school.

King's approach to the deeply emotional lyrics of "Sacred Heart of Stone" again calls to mind the work of Paul Simon, one of the greatest singer-songwriters of the rock era. Some did not find this attribute nearly as noticeable in his work with Art Garfunkel, but once Simon began a solo career in the 1970s, he established a decidedly and calculatedly understated singing approach. This cool emotional detachment added significantly to the irony of his observations of both his feelings and the feelings of the characters he created. There simply was no comparable American pop performer in the 1970s and 1980s. "Sacred Heart of Stone" finds Carole King working along the same lines. Although King would never devote herself as completely to this highly ironic and somewhat idiosyncratic approach to what might ordinarily be thought of as highly emotionally charged topics and personal situations as Simon, King clearly made it part of her repertoire. It would appear to excellent effect on her few subsequent recordings.

The album's title track follows. Gerry Goffin's text deals with the fear of the passing of time and the belief that the only escape is to prepare for the future and make the most of the present. There is a logical progression in his lyrics. The beginning of the song highlights the fear—even terror—that one can feel as one's days pass by; the middle of the poem warns the listener not to fall prey to the fear; and the end confirms that there is nothing one can do "except to try." King's musical setting remains at a fairly even keel throughout, although the arrangement does thicken a bit as the song progress. Goffin's text is in conventional pop song verse-chorus form, and King sticks to conventional strophic form in her musical setting. The progression of Goffin's text might have lent itself to the mix of strophic and through-composed writing that King had done on *Welcome Home*. Had she treated form a little more freely, she might have highlighted the changes of mood that unfold in the text; however, this also would have meant that "Speeding Time" would have been structurally different from the other songs on this album. By just adding the backing vocal chorus and thickening the synthesizer-based accompaniment, she brings out the hope in the now that is inherent in Goffin's text, despite the early focus on the inevitability of the passage of time, and she does so while maintaining the song's traditional structure.

Goffin and King's "Standin' on the Borderline" concerns the critical juncture in a relationship at which a couple might either fall in love or fall apart. King sets the text to a fairly static harmony and a melody that is not one of her most memorable. Compared with some of the best musical settings on *Speeding Time*, this song seems pedestrian. This is perhaps the sort of song that caused some critics to suggest that the best songs on the album were the ones for which King supplied both words and music.[4] Certainly, the songs for which she wrote the lyrics seem to be more fully integrated pieces. "Standin' on the Borderline" does not seem as organically whole.

King provided her own lyrics for the next song on *Speeding Time*, "So Ready for Love." As the title suggests, it is another love song. In fact, it can be understood as a lyrical companion to "Standin' on the Borderline"—perhaps a response by the other half of the couple—a confirmation that the fall will be in the direction of love and not "falling apart." By Carole King standards, this song is quite long, clocking in at 5 minutes 40 seconds. Although the song's phrase structure is a bit more elaborate and unpredictable than the typical pop song, it forms an ideal companion for "Standin' on the Borderline," both in lyrics and musical style. The song's structure and harmony have elements of jazz and soul ballad, which complements the relative stasis and more predictable structure of its predecessor. Robbie Kondor provides a synthesizer solo that sounds like an acoustic harmonica. This pseudo-harmonica solo cannot help but make the listener think of Stevie Wonder's jazz-influenced ballads of the 1970s, on which he would sometimes incorporate jazz harmonica solos.

"Chalice Borealis," a collaboration of King and Rick Sorensen, is based on abstract, nearly psychedelic lyrics. The lyrical style seems out of place on an album that generally is much more direct; however, at the background of the lyrics lies a statement in support of good environmental and social stewardship. King's melody is haunting in its detached mood.

Carole King's "Dancing" is somewhat open to interpretation; however, it is certainly much more straightforward lyrically than "Chalice Borealis."

Depending on the extent to which the listener deconstructs the piece, it can be understood literally or metaphorically. In its literal meaning, King is portraying a dancer (ballroom, disco, ballet—take your pick) who is conversing with a fellow dancer, pointing out their relationship on stage or on the dance floor, and the way in which her fellow dancer enjoys, and indeed needs, the attention of the audience, and needs to feel in control of the audience's mood. As a metaphorical song, it would seem to refer to the "dance" of love and the things that bring couples together and break them apart. The music and its arrangement are somewhat generic sounding and do not work particularly well, for Carole King is at her best when she writes distinctive-sounding songs.

Speeding Time concludes with "Alabaster Lady," a compositional tour de force for King. Composed in several distinct sections with contrasting tempos and harmonic and melodic styles, the song is more structurally complex than most of King's work. Her lyrics address the long-legged Alabaster Lady, who holds men in the palm of her hand, and whom King's character would like to emulate. By painting an impressionistic picture of the Alabaster Lady, and encouraging her to do what she has within her power to do, one learns as much about King's character as the character to whom she sings. There is a sense that King's character projects herself into the Alabaster Lady and lives out possibilities she will never have through this other character. It is a haunting song.

Critical reaction to *Speeding Time* was somewhat mixed, but certainly far more positive than that generated by King's late 1970s albums. *People Weekly*, for example, complained that "there's too much schlock on this album," but tempered that statement with the acknowledgment that some of the songs written by King alone "are the kind of thoughtful, danceable pop music she built her reputation on." This assessment is interesting, given the less-than-stellar reviews King had received back in the 1970s for her lyrics. The *People* review praises "Alabaster Lady" as an intricate combination of lyrics and music, as well as "Dancing" for its commentary.[5] In addition, *High Fidelity*'s Sam Sutherland gave the album a favorable review,[6] but *Stereo Review*'s Joel Vance did not.[7] Because of the heavier use of synthesizers and a more dance-oriented, techno-lite style, *Speeding Time* stands out in the Carole King canon. It was a bold move and generally is effective in its own right. It would seem, though, not to be the best-connected album to King's traditional audience.

CITY STREETS

Having explored a muted form of early-1980s techno in her previous album, *Speeding Time*, King turned to a harder-edged rock sound for her 1989 album, *City Streets*. As is the case with most of King's stylistic shifts, however, "harder-edged" is only relative here: she embraces elements of hard rock style on the album, without truly *becoming* a rocker. True, her performance is more thoroughly rock-oriented than anything she had ever done in the recording studio. And the edge that King's voice developed in the late 1970s remains, but works convincingly here in the context of the harder-edged feel of *City Streets* music. *City Streets* was co-produced by King and Rudy Guess, who continues to work with her as a guitarist and co-producer into the twenty-first century. Although King had done some of her own production work in collaboration with others—notably Mark Hallman—in the late 1970s and early 1980s, she and Guess click as a production team on this album. For one thing, King and Guess bring King's voice more forward in the recording mix than Lou Adler had done on *Speeding Time*. They also treat King's voice with considerably less artificial studio reverberation than Adler had used on King's previous album. The instrumental work, arrangements, and the placement of the instruments within the recording's mix all sound thoroughly up to date. The combination of vocal and instrumental treatment, then, are contemporary, but with a nice balance of the sort of immediacy found in King's classic work of the early 1970s.

Carole King had started her songwriting career at a time when the 45-rpm single ruled the record industry. By the time King's solo career took off with the 1971 album *Tapestry,* concept albums had been around for at least four years, but most of King's albums continued the individual song focus of her songwriting work in the 1960s. To be sure, there were some thematic connections and stylistic connections on several of her albums, including *Rhymes & Reasons, Touch the Sky,* and *One to One.* Few of her albums, however, had the kind of full writing, performance, production, and packaging focus of *City Streets.* The somewhat stark black-and-white cover art shows a leather jacket-clad King in an obviously urban environment. The theme of starkness and grittiness is enhanced by the photo of King leaning against a wall in what appears to be a bare urban apartment room; an electric guitar stands propped in the window frame. All of the album's songs can be interpreted as representatives of the moods—generally none too sunny—of city life. The playing of keyboardist Robbie Kondor, guitarist Rudy Guess, the several percussionists who appear (especially Steve Ferrone, late of the Average White Band), and guest guitarist Eric Clapton affirm the harder-edged nature of these songs, as does King and Guess's production, which emphasizes the drums to an extent never before heard on a Carole King album. About the only thing that keeps *City Streets* from being a fully integrated concept album is that the lyrics of some of the songs are general enough that they don't necessarily have to come from the urban landscape. In terms of King's impressive list of albums, *City Streets* is easily among the most unified packages. It is also a powerful album.

The song "City Streets," with words and music by King, establishes the album's theme. King paints the city streets, a metaphor for life in the city, as a tale of extremes: heaven/hell, icy/burning. King contrasts the "lovers with their arms entwined"—who have lived in the city all their lives—and their hope with her character's feelings of despair. Her melody is based primarily on short rhythmic motives, but with a fairly wide pitch range, dramatic upward leaps, and quite a bit of pitch direction variation from phrase to phrase. This is a style of melodic writing that becomes a distinctive feature of King's rock-oriented songs on *City Streets* and the 1993 album *Colour of Your Dreams*. It is particularly effective in songs of pain, such as this one.

The instrumental texture of "City Streets" is harder-edged than any previous album-opening song in Carole King's output, save possibly for "Spaceship Races," from *Writer*, nearly two full decades earlier. In the six years since King's previous album, *Speeding Time*, her approach (and that of additional keyboardist Robbie Kondor) to the synthesizer had matured considerably. Compared with the use of synthesizers on *Speeding Time*, here King blends the electronic timbres more fully into the overall texture; everything sounds fully integrated on "City Streets." Adding to the strength of the song and its overall texture are Eric Clapton's electric guitar solos and Michael Brecker's hard-edged tenor saxophone solo. Co-producers Carole King and Rudy Guess achieve an effective balance on the song (and throughout the rest of the album) between passion and detachment by mixing the recording so that it has a feeling of space. As King sings the chorus—and especially the dramatic lines about how the city streets can be heaven or hell—her passion is tempered by the cool detachment suggested by the recording's mix. This works effectively because it highlights the sharp contrasts and complexities of the emotions King presents in her text. To have used the kind of close miking and drier overall sound of King's singer-songwriter school recordings would have captured just the passion about the despair her character feels and not the almost eerie resignation that mixes with that passion in this production. In short, "City Streets," although unknown outside the context of this album, is one of the finest songs, and one of the most effective arrangements, performances, and productions Carole King ever created in her long solo career.

King and Rudy Guess collaborated as writers on the album's second song, "Sweet Life." Like "City Streets," this is a song of emotional extremes. In this case, however, the character King is addressing feels the despair, while King's character tells him that they are living "a sweet life." The musical setting is notable for a fair amount of contrast between the verses and the chorus. The lower pitch range of the verses seems to match the feelings of King's partner; the higher pitch range and less conjunct melodic writing of the chorus emphasize the exuberance King's character feels with life. King and Guess's rhythm guitar figures and the timbres they use suggest several prominent guitarists of the 1970s and 1980s. Especially noticeable is the style of George Harrison in the arpeggiated figures at the end of the song's chorus, and the timbre closely associated with U2's The Edge in the accompaniment work on the song. Guess's solo, although individualistic, carries on the feeling of passion heard in Eric Clapton's solo on "City Streets."

King's "Down to the Darkness" continues the feeling of high drama that especially characterizes the beginning of *City Streets*. Set to a tune with dramatic leaps and register changes, King's text deals with a potential lover who will take her "down to the darkness" with "just one kiss." The love that she senses she will feel represents both extreme pleasure and a look "down into the black abyss." As in the song "City Streets," the dramatic melodic writing, contradictory passionate/detached sound of the vocals, and the texture of the instrumental mix are all quite different from anything on earlier Carole King albums, but represent a style that King uses not only on this album, but also on *Colour of Your Dreams*. In fact, there are short melodic figures in "Down to the Darkness" that can be heard in the melodies of several songs on *Colour of Your Dreams*. These figures, especially the dramatic upward leaps, suggest the writing of U2 and the singing of U2's Bono, just as some of the guitar work and timbres on *City Streets* recall the instrumental work of the Irish band.

King's "Lovelight" presents the listener with a break from the lyrical intensity that defines the beginning of *City Streets*. In this song King's character tells her lover that she wants their relationship to return to the intensity that it had in former days. The music's pace is fast with a driving beat. And at the risk of the analyses of the songs of *City Streets* seeming too repetitious, it has a U2, *Joshua Tree*-like intensity to it.

Guitarist Paul Hipp collaborated with King on "I Can't Stop Thinking about You," the next cut on *City Streets*. In the lyrics of this slow ballad, King's character wishes for the return of a lover who she cannot get out of her mind. The song might fit with the album's overall theme of the ups and downs of city life—the lyrics do suggest that King's character lives in an urban environment—it is not the most memorable song on *City Streets*, mostly because of its melody and somewhat generic-sounding instrumental accompaniment.

In "Legacy," a collaborative effort of King and Rudy Guess, King addresses either an individual—or a whole group of people—who has/have left the idealism of their youth behind. They are now living in the "rat maze" of contemporary corporate America, and have lost their earlier concerns with equality and just generally leaving the world in a better place than they inherited it. King urges those to whom she sings to renounce their decision "to perpetuate the destruction" and to make a stand for the betterment of the world. She seems to be addressing the yuppies of the time, some of whom presumably were hippies back in the 1960s and early 1970s. Sonically, the song resembles the style of the mid-1980s Moody Blues, as best exemplified on the 1986 album *The Other Side of Life*. This similarity is fitting given that the Moody Blues was one of those 1960s bands whose somewhat trippy lyrics were popular among the young people of the late 1960s and early 1970s and who, 15 or 20 years later, may have become part of the young urban professional (yuppie) class. Of interest, King and Guess's use of a slow introduction to what is essentially a fairly fast-paced song suggests some of the Moody Blues's hits of the 1980s, most notably "Your Wildest Dreams," a popular single that was drawn from *The Other Side of Life*.

The reader undoubtedly will have noticed that I have compared Carole King's music, arrangements, record production on *City Streets* now with that of contemporary recordings by U2 and the Moody Blues. It should be noted, however, that in no way do I find *City Streets* to be a derivative-sounding album. King's work—exclusive of her lyrics, which revolve entirely around the dialectic of hope and despair that she finds in urban life—is more like a composite compendium of styles in the air in the second half of the 1980s. I suspect that casual listeners would not be aware so much of the resemblances to specific contemporary artists of the time as much as they might be aware that there was something more vaguely familiar—more reflective of the times in general—about the sound of *City Streets*. This represents a great achievement for Carole King. After all, she was a child of the 1960s who wrote highly successful top 40, R&B, rock, and easy listening hits during that decade. She rose to fame as part of the more acoustically based singer-songwriter movement in the early 1970s. She explored country-rock in the late 1970s—maybe a decade too late to have been truly innovative—and made a brief, but not entirely unsuccessful, foray into the new-wave-ish techo style in the early 1980s. Now here she was in her late forties still integrating contemporary musical styles into her compositional palette in 1989. *City Streets* comes off as "adaptive" much more than "derivative."

King's solo composition "Ain't That the Way" follows "Legacy." The music sounds vaguely religious, or at least "churchy," mostly because of King's organ playing. Curiously, the harmonic progression and the timbre of the organ recalls "A Whiter Shade of Pale" by Procol Harum. There are also harmonic and melodic relationships to songs of more recent days, such as a hint of Lionel Richie's 1985 hit "Say You, Say Me." But that is in no way meant to imply that "Ain't That the Way" steals from, or was even directly influenced by, a rock hit of the late 1960s or a Quiet Storm R&B-pop hit of the mid-1980s. The kind of sequential harmonic progression found in "Ain't That the Way," "Say You, Say Me," and "A Whiter Shade of Pale" has its roots and true inspiration in the music of the European Baroque era, more specifically in the organ compositions of Johann Sebastian Bach.

The lyrics of "Ain't That the Way" describe a bitter irony: just when things seem to be going right, huge problems arise. King also explores a subtheme of friendly empathy with those problems. In a way, the song's lyrics reaffirm the idea of a dialectic between positive and negative, a dialectic that drives the entire structure of the album.

In "Midnight Flyer," a product of Gerry Goffin and Carole King's ongoing songwriting partnership, King returns to hints of the country-rock music she had explored in the late 1970s. In contrast to the rural themes and country influences that defined her work of that earlier period, this song has more of a sophisticated urban feel to it, provided in large part by the technically virtuosic soprano saxophone work of Branford Marsalis and harmonica playing of Jimmy "Z" Zavala. Rudy Guess's mandolin playing suggests the prevailing contemporary acoustic folk style of the time more so than it does hardcore rural bluegrass. Goffin's text finds King's character singing about the promise of romance that she finds in going to the city to dance late into the night/early into morning. Without sounding disparaging, it is sort of an "urban cowgirl" themed song, both lyrically and musically. Although it plays a significant role in filling out the range of *City Streets* (not all cities are northern [hard rock] ones—some are southern [country rock] ones), it is not the most memorable song in the collection, as it is a genre piece, without the kind of easily remembered melodic hooks that define King's most commercially successful work.

The theme of alienation, which King seems to find in abundance in the city streets that form the structural basis for this album, returns in "Homeless Heart." The song is a rare collaboration between King and lyricist John Bettis, who is perhaps best known for songs such as "Yesterday Once More," "Goodbye to Love," and "Top of the World" for the Carpenters, and "Human Nature," a hit for Michael Jackson. King sings of her "homeless heart," which cannot seem to find love in the cold city. Actually, Bettis is a little coy in the way he works the urban theme into his lyrics: the fleeting reference that King's character makes to looking out on "icy roofs below" places her in what the listener might presume is an urban apartment building. By the end of the song, resignation turns to yearning for a missing lover. This change of mood is confirmed by the singing of King's daughter Sherry Goffin on a second lead vocal line. Because Sherry Goffin's voice is more stereotypically "beautiful," in the standard pop singing sense, than her mother's edgier voice, the overall feel of the song softens as the yearning for a matching heart appears in the lyrics that Goffin apparently improvises. It is a beautiful arranging and production touch for King and her co-producer Rudy Guess. King's composition is marked by a generally low register melody built on short motives in a minor key. In fact, the minor-key cadences at the end of each verse and at the end of the chorus add significantly to the feeling of resignation that pervades the first three-quarters of the song. During the extended coda section in which Goffin improvises and the subsequent instrumental fades out, King avoids the minor mode, raising the possibility that her character, and her heart, might find the missing love. This represents an important turning point in the overall feel of *City Streets*. The mood changes within the song from alienation (which had defined most of the first part of the album) to a vague sense of hope. That hope would be heightened and confirmed in the next song. Stylistically, King's music breaks some new ground for her, perhaps coming closer to the Quiet Storm subgenre of soul music than anything she has ever written. And it is more successful than the Quiet Storm soul music of her early twenty-first century album, *Love Makes the World*.

City Streets ends on a quiet and positive note with Goffin and King's "Someone Who Believes in You." The song, a gentle, piano-based ballad, is among the closest examples of a Carole King composition in the form and style of the traditional AABA form Tin Pan Alley pop song. In fact, it stands in especially sharp contrast to the rock orientation of most of the rest of the album. In its mainstream pop style, King's music resembles the work of such writers as Marvin Hamlisch and Burt Bacharach, whose ties to the pop/jazz standard have always been much more immediately apparent than those of Carole King, with her tendency toward R&B, rock, and other decidedly non-jazz standard styles and forms. Goffin's lyrics present the same basic sentiments as King's lyrics for her 1971 hit "You've Got a Friend." They assure the person to whom King sings that he or she will be able to overcome any obstacle and realize his/her dreams because the person has someone (King's character) who believes in him/her. Although some fans of King's harder-edged sound in the 1980s might believe that the song leans too much to the sappy side, it wraps up the album very well. The package's first song, "City Streets," set the "heaven" and "hell" of city life in opposition to one another. Throughout the album King explored the extremes of emotions that she observes in urban life. Ultimately, as she does consistently throughout her songwriting career, she chooses optimism over pessimism. "Someone Who Believes in You" confirms that spirit of optimism in the face of confusion.

Sonic references to the contemporary work of U2, the Moody Blues, and others can be found throughout *City Streets*. All of these, however, are so general that the listener is left with the sense that King was incorporating sounds that happened to be in the air at the time, rather than consciously imitating specific artists. It is hard to begrudge Carole King her desire to aim in the direction of optimism; however, after her exposure to some of the harshness of life in the city, the move toward optimism seems a bit too comfortable. And the dialectic of dark side/bright side also seems to be a bit too predictable. All in all, *City Streets* is one of Carole King's most emotionally powerful albums. From the standpoint of commercial acceptance, however, the main problem with *City Streets* is that it doesn't have the stylistic trappings of what a Carole King album is "supposed to" sound like. It is not so much personal and autobiographical as it is observational. If the album is evaluated as a product of someone entirely defined by the huge success of the songwriting, performance, and production style of *Tapestry,* it is a difficult sell. If, however, it is evaluated on its own merits, it is a highly successful package. In fact, I believe it ranks as one of King's best albums—the concept is well realized. About the only quibble is that *City Streets* tends to be structured too much like a two-sided, gloomy versus sunny, vinyl album. It extends the feeling of the Doors's *Morrison Hotel* (which is structured as Morrison Hotel [on one side], and Hard Rock Café [on the other side]) and Paul McCartney and Wings's *Back to the Egg* (which juxtaposes a post-punk rock side with a more conventional pop side) into the late 1980s.

FILM SOUNDTRACKS

By the 1980s, motion picture soundtracks often were of three principal types: (1) a movie-length score by a leading film composer such as John Williams or Danny Elfman;[8] (2) a collection of pop songs, either newly composed or oldies, that define the era depicted in the film's storyline; or (3) a hybrid type, in which a score is supported by perhaps a pop-style title song or a number of pop songs incorporated into the film as mood pieces. With her experience as a pop composer who could write accessible, commercially successful material in a variety of styles and developing a variety of moods, Carole King was well suited to provide songs to fit the second and third categories.

King had some experience outside of a purely musical medium from her *Really Rosie* project of the 1970s. Her settings of Maurice Sendak's poems originally were meant for a television cartoon. Eventually, the television program was adapted into a live staged version. King's first work in a more traditional motion picture soundtrack medium, however, came with her work for the 1985 film *Murphy's Romance,* a film in which she also performed a small walk-on role. For this film, she collaborated with the popular jazz saxophonist David Sanborn. However, King eventually found perhaps her greatest success in the area of film soundtracks, in the next phase of her career when she contributed individual songs to popular Hollywood movies such as *You've Got Mail, One True Thing,* and *A League of Their Own.*

Living the New and Celebrating the Old: 1991–2006

Carole King's output as singer and songwriter has slowed in the past 15 years, but she has continued to be a significant presence in the entertainment industry. During this period, a number of her songs have been included in benefit albums. For example, "Child of Mine" was included on the album *For Our Children* (Disney 60616, 1991), a CD produced to benefit the Pediatric AIDS Foundation, and "If I Didn't Have You to Wake up to" was included on the album *'Til Their Eyes Shine* (Columbia CK-52412, 1992). She contributed songs to the films *A League of Their Own, One True Thing,* and *You've Got Mail;* and she appeared at benefit concerts for children's causes, environmental causes, and in support of Democratic presidential candidates Gary Hart and John Kerry. Although King has released only two new studio albums during the period, one of these, *Colour of Your Dreams* (1993) ranks among her best. This period also saw the first official release of a live Carole King album. In fact, two live albums appeared in the mid-1990s (*In Concert* and *Carnegie Hall Concert: June 18, 1971*), and King's most recent album, the live *Living Room Tour* album, was issued in 2005.

COLOUR OF YOUR DREAMS

Although I would not go so far as to suggest that Carole King's 1993 album *Colour of Your Dreams* was exactly her *Tapestry* for the 1990s—any album by nearly any artist in popular music of the past half century would find it difficult to compare with King's 1971 classic, especially in terms of cultural, iconic status—*Colour of Your Dreams* is easily one of her best studio albums. It is personal, exudes social consciousness, finds a 50-year-old, exceedingly

well-established singer-songwriter taking musical risks, and in the end succeeds like no other Carole King studio album (aside from that famous 1971
one). She uses many of the musical and rhetorical styles that she had used on
her previous albums, but here King is altogether more convincing in her music,
arrangements, and lyrics than she had been in years. A lot of the groundwork for the overall rock sound of *Colour of Your Dreams* had been laid with
City Streets; however, the songs, and especially the stories in the lyrics, on
this album tend to stick in the listener's mind more thoroughly than those
of *City Streets.*

The album begins with King's composition (music and lyrics) "Lay Down
My Life." The song is a tale of a woman who has left her lover because
she knows that he needs to make a new life on his own. King's character
is consumed by the opposing feelings of desperation in loss ("My world
comes tumbling down") and a realization that the intensity of her love
("I would lay down my life for you") requires that she sever the bonds of
the couple's relationship for his good. Compared with her singing on "Tears
Falling Down on Me," "Hold out for Love," "Standing in the Rain," and
a couple of other songs on *Colour of Your Dreams,* her performance here
is somewhat understated in the verses and in the early statements of the
chorus. As the song nears its conclusion, however, she sings with believable
passion on the chorus line "I would lay down my life for you." However,
then she trails back off to a feeling of emotional detachment as the song's
volume drops. Ultimately, this speaks of the character's sad, dark sense of
resignation and highlights the complexity of her emotions as she realizes
that only through letting go can she truly give her partner what her love
for him demands.

As she often does on her most memorable songs, King provides plenty of
contrast between the melodic style of the verses and the chorus. The verse
sections consist primarily of short, motivically related phrases. These give
the effect of short declamations, as if her character is having difficulty coming up with words to say because of the intensity of the emotions she feels.
The chorus moves into the higher register and, although still built on related
melodic motives, they are longer phrases. Within the context of the lyrics, the
feel is that the one thing of which her character is certain—the one thing that
she can sing out about—is that, no matter what, she would indeed lay down
her life for her (soon to be) ex-partner. The combination of the emotional
complexity of King's lyrics with the music makes "Lay Down My Life" an
especially rich song.

One of the best features of *Colour of Your Dreams,* aside from the haunting and emotional nature of most of the songs, is the way in which so much
of the material matches the qualities of King's voice, and the way in which
she sings with a sense of passion missing from some of her albums. And on
the songs that are more introspective and feature lyrics that convey a sad
resignation, such as the verses of "Lay Down My Life," King sings in an

entirely appropriate, almost detached manner. Although her acting out of the emotions of the texts she sings is evident on more than a few tracks on the album, the package's second track, "Hold out for Love" provides an especially strong example.

In "Hold out for Love" King urges those who hear her words—she does not seem to be directing the message at any one particular individual—not to settle for anything less than true love. In other words, don't marry for money, for status, for mere security, or anything other than what you truly feel when you "listen to your heart." Also implicit in King's text is a sort of sexual empowerment: do only what you think is right, when you think it is right, and not in a way that makes you "sell your soul" to get through a dark night. It is a potent song, with a more complex structure than the prototypical rock song. The song's melody, harmony, and structure are all engaging; but what really makes it work are King's powerful, passionate singing and the expressive lead guitar playing of Slash, best known for his work as a member of the band Guns N' Roses.

The Goffin–King collaboration "Standing in the Rain" is perhaps King's best vocal performance on the album. Especially impressive are her multi-tracked backing vocals. King handles all the choral parts in a style that fully integrates, as opposed to imitates, gospel style. It is a tale of a woman's reaction to what amounts to little more than a one-night stand. The song's placement immediately after "Hold out for Love" is significant, as the story of "Standing in the Rain" provides a clear example of the ills that can come from not holding out for true love. In fact, Goffin's text can easily be read as a document of a very brief relationship that started out as an anonymous sexual encounter in a back alley between an unmarried woman and a married man. And King's character clearly did not believe that her partner was married when she initially hooked up with him.

King sets Goffin's "Standing in the Rain" text in a gospel rock style. As mentioned earlier, the multitracked backing "chorus" sounds like something out of the African American sacred tradition. Aside from Rudy Guess's blazing electric slide guitar solo, the song is in a conventional, Tin Pan Alley AABA structure. In the "B" section, which is heard only once in the song, King sets the part of the story where she discovers that her partner in passion is married to music that modulates from a remote key area back to tonic. Again, this is standard compositional procedure in early twentieth-century Tin Pan Alley American pop song writing. One of the highlights of the song is the way in which King uses a much tried and true form, but with a very non-Tin Pan Alley musical style. Because of the emotional power of King's performance, the song's perfect match of music to lyrics, and a melody that sticks in the listener's head, "Standing in the Rain" stands not only among Carole King's best recordings, but also among Goffin and King's best songs.

The album's next track, "Now and Forever," was the closest thing that *Colour of Your Dreams* had to a hit song. "Now and Forever" was featured in the hit Columbia Motion Picture *A League of Their Own*. At 3 minutes 13 seconds, it is the second shortest song on the album, which is significant because "Now and Forever" is the closest song on *Colour of Your Dreams* to a conventional, mainstrean top-40 song ready for radio airplay. King's lyrics speak of how much she misses a former lover, or friend; the specifics are vague enough that the nature of the relationship can be understood on several levels. Like several of the other songs on *Colour of Your Dreams* and, for that matter, *City Streets,* there is a touching mix of emotions both in the text and in the musical setting. There is a feeling of loss, but it is tempered in both lyrics and fairly upbeat music with a sense of happy memories of the past. Although it is a memorable song, and one that my own anecdotal evidence suggests played an important role in *A League of Their Own* for what seemed to be the film's biggest audience,[1] the commercial, accessible, don't-take-too-many-musical-chances nature of "Now and Forever," causes it to pale somewhat on *Colour of Your Dreams*. The highly emotional songs and the musically innovative songs on the album demand more attention.

"Wishful Thinking," for which King wrote both words and music, perhaps more than any other song she has recorded in her career, exhibits a clear link with jazz standard ballads more thoroughly than the *City Streets* album cut "Someone Who Believes in You" because of its greater jazz orientation. As a song that is clearly linked harmonically, melodically, and lyrically with the prerock-era ballad style, it invites comparison with several compositions of Stevie Wonder, who is the only pop music artist active in the 1960s through the present who has thoroughly integrated the jazz ballad into his compositional and performance repertoire. The main distinction between Carole King's jazz ballad and a Wonder composition such as "All in Love Is Fair" (from his 1973 *Innervisions* album), just to cite perhaps his best such work, is that Wonder sings this kind of song in a style of phrasing and with a vocal technique that indicates an understanding, appreciation, and technical mastery of the genre. In comparison, King's singing style is not "diva-esque" to suit the material. It is a beautifully composed ballad that could be highly effective in the hands of a jazz vocalist.

Strangely enough, King's song "Colour of Your Dreams" recalls some of the work of Moody Blues singer-songwriter Justin Hayward, both in his solo performances and in the 1980s and 1990s recordings of the Moody Blues. I do not mean to imply that the song is in some way derivative; in fact, it is less obviously "Moody Blues sounding" than a couple of the tracks on *City Streets*. The connections here to Justin Hayward's work are more oblique and come primarily from the emphasis on a harmonic *ostinato,* the acoustic rhythm guitar style, and the poetic use of impressionistic visual images. The compositional, poetic, and performance styles also resemble some of the contemporary work of Fleetwood Mac, a group that some of King's earlier work on *Simple Things* also called to mind. The specifics of King's lyrics suggest to her listeners that they follow their hearts and realize that not everything that one thinks they see in life is rooted in reality: sometimes appearances are just appearances. The verses are an interesting mix of conventional rhyme schemes (through the larger part of each verse) and a careful avoidance of obvious rhymes (at the conclusion of the verses). King's avoidance of rhyme at the end of the verses connects "Colour of Your Dreams" with "Standing in the Rain," in which the "B" section of Gerry Goffin's AABA-form lyrics ends without a rhyme. This is not an obvious connection on first hearing, but as the listener becomes more familiar with the songs of *Colour of Your Dreams,* it emerges as one of the subtle ways in which the album achieves the feeling of being an integrated whole. In the case of this song, the avoidance of conventional rhymes at the end of the verses gives the text an unresolved quality and might suggest the hazy nature of dreams in general, or the listener's dreams for the future; for example, one can dream about what one wishes to accomplish in life, but until it happens, one never knows exactly what will take place in the future.

As an album-defining title track, it is a little too vague, especially when compared with the earlier song "City Streets," which presents a much clearer thesis statement. Musically, the song is fast-paced, but the arrangement is somewhat low-key, particularly when compared with songs such as "Hold out for Love" and "Standing in the Rain," both of which include burning lead guitar parts. The melody contains a fair number of skips, which give it a somewhat unpredictable, disjunct feel. King's harmonic progressions, too, are a little unpredictable. The song is in a minor key but in several places in which the conventional expectation would be for the harmony to move to a minor chord, King briefly shifts to a major chord. The combination of lyrics, lyrical structure, melodic and harmonic surprises, and the acoustic, folklike nature of the arrangement all give "Colour of Your Dreams" a haunting quality. It may not be King's greatest album-defining title track—"Tapestry" and "City Streets" are more effective—nor, may it be the most memorable or singable song on this album (one should not expect to find "Colour of Your Dreams" in a Carole King karaoke collection), but it is an effective mood piece.

"Colour of Your Dreams" is followed by a couple of the album's highlights: "Tears Falling Down on Me" and "Friday's Tie-Dye Nightmare." Both songs feature both words and music by King. "Tears Falling Down on Me" finds King dealing with several contemporary social issues, including the low self-esteem felt by some young women, the use of women for the sexual pleasure of men, and racism. Partially because the verses are set to a fairly rapid patter-type rhythm within the context of a slow rock beat, and because the lyrical style is essentially narrative, the song tends to seem a little wordy; however, this does not detract from the powerful message of how "man's unkindness to man" brings tears to King, and tears to the world. The image of tears in itself is significant. In the context of her text, the tears symbolize the sorrow that King feels over sexism and racism and the serious problems these social ills bring, and they also symbolize the power to wash away social ills that King feels we possess. The image connects this song with "Standing in the Rain," in which King's character was not only drenched by the physical rain, but by the mistreatment she received at the hands of the man who essentially used her solely for his sexual pleasure. "Tears Falling Down on Me" is also connected to "Hold out for Love" insofar as the character Vera, who is used sexually when she is in a state of drunkenness, does not "hold out for love." Both the stonemason's son, "who had his way with her," and her own low self-esteem play a role in her violation.

King sets "Tears Falling Down on Me" to music that fits the text very well. The verses, which include the story of Vera and the stone mason's son and the story of a "pack of jokers" who beat up a "black kid,"[2] are set to a melody in a *parlando* (speechlike rhythms) style and in a low-pitch range. In the chorus of "Tears Falling Down on Me" King sings in the upper part of her vocal range, with the line set to a much slower rhythm. In "Tears Falling Down on Me," King plays acoustic guitar. Although she has focused almost exclusively on her primary instrument, the piano, throughout her recording career, King proves to be a fully credible rhythm guitarist on this track. "Tears Falling Down on Me" is a memorable song with an immediately recognizable melodic hook. It is not, however, a conventionally commercial song primarily because of the serious nature of the lyrics, but also because there is not much about the general tenor of the lyrics or musical setting that does not sound like socially conscious music of the late 1960s.

The decade of the 1960s emerges in full force on the album's next track, "Friday's Tie-Dye Nightmare." Although the song is thoroughly derivative, it is also one of Carole King's greatest compositions and performances in terms of the way she crafts something that is simultaneously humorous and full of serious social commentary. This song is a full-fledged send-up of the 1960s work of Bob Dylan. King's song includes the internal rhymes and the short, staccato rhymed lines of Dylan's lyrics, as well as the *parlando* and near-*sprechstimme* (speech-song)[3] singing style that marked Dylan's recorded performances, especially before his country recordings of the late-1960s *Nashville Skyline* period. Considering that King's customary audience had probably been following her work from some time, it would logically follow that they could not help but catch the obvious references to Dylan.

King uses this Dylan parody to tell a tale of her journey on a subway train. Along the way, she witnesses overt racism and society's abandonment of the poor and disenfranchised. She also finds fault with her character's inability to take positive action when the situation calls for it. Although it may be reading too much into King's music and the title of the song, I find "Friday's Tie-Dye Nightmare" to be an indictment of American society and just how little it had truly evolved since the idealistic 1960s. In the 1960s, the tie-dye era of idealism, people of Carole King's generation tried to solve problems such as racism, sexism, and the world's seeming addiction to war as an answer to international political conflicts. By referring to the dreamlike images of her text as a nightmare, it would seem to acknowledge the harsh reality that the battles of the 1960s and early 1970s had resulted in far fewer positive social changes in America than what might have been accomplished.

King's "Just One Thing" is another highlight, not only of *Colour of Your Dreams*, but also of her solo recording career. First, I must admit that "Just One Thing" is by no means among my favorite Carole King songs, or even among my favorite songs on *Colour of Your Dreams*. In context, however, it is a near perfect song because of the way it essentially "debriefs" King's observations in "Friday's Tie-Dye Nightmare." King portrays a character with strong connections to the disenfranchised people she observes in "Friday's Tie-Dye Nightmare." Her character is a person of the streets, to whom "trust is unknown" and whose life is filled with fantasies about her situation; these stand in sharp contrast to reality. For example, in the character's fantasies she is "a child running wild and free." This, however, is simply a mask for the harsh reality of homelessness. King's character has come to realize that the one last thing in which she could believe, and in which she had placed all her hope—her fantasy world—is a lie; therefore, she is completely without hope. King portrays the character convincingly by varying her voice from moods of sadness, to despair, to longing.

Part of the success of "Just One Thing" lies in the song's musical setting. King sets the verses, in which her character comes to realize that her fantasies are all an illusion, to a melody in the lower part of her vocal range. The rhythms are more speechlike than what one might ordinarily expect to hear in a pop song, as if King's character is having a conversation with herself in which she is finally forced to admit her hopelessness. The chorus, in which she begs for "just one thing [she] can believe in," is pitched higher, but features short descending phrases. This combination of higher range with descending lines suggests that her character's soul is torn between hope and a fear that hope will never be found.

Because some of the success of the individual songs of both *City Streets* and *Colour of Your Dreams* relies on their context within the album (as opposed to their instant commercial hit potential), it would seem appropriate to raise the issue of how these albums were received by album-oriented FM radio, the arm of the entertainment industry that might have latched onto King's work in the late 1980s and early 1990s but failed to do so.. *Rolling Stone* magazine's Kara Manning asked in her review of *Colour of Your Dreams* whether sexism might be the reason that this deserving album was largely ignored by album-oriented FM radio.[4] The reasons behind the lack of FM radio attention are probably more complex than sexism alone; King was at the time an over-50 pop star, so perhaps there was some age discrimination, too. I suspect, however, that part of the reason that both *City Streets* and *Colour of Your Dreams* received less attention than they merit has to do with musical expectations and the way in which audiences (and radio program-mers) seem to pigeon-hole performers into narrow categories. Because of the enormous success of, and the continuing interest in, *Tapestry,* King was defined as a largely acoustically based songwriter and singer of easily accessi-ble material about one-on-one interpersonal relationships. More so than any of her other recordings—with the exception of the techno/dance-influenced album *Speeding Time*—*City Streets* and *Colour of Your Dreams* break with the *Tapestry*-driven stereotypes of what Carole King songs and recordings should sound like. The albums are more fully realized as concept albums than *Tapestry,* the issues revolve around a larger social picture, the emotions and political points are more pointed, King's vocal style is more dramatic, and the music (generally) is harder-edged.

The penultimate song on *Colour of Your Dreams,* "Do You Feel Love," signals a return to the themes of self-image and self-respect that drove the beginning of the album. It is also a song that would seem to have the kind of potential for radio airplay described by *Rolling Stone*'s Kara Manning, in that the music and the arrangement is closer to early 1990s standards than to the music of *Tapestry.* Also, it is representative of the extent to which King had moved from songs that *sounded* autobiographical (whether or not her *Tapestry*-era songs truly were autobiographical) to songs that find her either portraying obviously fictional characters or observing the harsher side of life with a touch of cool detachment. Here, King portrays three people who suf-fer from unfulfilled lives—one because of poverty, one because of living too fast in her youth, and the third who tries to find true love through a variety of basically meaningless sexual encounters. The almost narrative, *parlando*-ish style that King uses in the verses of "Do You Feel Love" and several of the other tracks on *Colour of Your Dreams,* incidentally, is not entirely without precedent in the Carole King canon; it is reminiscent of her jazz-influenced work on *Rhymes & Reasons.*

Colour of Your Dreams concludes with the gospel-infused Goffin and King song "It's Never Too Late." Coming, as it does, after four consecutive songs that deal primarily with alienation, "It's Never Too Late" is a difficult album-closer to assess. It is a nice technical display for King as a gospel-style singer, and it shows how well she can integrate the musical attributes of gospel music into her accessible pop writing. The problem is that a song that glorifies love found later in life does not bring a full sense of closure to *Colour of Your Dreams* as an album with a significant focus on issues such as low self-esteem, poverty, racism, and sexism. It seems almost as though the listener is presented with the idea that romantic and physical love is the answer to the problems with which King deals throughout most of the rest of the album; it might solve some of them, but not all of them. This is a weakness in the structure of the album, at least to the extent that the listener hears *Colour of Your Dreams* as a concept album. Carole King's liner notes would seem to suggest that *Colour of Your Dreams* was not originally designed as a concept album. She writes, "This collection of songs began as a 'record' of songs as they were being written. We had no deadlines, no commercial pressures, only creative energy."[5] Indeed, the copyright dates of the songs span three years. Although King's words and the long span over which she wrote the material would suggest that *Colour of Your Dreams* is more of a confederation of songs than a fully integrated concept album, the fact remains that there is a discernible rhetorical focus throughout most of the album. The other challenging feature of "It's Never Too Late" is that it alone on *Colour of Your Dreams* re-creates a composing and arranging approach that defined King in the period just after the success of *Tapestry*, back in the early 1970s. It is a fine love song, but it does not fit what would seem to be the overall program of this album.

City Streets and *Colour of Your Dreams* form a stylistically connected subset of Carole King's output. Although *City Streets* is more immediately recognizable as a concept album—the ups and downs of life in the city theme is integrated into every song, and usually obviously so—the individual songs of *Colour of Your Dreams* are more memorable and more haunting. The range of emotions is not quite so stark, not so black and white (even some of the situations that appear on the surface to revolve around black-and-white issues are more complex). Insofar as one believes that much of life is illustrated in shades of gray, the complex songs of *Colour of Your Dreams* ring a little more true than the either/or songs of *City Streets*. And once the listener starts to recognize the structural connections (rhyme schemes) and lyrical and metaphorical connections (rain and holding out for love, for example) between the songs, the appreciation of the cohesive, concept-album nature of *Colour of Your Dreams* grows.[6] One of the curiosities of the album, which perhaps reflects the fact that it was not released on a major label, is the carelessness with which the CD booklet is prepared: artist listings and lyrics contain line breaks and the occasional typographical error that are otherwise inexplicable.

IN CONCERT

Considering the fact that King had been taking increasingly longer periods of time to issue albums in the 1980s and the early 1990s, the 1994 live album *In Concert* appeared quickly, following hot on the heels of *Colour of Your Dreams*. That being the case, it is important to note that most of the material on the album comes from the 1971–1974 period: "Hold out for Love," which features the guitar work of Slash, is the sole *Colour of Your Dreams* track to reappear on the live package. King's backup band, however, does include some of performers who helped to make *Colour of Your Dreams* a powerful studio album, including the aforementioned Slash, and guitarist Rudy Guess. *All Music Guide* reviewer Charles Donovan sums up the highs and lows of the album very well: King is "an abundantly confident, slick professional, with all the timing, glitz, and glamour of a Las Vegas pro," but "the blandly flawless band plays as if in a recording studio, rather than on stage."[7] Despite the highs and lows of this live album that were created by an emphasis on precision and perfection at the expense of passion on some tracks, it was an important album because it was the first live Carole King album ever, and it did represent her in top form as a seasoned performer.

The 1993 album *Colour of Your Dreams* and the 1994 concert album were not the only opportunities the public had to hear new Carole King songs during the period. The *Colour of Your Dreams* track "Now and For-ever" had been used as the opening and closing music in Penny Marshall's film *A League of Their Own*. And in 1994, Whittni Wright's recording of King's composition "You Are the Best" was part of the soundtrack of the film *I'll Do Anything*.

CARNEGIE HALL CONCERT: JUNE 18, 1971

Carole King's former manager and producer Lou Adler and the Ode orga-nization had control of the recordings that were made at King's June 18, 1971 concert at Carnegie Hall. Summer 1971 was an especially interesting time in Carole King's career. She was, of course, already a well-established songwriter. She was also a solo artist who was on the edge of becoming a household name, and not just as part of a hit songwriting team, in connec-tion with her former husband, Gerry Goffin.

A quarter-century after King's important return to New York City for her performance at Carnegie Hall, Ode was now part of the Sony organiza-tion, the company that finally released the recordings of the concert. This album contains the newly composed *Tapestry* tracks "I Feel the Earth Move," "Home Again," "Smackwater Jack," "So Far Away," "It's Too Late," "Way Over Yonder," and "Beautiful." Also represented are *Tapestry* tracks "You've Got a Friend," best known at the time in its James Taylor performance, and the true oldies that had found their way onto *Tapestry:* "(You Make Me Feel Like) A Natural Woman" and "Will You Love Me Tomorrow?" The album also finds King bringing several *Writer* and *Now That Everything's Been Said* songs to the public. This in itself is interesting in that part of the reason that King's two pre-*Tapestry* albums probably were not successful was because of King's reluctance to perform live.

The Carole King of *Carnegie Hall Concert: June 18, 1971* is far from the polished entertainer of the mid-1990s. In fact, given the way in which King's "authorized" live album, *In Concert,* presented her, it is difficult to imagine that she would have wanted this 25-year-old historical document to come out at all. King had battled with former manager/producer Lou Adler back in the mid-1980s over recordings of King that Adler controlled. Still, *Carnegie Hall Concert: June 18, 1971* is an important historical document, and despite King's apparent shyness, the recording captures the spirit of the singer-songwriter movement in its early days and King's career at a crucial turning point.

The release of King's historic June 1971 Carnegie Hall concert recordings was not the only nod to the past that marked the twenty-fifth anniversary of *Tapestry* in the mid-1990s. The album *Tapestry Revisited* (Lava Records 92604–2) appeared in 1995. This recording featured a mix of long-established performers such as Rod Stewart, Aretha Franklin, and the Bee Gees, along with new chart favorites, such as All-4-One and Faith Hill. Because of the never-to-be-duplicated nature of *Tapestry, Tapestry Revisited* was almost universally negatively compared with the original.[8]

Tapestry Revisited was not, however, the only Carole King tribute tied to the historical impact of *Tapestry* a quarter-century before. The year 1997 saw the release of saxophonist Bob Belden's *Tapestry* (Blue Note 57891) and the Overtures's *A Tribute to Carole King* (Master Tone 8026). Neither of these packages made a huge commercial impact; however, they are indicative of the appeal that King's early 1970s material still held for musicians. The Belden album is also significant in that it represents a fairly rare focus on the music of King by a jazz performer.

Carole King's life and career received a tribute of a far different and less flattering sort with the 1996 film *Grace of My Heart*. Although this film was a work of fiction, the lead character, Denise Waverly (pseudonym of Edna Buxton), who was a Jewish girl from Philadelphia who moved to New York to become a hit Brill Building songwriter after an unsuccessful early attempt at a singing career, was widely viewed as pseudo-Carole King. Along the way, Waverly/Buxton suffered several unsuccessful relationships with men in the music industry, moved to hippie-era California, and finally recorded a break-through solo album. From the very start of her career, Carole King is one of those rare celebrities who guarded her private life. This careful approach can be a double-edged sword, though, when it comes to a film such as *Grace of My Heart*. Because the general public know so little about the real-life Carole King, it could easily assume that the details of *Grace of My Heart* somehow represent those of King's life.

In the late 1990s, Carole King performed at various benefits, lending her name and talents to various progressive political and social causes. She was not entirely quiet on the recording front either. In 1998, her songs "Anyone at All" and "My One True Friend" were part of the soundtracks of the popular films *You've Got Mail* and *One True Thing,* respectively. Among her most notable performances in the late 1990s were the 1998 Nicollette Larson Memorial Concert, James Taylor's 1998 concert at the Universal Amphitheater in Los Angeles, and the 1998 benefit concert for Paul Newman's Barretstown Camp. Also notable was an October 14, 1999 benefit concert at New York City's Madison Square Garden that featured King's music, as performed by James Taylor, Babyface, Reba McEntire, Rickie Lee Jones, Trisha Yearwood, Chrissie Hynde, Mavis Staples, and Luther Vandross, among others. This Madison Square Garden event celebrated the twenty-fifth anniversary of *People* magazine, as well as King's four decades as a hit songwriter. King continued to perform at benefits into the twenty-first century, including a concert to aid victims of the September 11, 2001 terror attacks on New York City and Washington, D.C.

LOVE MAKES THE WORLD

The guest appearances that King made at the end of the twentieth century and the start of the new millennium at various benefits and other concerts, as well as the appearance of her songs in the films *You've Got Mail* and *One True Thing*, probably whetted her fans' appetites for more new material. The fans would not have to wait long: King's *Love Makes the World* was released in 2001. Of all of King's recordings, *Love Makes the World* uses the most guest stars and King collaborates with the most co-writers. This allows King to explore a wide variety of styles, as she duly notes in the album's liner notes.[9] As one might logically expect, a package predicated on the concept of musical diversity can at once show an artist's range and have a certain lack of musical coherence as an album. Certainly, this is the case with *Love Makes the World*. King demonstrates an impressive range as a performer and writer. The album's overarching theme of "love," in its many forms, is general enough that the various musical styles work; however, the album does not have an overall "sound" in the way that King's best albums do.

The album's title cut, "Love Makes the World," leads off. King collaborated with Dave Schommer (who did the programming on the track) and Sam Hollander in writing the song. Although from the instrumental introduction it is evident that this song is a slow ballad, the hip-hop beat in the bass drum tells the listener that this album will not represent your mother and father's Carole King. The *parlando* feel in the rhythm of the verses, too, owes a debt to hip-hop, as well as being reminiscent of the jazz-influenced style King explored on her 1972 album *Rhymes & Reasons*. More than anything else, though, in its musical arrangement and performance, "Love Makes the World" recalls the Quiet Storm R&B style of the 1990s. It is a credible representative of the style; however, like mainstrean pop and R&B material sometimes, "Love Makes the World" tends to sound pretty, somewhat slick, and fairly anonymous. This is especially true when the song is compared with the best of the songs King had written over the years for her own performance.

"You Can Do Anything," a collaboration of King, Carole Bayer Sager, and Babyface, is a more memorable song. Like "Love Makes the World," however, it also falls into the soulful R&B style of the late 1990s. It is a song of the need for self-confidence and self-love. King is joined on vocals by Babyface (Kenny Edmonds), who also plays keyboards, guitar, and drums, and who co-produced the song with King. Although it is a memorable piece with a beautiful melody in the verses and chorus (although the tune through the song's middle eight section tends to meander a bit), it exhibits some of the anonymous quality of the song "Love Makes the World."

"The Reason," a collaborative effort of King, Mark Hudson, and Greg Wells, continues the theme of soulfulness, but this time with different timbres (tone colors) and more of a rock-ballad orientation. The difference in timbres results from the guest appearance of singer Celine Dion, the instrumental emphasis on King's acoustic piano, and the burning electric guitar solos. King's backing vocal arrangement incorporates the kind of tight, barbershop-ish harmonies associated with the Beach Boys, mixed with a touch of the Beatles; Crosby, Stills, Nash and Young; and Queen's famous "Bohemian Rhapsody." Throughout its 4½ minutes, the song undergoes a stylistic metamorphosis from gentle pop ballad, to rock ballad, to power-rock ballad, to soulful-rock ballad, to gentle pop ballad. As that roll call of styles implies, it is song on which it is impossible to hang a single stylistic moniker. That is not to say that it is not a successful song. In fact, the stylistic progression is truly interesting and highlights the intensity of the love described in the lyrics.

The muted hip-hop, Quiet Storm feel returns in "I Wasn't Gonna Fall in Love," a collaboration of King and lyricist Carole Bayer Sager. Structurally, the song is classic Carole King: the verses, chorus, and middle eight sections are clearly distinguished from one another through contrasting melodic, harmonic, and rhythmic material. King bases the melodies of all three sections on short motives that she develops through repetition and sequence (repetition on higher or lower pitch levels). The jazzy rhythms of the verses and the inner rhymes of Sager's lyrics recall the songs on *Rhymes & Reasons*. Unlike the songs of King's 1972 album, however, the somewhat generic nature of the sentiments of the chorus of "I Wasn't Gonna Fall in Love" makes less of an autobiographical connection. The muted trumpet work of Wynton Marsalis adds a jazzy touch to the song, although it would have been nice to hear more of the trumpeter on the track.

A slightly heavier (albeit, still fairly slow) hip-hop beat introduces the next track on *Love Makes the World,* "I Don't Know." Strangely enough, it works. This collaboration of King, Gary Burr, Paul Brady, and Mark Hudson is more interesting musically than lyrically. The melodic, harmonic, and rhythmic material reflects the influence of gospel music and would not have been out of place in a late-1960s or early-1970s good-time gospel-rock song. Like the album's previous songs, "I Don't Know" is well crafted, with memorable music that could make sense as an album track on packages by any one of a huge number of pop/R&B performers.

Early in her career as an album artist—on *Now That Everything's Been Said, Writer, Tapestry,* and *Music,* in particular—Carole King had established a pattern of including one of her old 1960s hit Brill Building collaborations with Gerry Goffin on each album. By the end of the 1970s, King would less frequently present her own interpretations of songs that originally had been made famous by other performers. The next track on *Love Makes the World,* "Oh No, Not My Baby," had been a no. 24 pop hit for R&B singer Maxine Brown in 1964. Although Brown's recording was the most commercially successful single release of the song in the United States, Manfred Mann's 1965 cover version made it all the way to no. 11 in the British *New Musical Express* charts. And this was not even Carole King's first recording of the song; it appeared on her 1980 album *Pearls: The Songs of Goffin and King.* King's *Love Makes the World* arrangement calls for solo voice, piano, and acoustic bass (played by King's former husband and long-time bassist Charles Larkey). This texture suggests that introspective, personal sound of some of King's early 1970s treatments of her old Brill Building compositions. It gives the listener the impression that she or he is hearing the song as Gerry Goffin and Carole King originally conceived of it, before a formal arrangement or demo version had been put together. Her arrangement is so utterly different from any other on *Love Makes the World* that "Oh No, Not My Baby" stands out as a nod to nostalgia. This acknowledgment of the past is not a bad thing: the track lends a personal touch that is missing on some of the other *Love Makes the World* songs.

King, Carole Bayer Sager, and David Foster collaborated in writing the next *Love Makes the World* song, "It Could Have Been Anyone." The song is a gentle pop ballad. Perhaps the closest comparable earlier King composition and recording is "Now and Forever." "Now and Forever," however, is a much better-known (particularly as a result of its exposure in Penny Marshall's film *A League of their Own*) and much more memorable song.

Following "It Could Have Been Anyone" is "Monday Without You," a collaboration of King, Paul Brady, and Mark Hudson. This song definitely comes out of the late 1970s/early 1980s rock tradition. Carole King does not exactly sound like Chrissie Hynde (the Pretenders) or Joan Jett (Joan Jett and the Blackhearts), but the style of those early 1980s rockers is certainly here vocally and in the instrumental arrangement, which is driven by the prototypical straight-eighth-note electric rhythm guitar style associated with the new wave era. Carrying on the references to the rock music of the 1970s, the opening of the song includes an electric guitar melodic figure that suggests the Bruce Springsteen song "Born to Run," which, although it shared some of the back-to-basics nature of the music of the punk and post-punk late 1970s and early 1980s, was a product of the mid-1970s. "Monday Without You" is closer in style to the work King had done on her previous two albums (*City Streets* and *Colour of Your Dreams*) than anything else on *Love Makes the World.* It is also the most effective song on this album for a variety of reasons. First, as she proved on *City Streets* and *Colour of Your Dreams,* Carole King is a good rock singer. A song such as "Monday Without You" suits her voice much better than the more mainstrean pop ballads that populate the second half of this album. Second, this is the one full energy cut on *Love Makes the*

World. King's adoption of some of the rhythmic materials of hip-hop gives the songs of the first half of the album some potential for power, but they are largely of the Quiet Storm brand of R&B that emphasizes mood over power. Even outside the context of *Love Makes the World*, "Monday Without You" is a catchy song that exhibits a clear exuberance with love. It follows in the tradition of King's best rock compositions of the 1960s.

"An Uncommon Love" is perhaps the most intriguing song on *Love Makes the World*. This collaborative effort of King, Rob Hyman, and Rich Wayland features lead vocals by King and k.d. lang. King's string writing features voicings and counterpoint that show the influence of classical music, in the tradition of George Martin's string writing on the Beatles's "Eleanor Rigby." It is easily the most classically inspired string writing King has recorded to date. The melodic and harmonic writing has the kind of organic simplicity associated with country and folk music, but the style, largely as defined by the instrumental accompaniment, has nothing to do with folk or country.

Probably more interesting than the music or the arrangement on "An Uncommon Love," however, is the pairing of co-lead vocalists Carole King and k.d. lang. The song's lyrics find one (or possibly two) character(s) asking why the differences between her and her lover seem to play a bigger role in their relationship than the fact that they share "an uncommon love." Or, at least, that is what seems to be the case when the lyrics are taken as words on a page, or if one lead vocalist were to sing the song. The interplay between the two lead singers on this recording suggests that the characters portrayed by King and lang could in fact be singing to each other. In this context, the "uncommon love" about which the two sing would appear to be a love that binds two women in a lesbian relationship. A listener could easily read the song this way, especially given k.d. lang's public openness about her homosexuality.

In some respects, "An Uncommon Love" might be one of the most profound—and certainly one of the most sensitive—songs Carole King ever wrote and recorded. Aside from the description of the relationship of the characters portrayed by King and lang as "an uncommon love," the relationship is treated as one that is completely natural and mainstream. If the listener takes the song as a confirmation of the full validity of homosexual love, then "An Uncommon Love" serves an important sociological and political role on *Love Makes the World*. The sensitive musical setting makes it clear that the relationship of the two characters may be "uncommon" (that is a kind of relationship that is not experienced by a majority of the population), but it should be fully accepted as natural, normal, loving, and totally without stigma. This acknowledgment of homosexual relationships adds to the breadth of the kinds of love that King explores throughout *Love Makes the World*.

The album's next track, "You Will Find Me There," begins a mini-set of three songs with words and music by King. Inspired by a track by Allstar and Joel Campbell, this pop ballad reiterates the sentiments King expressed in one of her most famous compositions, "You've Got a Friend." It is an expression of total acceptance and unconditional love. The exact context of the love is left intentionally vague—it could be platonic love, romantic love, love for a child, or another kind of love King's music is tuneful, with beautiful harmony that suggests mainstrean R&B ballads. Although the song is a muted ballad with an instrumental backing track that does not reference hip-hop, King's melodic writing in the song's verses includes some double-time rhythmic figures that suggest the influence of the style.

"Safe Again" finds King playing the role of a woman who has lost her lover and wants to "feel safe again" with his return. The mournful melodic and harmonic writing suggests that, despite her hope that she will be "safe again," the relationship really has no chance at ever being rekindled. This mournful feeling is supported by the orchestration, which includes flute, oboe, and French horn. It is a more memorable piece—and much less repetitious-sounding—than "You Will Find Me There." For one thing, it is more interesting harmonically, with King including sophisticated chromatic harmonic shifts that reflect the influence of classical music and would not sound completely out of place in a late twentieth-century Broadway musical. At 2 minutes 41 seconds, "Safe Again" is the briefest song on *Love Makes the World*, but it is also one of the most beautiful; it leaves the listener wanting more.

The listener will not feel wanting for long, though; the next track, "This Time," shares motivic relationships with "Safe Again," both in its instrumental accompaniment and in the melodic line of the lead vocal. Musically, this creates a sense of variation and progression from one song to the next. King's lyrics, too, reflect a sense of progression. In "This Time," her character is telling her lover that this will be the last time she leaves—that this time "I mean to stay." This does not provide a crystal-clear sense of completion from "Safe Again," as in the earlier song it is King's character who is home and the lover who is not. It does, however, move the spirit from loss to hope for a brighter future. "This Time" includes some annoying spoken phrases that obscure the lead vocal line (something found in some contemporary R&B songs, but completely unnecessary here), but the song is distinguished by some of the best lead and backing vocals King has produced in years.

The limited edition of *Love Makes the World* (only available through some retail outlets) concludes with a bonus track, "Birthday Song." The album's liner notes do not make it clear why this is considered a "bonus track," but the lyrics are not included in the CD's booklet. It is a simple love song addressed to someone on his or her birthday. It is tuneful and simple. The main distinguishing feature of the song, though, is King's backing vocal arrangement and multitracked performance. Her arrangement features the same full, close-harmony style found to good effect on several other *Love Makes the World* cuts.

The touches of hip-hop that mark several of the first songs on the album give *Love Makes the World* a contemporary, early twentieth-century sound; however, the style is so different from the various musical styles with which King had been associated that these songs have a surface-level lack of connection with

King's previous work. Although King incorporates other styles on the album, there is enough of this turn-of-the-century soul style that it can gnaw on the nerves of the listener who associates Carole King with something other than a preprogrammed, thumping synth-bass drum thud. More important, however, some of the lyrics are general to the point of not having the feel of the kind of personal connection that marks King's best-remembered songs. That being said, the production is clean and clear, and King provides convincing performances of the newer-style material.

The presence of so many guest performers, from across so many stylistic categories and representing so many different tone colors (male singers, female singers, a trumpet player, a saxophone player) on the individual tracks, means that, despite the heavy amount of Quiet Storm-ish hip-hop rhythmic references, *Love Makes the World* does not have a clearly defined "sound." Perhaps another reason for this lack of clear album-defining sound and style is that the songs were written over several years.

Love Makes the World generally is organized so that the first half contains the hip-hop references and the second half represents mostly peaceful ballads, along with one early 1980s-style rock number. This adds to the album's feel of a collection of individual songs held together by a lyrical focus on love in its various forms (as opposed to a fully integrated concept album). It is the sort of approach implied by the Doors's 1970 album, *Morrison Hotel,* which has a "Morrison Hotel" side and a "Hard Rock Café" side. Wings's 1979 album, *Back to the Egg,* is an even more explicit example of the same sort of hard-soft, side-A/side-B contrast with its "sunny side up" (the more rock-oriented side) and "over easy" (the more pop-oriented side) designations. In this Carole King compact disc, the contrast between the first set of songs and the second half of the album makes less sense. It does tend to make the album gradually mellow out; however, there is no sense of an overall logical musical progression. It probably is no accident that on King's 2005 live album, *The Living Room Tour,* only one *Love Makes the World* song (the title track) would appear, and then without the vestiges of hip-hop of the original version. It's not that the individual songs on *Love Makes the World* are not up to Carole King's usual high standards as compositions, it's just that generally the combinations of words and music are too generic sounding for any of them to have "instant classic" stamped on them and the entire album suffers from too great a diversity of styles, timbres, and from too great a feeling of loss of energy as it reaches its conclusion.

THE LIVING ROOM TOUR

Carole King has rarely toured. The only officially sanctioned live recordings of her concerts released in the twentieth century were released in the mid-1990s. It would come as a pleasant surprise to King's fans, then, when a two-CD set culled from her 2004 "Living Room Tour" was issued in 2005.

The recording (and the concerts on the tour) begins with a brief new song, "Welcome to My Living Room." Although this opener could be filed away as a trifle, I believe that it deserves some discussion. King accompanies her singing with her solo piano—none of the other accompanying musicians appear on stage with her at the start of the concert. She is seated at the piano in what appears to be her living room (chairs, carpeting, a lamp, table, plants all graced the stage at each stop on the tour). The brief song introduces the "unplugged" nature of the concert and the fact that King will be presenting an overview of her four decades as a pop songwriter. Although much of the song has an easy-going waltz (triple meter) feel, there is a *parlando* (speech rhythm) feel that suggests to the listener that King is improvising the song for her individual concert. It is a nicely effective touch that meets with the obvious approval of audience members at the Cape Cod Melody Tent in Hyannis, Massachusetts, which is the source for the recording on the tour album.[10]

King includes the following songs that she had previously recorded on her albums between 1971 and 2003: "Peace in the Valley," "Love Makes the World," "Now and Forever," "Where You Lead I Will Follow" (the mother-daughter version used as the theme of the television program *Gilmore Girls*), "Lay Down My Life," "Jazzman," "Smackwater Jack," "Wishful Thinking," "It's Too Late," "So Far Away," "Sweet Seasons," "Being at War with Each Other," "I Feel the Earth Move," "(You Make Me Feel Like) A Natural Woman," and, perhaps her best-loved composition, "You've Got a Friend." In addition, King performed in their entirety "The Loco-Motion," "Pleasant Valley Sunday," and "Chains," as well as a Goffin and King medley consisting of "Take Good Care of My Baby," "It Might As Well Rain Until September," "Go Away, Little Girl," "I'm into Something Good," "Hey Girl," "One Fine Day," and "Will You Love Me Tomorrow." There is even a brand new Carole King–Gary Burr collaboration, "Loving You Forever." In short, it is a formidable collection of compositions that represent nearly 45 years of success in the pop music industry.

The Living Room Tour is an important chronicle of a career; however, it is not an album without flaws. For example, the medley of old Goffin–King hits goes by far too quickly, and King's voice sounds strained. Some of the songs, "Jazzman" in particular, beg for at least slightly fuller arrangements than the three acoustic musicians. It is, however, completely personal and completely different in focus, spirit, and presentation than either of the two Carole King live albums that had been released in the early 1990s. For a listener who is looking for an answer to the question, "Just what contribution did this woman make to popular music," this two-compact disc collection says everything that needs to be said.

Conclusions

One measure of the commercial and critical impact of pop musicians is the number of times other artists record their material. The songs that Carole King wrote back in the 1960s in collaboration with Gerry Goffin have become true standards of their era and have been covered by numerous artists. For example, although "Will You Love Me Tomorrow," was so closely linked to the Shirelles, it has been recorded by artists as diverse as Dave Mason, Cissy Houston, Millie Jackson, Bryan Ferry, Frankie Valli & the Four Seasons, Linda Ronstadt, Neil Diamond, the Righteous Brothers, and Dusty Springfield. The Goffin–King songs "One Fine Day" and "Go Away, Little Girl" are much more gender specific, so the range of artists covering the song is not as wide; however, both songs found their way onto numerous albums by a fairly large number of pop singers and mainstrean instrumentalists. Perhaps the most frequently covered Goffin–King hit, however, was "Up on the Roof." In addition to the original recording by the Drifters, such artists as James Taylor, Laura Nyro, Dawn, 101 Strings, the Nylons, Little Eva, the Cryan' Shames, II D Extreme, Billy Joe Royal, and Kenny Rankin have all recorded the song.

Once King began writing mostly for her own performance beginning in the 1970s, her material increasingly became more album-oriented than any of her work had been in the previous decade. As a result, it was mostly her bigger hits that were covered by other artists. As one might imagine, the songs of *Tapestry* were especially attractive for artists; these songs were well known to a wide variety of audiences, not just because of the enormous sales King's album enjoyed, but also because of the extensive radio airplay many of the songs (and not just the singles) enjoyed on top-40 stations.

As an example of the kind of coverage that King's *Tapestry* hits enjoyed, let us consider just two songs: "So Far Away," and perhaps the best-known song Carole King has ever written, "You've Got a Friend." Hot on the heals of the success of *Tapestry*, arrangements of their tracks for instrumental ensembles emerged. "So Far Away," for example, was scored by noted jazz and concert band arranger Bill Holcombe for concert band. The easy listening group, the New Generation, included the song on their 1973 album *"It's Too Late"/ "You've Got a Friend" and Other Carole King Songs* (RCA Camden ACL 1–0304). Well-known groups, too, found favor with "So Far Away." For example, the Crusaders, a significant jazz group, included the song on their album *Scratch* (Blue Thumb Records BTS 6010, 1974).

Both James Taylor's Grammy Winning recording of "You've Got a Friend" and King's *Tapestry* version received significant radio airplay in the 1970s. As perhaps Carole King's best-loved composition, and one that lyrically and stylistically is particularly open to a wide audience, it is natural that "You've Got a Friend" is King's most covered song. Performers from Broadway favorite Barbra Streisand, to soul singers Roberta Flack and Donny Hathaway, to easy listening acts such as pianist-orchestra leader Peter Nero, 101 Strings, and the Montovani Orchestra have all recorded the song. It has also found favor among jazz musicians, with recorded versions by Rob McConnell and the Boss Brass, Ella Fitzgerald, Phil Upchurch, and Bob Belden. Well-known singers, including Aretha Franklin, Petula Clark, and Michael Jackson, have also issued recordings of "You've Got a Friend." In addition to piano-vocal sheet music, the song has also been available in arrangements for SATB choir, women's chorus, concert band, marching band, and jazz ensemble.

Although it was not as commercially successful as the songs of *Tapestry*, King and Stern's "It's Going to Take Some Time" (a track from *Music*) was covered by easy listening, R&B, and light jazz artists. Karen and Richard Carpenter (The Carpenters) a popular act in the early 1970s, released the song as a single (No. 12 on the *Billboard* pop charts) and on their 1972 album, *A Song for You*. The Carpenters's recording later found its way onto several reissues of older material. Other artists who recorded the song include Richard "Groove" Holmes, Bob James, the Shirelles, and 101 Strings.

When considering cover versions of Carole King's compositions, special mention needs to be made of big band jazz musician Woody Herman. Herman (1913–1987), a clarinetist and saxophonist who rose to prominence during the swing era of the 1930s and 1940s, was one of the few jazz musicians of his generation to continue to lead a big band into the 1970s. Not only did his band remain active, but unlike most of the bands that had enjoyed their initial popularity in the 1930s and 1940s, Woody Herman's Thundering Herd changed with the times and refused to keep performing and recording only their old swing-era hits. This band recorded new material, including modern-sounding arrangements of pop and rock hits. Herman's band recorded two Carole King songs in the 1970s, "Jazzman" (on the album *King Cobra*, Fantasy F-9499, 1975) and "Corazón" (on the album *Thundering Herd*, Fantasy F-9452, 1974). At the time, Herman's band and its recordings were quite popular among younger jazz musicians and fans, including this author. The arrangements that the Herman band recorded were available for purchase and quickly became popular among high school and university jazz ensembles.

Not only has Carole King been recognized by fellow musicians through covers of her most famous compositions, she has also been given official recognition by her peers, leading figures in the entertainment industry. Of course, 1971 was *the* year of Carole King. Not only was *Tapestry* a huge commercial success, but the album and King's compositions generated recognition from the National Academy of Recording Arts and Sciences, the organization that presents the Grammy Awards. King won Grammys for Record of the Year ("It's Too Late"), Album of the Year (*Tapestry*), Song of the Year ("You've Got a Friend"), and Best Female Vocal Performance (*Tapestry*). To top it off, James Taylor won the Grammy for Best Male Vocal Performance for his recording of King's "You've Got a Friend."

The late 1980s saw a resurgence of official recognition of Carole King's work as a composer. She was inducted into the Songwriters Hall of Fame in 1986. In 1988, the National Academy of Songwriters presented King and her one-time husband and long-time musical collaborator Gerry Goffin with the Lifetime Achievement Award. For their songwriting contributions, Goffin and King were inducted into the Rock and Roll Hall of Fame as nonperformers in 1990. In addition, because of her popularity as a singer-songwriter-pianist in the 1970s and because of her longstanding association with the music publishing establishment, Carole King remains one of, if not *the*, best represented composer of the rock era in sheet music publications.

If one were forced to pick Carole King's best handful of albums as pertains to her career as a singer-songwriter, it would be a difficult task. Certainly *Tapestry* would have to be on the list: this album was one of the most significant "coming of age" albums for a large segment of the American population in the early 1970s, and its songs are King's best-remembered into the twenty-first century. The story of singer-songwriter Carole King, however, does not end with *Tapestry*. Based on the quality of the albums as packages and the quality of the individual songs (and attempting to present the fullest possible range of King's impressive output as far as style), my personal unranked list of King's top five albums include the following (in chronological order): *Tapestry* (1971), *Rhymes & Reasons* (1972), *Touch the Sky* (1979), *City Streets* (1989), and *Colour of Your Dreams* (1993). This list does not begin to cover all the great songs Carole King has written and recorded (in particular "Jazzman," from *Wrap Around Joy*, one of King's best-selling songs ever), but these five albums would certainly give any new listener an inspiring and wide-ranging introduction to Carole King's fascinating and enduringly popular body of work.

Discography

The Albums of Carole King

Now That Everything's Been Said. The City (Carole King, piano, keyboards, and vocals; Danny Kortchmar, guitar and vocals; Charles Larkey, bass; Jim Gordon, drums). "I Wasn't Born to Follow" (Gerry Goffin, King), "A Man without a Dream" (Goffin, King), "Now That Everything's Been Said" (King, Toni Stern), "Paradise Alley" (King, David Palmer), "I Don't Believe It" (King, Stern), "That Old Sweet Roll (Hi-De-Ho)" (Goffin, King), "Snow Queen" (Goffin, King), "Why Are You Leaving?" (King, Stern), "Victim of Circumstance" (King, Palmer). 33–1/3 rpm phonodisc. Ode 1244012, 1969. Reissued on compact disc, Sony International 65851, 1999.

Writer. Carole King, piano, keyboards, and vocals; various assisting instrumentalists and vocalists. "Spaceship Races" (Gerry Goffin, King), "No Easy Way Down" (Goffin, King), "Child of Mine" (Goffin, King), "Goin' Back" (Goffin, King), "To Love" (Goffin, King), "What Have You Got to Lose?" (Goffin, King, Toni Stern), "Eventually" (Goffin, King), "Raspberry Jam" (King, Stern), "Can't You Be Real?" (Goffin, King), "I Can't Hear You No More" (Goffin, King), "Sweet Sweetheart" (Goffin, King), "Up on the Roof" (Goffin, King). Produced by John Fischbach. 33–1/3 rpm phonodisc. Ode/A&M 77006, 1970. Reissued as Columbia/Legacy 34944. Reissued on compact disc, Epic EK-34944. Reissued on compact disc with *Rhymes & Reasons,* Sony International, 2002.

Tapestry. Carole King, piano, keyboards, and vocals; various assisting instrumentalists and vocalists. "I Feel the Earth Move" (King), "So Far Away" (King), "It's Too Late" (King, Toni Stern), "Home Again" (King), "Beautiful" (King), "Way over Yonder" (King), "You've Got a Friend" (King), "Where You Lead" (King, Stern), "Will You Love Me Tomorrow?" (Gerry Goffin, King), "Smackwater Jack" (Goffin, King), "Tapestry" (King), "(You Make Me Feel Like) A Natural Woman" (Goffin, King, Jerry Wexler). Produced by Lou Adler. 33–1/3 rpm phonodisc. Ode 34946, 1971. Reissued as Ode 77009, 1972. Reissued on compact disc, Ode EK 34946, 1986. Reissued on compact disc, Sony 66226, 1995. Reissued on compact disc with *Really Rosie* and *Her Greatest Hits,* Ode/Epic/Legacy, 2000.

Music. Carole King, piano, keyboards, and vocals; various assisting instrumentalists and vocalists. "Brother, Brother" (King), "It's Going to Take Some Time" (King, Toni Stern), "Sweet Seasons" (King, Stern), "Some Kind of Wonderful" (Gerry Goffin, King), "Surely" (King), "Carry Your Load" (King), "Music" (King), "Song of Long Ago" (King), "Brighter" (King), "Growing away from Me" (King), "Too Much Rain" (King, Stern), "Back to California" (King). Produced by Lou Adler. 33–1/3 rpm phonodisc. Ode 77013, 1971. Reissued on compact disc, Ode SQ-88013; Epic 982 595 2, 1995. Also issued on compact disc as Epic EK-34949. Reissued on compact disc with *Fantasy,* Sony International, 2002.

Rhymes & Reasons. Carole King, piano, keyboards, and vocals; various assisting instrumentalists and vocalists. "Come Down Easy" (King, Toni Stern), "My My She Cries" (King, Stern), "Peace in the Valley" (King, Stern), "Feeling Sad Tonight" (King, Stern), "First Day in August" (King, Charles Larkey), "Bitter with the Sweet" (King), "Goodbye Don't Mean I'm Gone" (King), "Stand Behind Me" (King), "Gotta Get through Another Day" (King), "I Think I Can Hear You" (King), "Ferguson Road" (Gerry Goffin, King), "Been to Canaan" (King). Produced by Lou Adler. 33–1/3 rpm phonodisc. Columbia 34950/Ode 77016, 1972. Reissued on compact disc, Epic EK-34950. Reissued on compact disc with *Writer,* Sony International, 2002.

Fantasy. Carole King, piano, keyboards, and vocals; various assisting instrumentalists and vocalists. "Fantasy Beginning" (King), "You've Been Around Too Long" (King), "Being at War with Each Other" (King), "Directions" (King), "That's How Things Go Down" (King), "Weekdays" (King), "Haywood" (King), "A Quiet Place to Live" (King), "Welfare Symphony" (King), "You Light Up My Life" (King), "Corazón" (King), "Believe in Humanity" (King), "Fantasy End" (King). Produced by Lou Adler. 33–1/3 rpm phonodisc. Ode 77018, 1973. Reissued on compact disc, Epic EK-34962. Reissued on compact disc with *Music,* Sony International, 2002.

Wrap Around Joy. Carole King, piano, keyboards, and vocals; various assisting instrumentalists and vocalists. "Nightingale" (King, David Palmer), "Change in Mind, Change in Heart" (King, Palmer), "Jazzman" (King, Palmer), "You Go Your Way, I'll Go Mine" (King, Palmer), "You're Something New" (King, Palmer), "We Are All in This Together" (King, Palmer), "Wrap Around Joy" (King, Palmer), "You Gentle Me" (King, Palmer), "My Lovin' Eyes" (King, Palmer), "Sweet Adonis" (King, Palmer), "A Night This Side of Dying" (King, Palmer), "The Best Is Yet to Come" (King, Palmer). Produced by Lou Adler. 33–1/3 rpm phonodisc. Ode 77024, 1974. Reissued as Columbia/Legacy 34953, 1974. Reissued on compact disc, Epic EK-34953. Reissued on compact disc with *Thoroughbred,* Sony International, 2002.

Really Rosie. Carole King, piano and vocals; various assisting instrumentalists and vocalists. "Really Rosie" (King, Maurice Sendak), "One Was Johnny" (King, Sendak), "Alligators All Around" (King, Sendak), "Pierre" (King, Sendak), "Screaming and Yelling" (King, Sendak), "Ballad of Chicken Soup" (King, Sendak), "Chicken Soup with Rice" (King, Sendak), "Ave. P" (King, Sendak), "My Simple Humble Neighborhood" (King, Sendak), "Awful Truth" (King, Sendak), "Such Sufferin'" (King, Sendak), "Really Rosie" [reprise]

(King, Sendak). Produced by Lou Adler. 33–1/3 rpm phonodisc. Caedmon TRS-368/Columbia 34955, 1975. Reissued as CBS 34955/Ode 77027, 1979. Reissued on compact disc, Ode/Epic/Legacy EK-65742, 1999. Reissued on compact disc with *Tapestry* and *Her Greatest Hits*, Ode/Epic/Legacy, 2000.

Thoroughbred. Carole King, piano, keyboards, and vocals; various assisting instrumentalists and vocalists. "Ambosia" (King, David Palmer), "Daughter of Light" (Gerry Goffin, King), "High Out of Time" (Goffin, King), "Only Love Is Real" (King), "So Many Ways" (King), "I'd Like to Know You Better" (King), "There's a Space Between Us" (King), "It's Gonna Work Out Fine" (King), "Still Here Thinking of You" (Goffin, King), "We All Have to Be Alone" (Goffin, King). Produced by Lou Adler. 33–1/3 rpm phonodisc. Ode 77034, 1975. Also issued as Columbia/Legacy 34963, 1976. Reissued on compact disc, Epic EK-34963. Reissued on compact disc with *Wrap Around Joy*, Sony International, 2002.

Simple Things. Carole King, piano, keyboards, and vocals; various assisting instrumentalists and vocalists. "Simple Things" (King, Rick Evers), "Hold On" (King, Evers), "In the Name of Love" (King), "Labyrinth" (King), "You're the One Who Knows" (King), "Hard Rock Café" (King), "Time Alone" (King), "God Only Knows" (King), "To Know That I Love You" (King, Evers), "One" (King). Produced by Carole King and Norm Kinney. 33–1/3 rpm phonodisc. Capitol SMAS-11667, 1977.

Her Greatest Hits. Carole King, piano, keyboards, and vocals; various assisting instrumentalists and vocalists. "Jazzman" (King, David Palmer), "So Far Away" (King), "Sweet Seasons" (King, Toni Stern), "Brother, Brother" (King), "Only Love Is Real" (King), "I Feel the Earth Move" (King), "It's Too Late" (King, Stern), "Nightingale" (King, Palmer), "Been to Canaan" (King), "Smackwater Jack" (Gerry Goffin, King), "Corazón" (King), "Believe in Humanity" (King). Produced by Lou Adler. 33–1/3 rpm phonodisc. Epic/Ode 34967, 1978. Reissued on compact disc, Epic EK-34967, 1986. Reissued on compact disc with *Tapestry* and *Really Rosie*, Ode/Epic/Legacy, 2000. Note: The compact disc reissued includes live recordings of "Eventually" and "(You Make Me Feel Like) A Natural Woman" as bonus tracks.

Welcome Home. Carole King, piano and vocals; various assisting instrumentalists and vocalists. "Main Street Saturday Night" (King), "Sunbird" (King, Rick Evers), "Venusian Diamond" (King, Evers, Robert McEntee, Mark Hallman, Robb Galloway, Michael Hardy, Miguel Rivera, Michael Wooten), "Changes" (King), "Morning Sun" (King), "Disco Tech" (King, McEntee, Hallman, Galloway, Hardy, Rivera, Wooten), "Wings of Love" (King, Evers), "Ride the Music" (King), "Everybody's Got the Spirit" (King), "Welcome Home" (Gerry Goffin, Howard Greenfield, King). Produced by Carole King and Norm Kinney. 33–1/3 rpm phonodisc. Avatar/Capitol SW-11785, 1978.

Touch the Sky. Carole King, piano, acoustic guitar, keyboards, and vocals; various assisting instrumentalists and vocalists. "Time Gone By" (King), "Move Lightly" (King), "Dreamlike I Wander" (King), "Walk with Me (I'll Be Your Companion)" (King), "Good Mountain People" (King), "You Still Want Her" (King), "Passing of the Days" (King), "Crazy" (King), "Eagle" (King), "Seeing Red" (King). Produced by Carole King and Mark Hallman. 33–1/3 rpm phonodisc. Capitol SWAK-11953, 1979.

Pearls: The Songs of Goffin and King. Carole King, piano, keyboards, and vocals; various assisting instrumentalists and vocalists. "Dancin' with Tears in My Eyes" (Gerry Goffin, King), "The Loco-Motion" (Goffin, King), "One Fine Day"

(Goffin, King), "Hey Girl" (Goffin, King), "Snow Queen" (Goffin, King), "Chains" (Goffin, King), "Oh No, Not My Baby" (Goffin, King), "Hi-De-Ho" (Goffin, King), "I Wasn't Born to Follow" (Goffin, King), "Goin' Back" (Goffin, King). Produced by Carole King. 33–1/3 rpm phonodisc. Capitol SOO-12073, 1980. Reissued as Fame 3014, 1982. Reissued on compact disc, Scarface 53879, 1994.

One to One. Carole King, piano, keyboards, and vocals; various assisting instrumentalists and vocalists. "One to One" (King, Cynthia Weil), "It's a War" (King), "Looking Out for Number One" (King), "Life without Love" (Gerry Goffin, Louise Goffin, Warren Pash), "Golden Man" (King), "Read Between the Lines" (King), "(Love Is Like a) Boomerang" (King), "Goat Annie" (King), "Someone You Never Met Before" (Gerry Goffin, King), "Little Prince" (King). Produced by Carole King and Mark Hallman. 33–1/3 rpm phonodisc. Atlantic SD 19344, 1982. Reissued on compact disc, Wounded Bird Records WOU-9344, 2005.

Speeding Time. Carole King, piano, keyboards, and vocals; various assisting instrumentalists and vocalists. "Computer Eyes" (Gerry Goffin, King), "One Small Voice" (King), "Crying in the Rain" (King, Howard Greenfield), "Sacred Heart of Stone" (Goffin, King), "Speeding Time" (Goffin, King), "Standin' on the Borderline" (Goffin, King), "So Ready for Love" (King), "Chalice Borealis" (King, Rick Sorensen), "Dancing" (King), "Alabaster Lady" (King). Produced by Lou Adler. 33–1/3 rpm phonodisc. Atlantic 7 80118, 1983. Reissued on compact disc, Wounded Bird Records WOU-118, 2004.

City Streets. Carole King, piano, keyboards, and vocals; various assisting instrumentalists and vocalists. "City Streets" (King), "Sweet Life" (King, Rudy Guess), "Down to the Darkness" (King), "Lovelight" (King), "I Can't Stop Thinking about You" (King, Paul Hipp), "Legacy" (King, Guess), "Ain't That the Way" (King), "Midnight Flyer" (Gerry Goffin, King), "Homeless Heart" (King, John Bettis), "Someone Who Believes in You" (Goffin, King). Produced by Carole King and Rudy Guess. Simultaneously issued on 33–1/3 rpm phonodisc, Capitol 2092; and compact disc, Capitol CDP 7 90885 2, 1989.

Colour of Your Dreams. Carole King, piano, keyboards, guitar, and vocals; various assisting instrumentalists and vocalists. "Lay Down My Life" (King), "Hold Out for Love" (King), "Standing in the Rain" (Gerry Goffin, King), "Now and Forever" (King), "Wishful Thinking" (King), "Colour of Your Dreams" (King), "Tears Falling Down on Me" (King), "Friday's Tie-Dye Nightmare" (King), "Just One More Thing" (King), "Do You Feel Love?" (King), "It's Never Too Late" (Goffin, King). Produced by Carole King and Rudy Guess. Compact disc. King's X/Rhythm Safari P2 57197, 1993.

In Concert. Carole King, piano and vocals; various assisting instrumentalists and vocalists. "Hard Rock Café" (King), "Up on the Roof" (Gerry Goffin, King), "Smackwater Jack" (Goffin, King), "So Far Away" (King), "Beautiful" (King), "(You Make Me Feel Like) A Natural Woman" (Goffin, King, Jerry Wexler), "Hold Out for Love" (King), "Will You Love Me Tomorrow?" (Goffin, King), "Jazzman" (King, David Palmer), "It's Too Late" (King, Toni Stern), "Chains" (Goffin, King), "I Feel the Earth Move" (King), "You've Got a Friend" (King), "The Loco-Motion" (Goffin, King). Produced by Rudy Guess; Executive producer, Hilton Rosenthal. Compact disc. King's X/Rhythm Safari P2 53878, 1994.

A Natural Woman: The Ode Collection (1968–1976). Carole King, piano, keyboards, and vocals; various assisting instrumentalists and vocalists. "Hi-De-Ho (That Old Sweet Roll)" (Gerry Goffin, King), "I Wasn't Born to Follow" (Goffin, King), "Up on the Roof" (Goffin, King), "Child of Mine" (Goffin, King), "I Feel the Earth Move" (King), "So Far Away" (King), "It's Too Late" (King, Toni Stern), "Home Again" (King), "Beautiful" (King), "Way Over Yonder" (King), "You've Got a Friend" (King), "Where You Lead" (King, Stern), "Will You Love Me Tomorrow?" (Goffin, King), "Smackwater Jack" (Goffin, King), "Tapestry" (King), "(You Make Me Feel Like) A Natural Woman" (Goffin, King, Jerry Wexler), "Music" (King), "Brother, Brother" (King), "Sweet Seasons" (King, Stern), "Pocket Money" (King), "It's Going to Take Some Time" (King, Stern), "Bitter With the Sweet" (King), "Goodbye Don't Mean I'm Gone" (King), "At This Time in My Life" (King), "Been to Canaan" (King), "Ties That Bind" (King), "Corazón" (King), "Believe in Humanity" (King), "Jazzman" (King, David Palmer), "Wrap Around Joy" (King, Palmer), "Nightingale" (King, Palmer), "Really Rosie" (King, Maurice Sendak), "Alligators All Around" (King, Sendak), "There's a Space Between Us" (King), "Only Love Is Real" (King), "You've Got a Friend" (King). Produced by Lou Adler. Two compact discs. Ode 48833, 1994. Contains previously released material.

Time Gone By. Carole King, piano, keyboards, and vocals; various assisting instrumentalists and vocalists. "Hard Rock Café" (King), "In the Name of Love" (King), "Morning Sun" (King), "Simple Things" (King, Rick Evers), "Time Gone By" (King), "You Still Want Her" (King), "Passing of the Days" (King), "Time Alone" (King), "Main Street Saturday Night" (King), "Welcome Home" (Gerry Goffin, Howard Greenfield, King). Compact disc. King's X/Priority 53880, 1994. Also issued on compact disc with *Pearls: The Songs of Goffin and King*, Alex VSOP199, 1995. Contains previous released material.

Carnegie Hall Concert: June 18, 1971. Carole King, piano and vocals; various assisting instrumentalists and vocalists. "I Feel the Earth Move" (King), "Home Again" (King), "After All This Time" (King), "Child of Mine" (Gerry Goffin, King), "Carry Your Load" (King), "No Easy Way Down" (Goffin, King), "Song of Long Ago" (King), "Snow Queen" (Goffin, King), "Smackwater Jack" (Goffin, King), "So Far Away" (King), "It's Too Late" (King, Toni Stern), "Eventually" (Goffin, King), "Way Over Yonder" (King), "Beautiful" (King), "You've Got a Friend" (King), "Will You Love Me Tomorrow?" (Goffin, King), "(You Make Me Feel Like) A Natural Woman" (Goffin, King, Jerry Wexler). Produced by Lou Adler. Compact disc. Sony Music EK-64942, 1996.

Goin' Back. Carole King, piano, keyboards, and vocals; various assisting instrumentalists and vocalists. "Jazzman" (King, David Palmer), "Child of Mine" (Gerry Goffin, King), "Back to California" (King), "So Far Away" (King), "Corazón" (King), "Will You Love Me Tomorrow?" (Goffin, King), "Brother, Brother" (King), "Home Again" (King). Produced by Lou Adler. Compact disc. Sony Music A-28556, 1997. Contains previously released material.

Love Makes the World. Carole King, piano, keyboards, and vocals; various assisting instrumentalists and vocalists. "Love Makes the World" (King, Dave Schommer, Sam Hollander), "You Can Do Anything" (King, Carole Bayer Sager, Babyface), "The Reason" (King, Mark Hudson, Greg Wells), "I Wasn't Gonna Fall in Love" (King, Carole Bayer Sager), "I Don't Know" (King, Gary

Burr, Paul Brady, Mark Hudson), "Oh No Not My Baby" (Gerry Goffin, King), "It Could Have Been Anyone" (King, Carole Bayer Sager, David Foster), "Monday Without You" (King, Paul Brady, Mark Hudson), "An Uncommon Love" (King, Rob Hyman, Rich Wayland), "You Will Find Me There" (King), "Safe Again" (King), "This Time" (King). Produced by Carole King and Humberto Gatica. Compact disc. Rockingale Records RKGL/ KOC-CD8346, 2001.

The Living Room Tour. Carole King, piano, keyboards, guitar, and vocals; various assisting instrumentalists and vocalists. "Welcome to My Living Room" (King), "Peace in the Valley" (King, Toni Stern), "Love Makes the World" (King, Sam Hollander, Dave Schommer), "Now and Forever" (King), "Where You Lead, I Will Follow" (King, Stern), "Lay Down My Life" (King), "Jazzman" (King, David Palmer), "Smackwater Jack" (Gerry Goffin, King), "Wishful Thinking" (King), Medley: "Take Good Care of My Baby"/"It Might As Well Rain Until September"/"Go Away, Little Girl"/"I'm into Something Good"/"Hey Girl"/"One Fine Day"/"Will You Love Me Tomorrow" (Goffin, King), "Loving You Forever" (King, Gary Burr), "It's Too Late" (King, Stern), "So Far Away" (King), "Sweet Seasons" (King, Stern), "Chains" (Goffin, King), "Pleasant Valley Sunday" (Goffin, King), "Being at War with Each Other" (King), "I Feel the Earth Move" (King), "(You Make Me Feel Like) A Natural Woman" (Goffin, King, Jerry Wexler), "You've Got a Friend" (King), "The Loco-Motion" (Goffin, King). Produced by Carole King and Rudy Guess. Two compact discs. Rockingale Records RCD2–6200-2, 2005.

THE SINGLES OF CAROLE KING

"The Right Girl" (King), "Goin' Wild" (King). 45 rpm phonodisc. ABC-Paramount 9921, 1958.

"Babysittin'" (King), "Under the Stars" (Gerry Goffin, King). 45 rpm phonodisc. ABC-Paramount 9986, 1959.

"Short Mort" (Gerry Goffin, King), "Queen of the Beach" (Goffin, King). 45 rpm phonodisc. RCA 7560, 1959.

"Oh Neil" (Gerry Goffin, Howard Greenfield, Neil Sedaka), "A Very Special Boy" (Goffin, King). 45 rpm phonodisc. Alpine 57, 1959.

"It Might As Well Rain until September" (Gerry Goffin, King), "Nobody's Perfect" (Goffin, King). 45 rpm phonodisc. Companion 2000, 1962. Also issued as Dimension 2000, 1962.

"School Bells Are Ringing" (Gerry Goffin, King), "I Didn't Have Any Summer Romance" (Goffin, King). 45 rpm phonodisc. Dimension 1004, 1962.

"He's a Bad Boy" (Gerry Goffin, King), "We Grew up Together" (Goffin, King). 45 rpm phonodisc. Dimension 1009, 1963.

"A Road to Nowhere" (Gerry Goffin, King), "Some of Your Lovin'" (Goffin, King). 45 rpm phonodisc. Tomorrow 7502, 1966.

"Snow Queen" (Gerry Goffin, King), "Paradise Alley" (King, David Palmer). The City (Carole King, keyboards and vocals). 45 rpm phonodisc. Ode 113, 1969.

"That Old Sweet Roll (Hi-De-Ho)" (Gerry Goffin, King), "Why Are You Leaving?" (King, Toni Stern). The City (Carole King, keyboards and vocals). 45 rpm phonodisc. Ode 119, 1969.

"Up on the Roof" (Gerry Goffin, King), "Eventually" (Goffin, King). 45 rpm phonodisc. Ode 66006, 1970.

"It's Too Late" (King, Toni Stern), "I Feel the Earth Move" (King). 45 rpm phonodisc. Ode 66015, 1971.

"So Far Away" (King), "Smackwater Jack" (Gerry Goffin, King). 45 rpm phonodisc. Ode 66019, 1971.

"Sweet Seasons" (King, Toni Stern), "Pocket Money" (King). 45 rpm phonodisc. Ode 66022, 1972.

"Brother, Brother" (King), "It's Going to Take Some Time" (King, Toni Stern). 45 rpm phonodisc. Ode 66026, 1972.

"Bitter with the Sweet" (King), "Been to Canaan" (King). 45 rpm phonodisc. Ode 66031, 1972.

"Believe in Humanity" (King), "You Light Up My Life" (King). 45 rpm phonodisc. Ode 66035, 1973.

"Corazón" (King), "That's How Things Go Down" (King). 45 rpm phonodisc. Ode 66039, 1973.

"Jazzman" (King, David Palmer), "You Go Your Way, I'll Go Mine" (King, Palmer). 45 rpm phonodisc. Ode 66101, 1974.

"Nightingale" (King, David Palmer), "You're Something New" (King, Palmer). 45 rpm phonodisc. Ode 66106, 1975.

"Only Love Is Real" (King), "Still Here Thinking of You" (Gerry Goffin, King). 45 rpm phonodisc. Ode 66119, 1976.

"Hard Rock Café" (King), "To Know that I Love You" (King, Rick Evers). 45 rpm phonodisc. Capitol 4455, 1977.

"One Fine Day" (Gerry Goffin, King), "Rulers of this World" (Goffin, Barry Goldberg, King). 45 rpm phonodisc. Capitol 4864, 1980.

Notes

INTRODUCTION

1. Robert Christgau, "Carole King: Five Million Friends," *Newsday,* November 1972. Reprinted in Christgau, Robert, *Any Old Way You Choose It* (Baltimore, MD: Penguin Books, 1973).

2. *Welcome to the NREPA Network,* http://www.nrepanetwork.org, Accessed July 29, 2005.

CHAPTER 1

1. Although the actual Brill Building was located at 1619 Broadway in Manhattan, and although much of the publishing activity was centered around companies located in the building, some were housed in other office buildings in the immediate vicinity. For example, Aldon Music, where Gerry Goffin and Carole King worked, had its first offices across the street from the Brill Building at 1650 Broadway.

2. Virginia L. Grattan, "King, Carole," *American Women Songwriters* (Westport, CT: Greenwood Press, 1993).

3. Ron Fell, "Carole King: Rewriting Her Legacy," *The Gavin Report,* April 21, 1989, p. 2.

4. Brian Gari, notes for *The Colpix-Dimension Story,* Two compact discs, Rhino R2–71650, 1994.

5. Discussion of King's own 1950s and 1960s recordings can be found in the chapter "Before *Tapestry.*"

6. A secondary dominant chord tends to pull the music—and the listener—toward the chord that follows. Unlike the dominant chord, which sounds as if it will lead back to the tonic chord (the principal key center of the song, built on the first scale-step), a secondary dominant pulls in the direction of some other chord.

7. Fred Bronson, *The Billboard Book of Number 1 Hits,* 5th ed. (New York: Billboard Books, 2003), p. 83.

8. "King as Queen?," *Time* 98, July 12, 1971, p. 52.

9. James E. Perone, *Carole King: A Bio-Bibliography* (Westport, CT: Greenwood Press, 1999), p. 3.

10. Al Kasha and Joel Hirschhorn, "Anatomy of a Hit: 'Up on the Roof,'" *Songwriter Magazine* 5, March 1980, pp. 14–15.

11. One of the unfortunate ironies of Nyro's career was that this talented singer-songwriter, who wrote songs that were significant hits for the 5th Dimension and Blood, Sweat and Tears, among others, only had one *Billboard* Top 100 single—this composition by Gerry Goffin and Carole King.

12. Not to be confused by the better-known British band of the same name of the early 1960s.

13. Reproduced in Roy Carr and Tony Tyler, *The Beatles: An Illustrated Record* (New York: Harmony Books, 1975), p. 25.

14. Ian Inglis, "'Some King of Wonderful': The Creative Legacy of the Brill Building," *American Music,* Summer 2003, p. 222.

15. Incidentally, both the lasting power of "I'm Into Something Good" and the song's adaptability to male and female singers is confirmed by its appearance in a television commercial for Cheerios cereal that was aired in late 2005.

16. Aniko Bodroghkozy, *Groove Tube: Sixties Television and the Youth Rebellion* (Durham, NC: Duke University Press, 2001), p. 72.

17. Andrew Sandoval, Liner notes for *Pisces, Aquarius, Capricorn & Jones Ltd.,* Compact disc reissue, Rhino R2–71793, 1995. Sandoval quotes former Monkee Michael Nesmith as crediting Douglas with creating the riff and then teaching it to Nesmith, who plays lead electric guitar on the track.

18. Chip Douglas, quoted in Andrew Sandoval, "Song Stories," liner notes for *The Monkees Music Box,* Four-compact disc set, Rhino R2–76706, p. 54.

19. Carole King, Liner notes for *The Living Room Tour,* Rockingale Records RCD2–6200–2, 2005.

CHAPTER 2

1. King's liner notes to her 2005 album *The Living Room Tour* describe Goffin as such. Carole King, Liner notes for *The Living Room Tour,* two compact discs, Rockingale RDC2–6200–2, 2005.

2. Although the title is often given as "Wasn't Born to Follow" (on the *Easy Rider* soundtrack album, for example), this release includes the personal pronoun "I."

3. The fact that Blood, Sweat and Tears' recording of "Hi-De-Ho" made it to No. 14 on the pop charts is significant and speaks both to the strength of the song and the band's jazzy arrangement of it, considering the irreparable harm to their standing within the rock community that had just been done by their U.S. State Department-sponsored concert tour of Europe. The tour placed the band in the unfortunate position of appearing to support the U.S. war in Vietnam, thereby alienating part of their potential audience base.

4. Danny "Kootch" Kortchmar, Preface to the liner notes for *Now That Everything's Been Said,* Compact disc reissue, Ode-Epic-Legacy EK-65851, 1999.

5. These acoustic guitar fills are best heard in 1968–1970 Taylor songs such as "Carolina on My Mind," "Fire and Rain," and "Country Road." Incidentally, Carole

King played piano on James Taylor's December 1969 recording sessions for the last two songs.

6. Photographer Jim McCrary explains the rumpled, startled look of King's cat on his Web site: "I moved the Cat on the pillow from accross [*sic*] the room into my shot." Jim McCrary, *Presenting . . . Samples from a Half-Century of Works by Jim McCrary, Photographer,* "Carole King," http://www.jimmccrary.com/pages/page3/index.htm, Accessed February 15, 2006.

7. Melissa Mills, "*Writer,*" *Rolling Stone* no. 69, 29 October 1970, pp. 46ff.

8. Jon Landau, "Records: Carole King, *Writer, Tapestry,*" *Rolling Stone* no. 81, April 29, 1971, pp. 40–41.

9. "Recordings of Special Merit: Writer," *Stereo Review* 26, February 1971, pp. 119–120.

10. Ibid.

CHAPTER 3

1. Betty Friedan, *The Feminine Mystique* (New York: Norton, 1963).

2. Shulamith Firestone, *The Dialectic of Sex: The Case for Feminist Revolution* (New York: Morrow, 1970).

3. The Boston Women's Health Book Collective, *Our Bodies, Ourselves: A Book by and for Women* (New York: Simon and Schuster, 1971).

4. Susan Brownmiller, *Against Our Will: Men, Women, and Rape* (New York: Simon and Schuster, 1975).

5. Debra Michals, "From 'Consciousness Expansion' to 'Consciousness Raising': Feminism and the Countercultural Politics of Self," in Peter Braunstein and Michael William Doyle, eds., *Imagine Nation: The American Counterculture of the 1960s and '70s* (New York: Routledge, 2002).

6. "Library," *The Official Carol Kaye Website,* http://www.carolkaye.com/www/library/index.htm. Accessed December 23, 2005.

7. Robert Christgau, "Carole King: Five Million Friends," *Newsday,* November 1972, reprinted in Robert Christgau, *Any Old Way You Choose It* (Baltimore: Penguin Books, 1973).

8. These albums were remastered from the original master tapes at half the normal speed, which resulted in greater audio fidelity and less compression of volume range. The vinyl that was used for these records was of higher quality than what was routinely used both at the time of the albums' original release and at the time the audiophile recordings were issued.

9. See, for example, Dave DiMartino, et al., "The Record That Changed My Life," *Musician,* no. 192, October 1994, p. 42.

10. James E. Perone, *Carole King: A Bio-Bibliography* (Westport, CT: Greenwood Press, 1999).

CHAPTER 4

1. Liner notes to *Music,* 33–1/3 rpm phonodisc, Ode 34949, 1971.

2. Specifically, the melodic progression of the lowered seventh scale step, sixth scale step, fifth scale step, and its associated harmony echoes too closely keyboard and rhythm guitar figures of "Get Back."

3. "Albums: *Rhymes & Reasons,*" *Melody Maker* 47, November 18, 1972, p. 25.

4. Stephen Holden, "Records: *Rhymes & Reasons*," *Rolling Stone* no. 121, 21 December 1972, p. 61.

5. Ellen Wolff, "*Rhymes & Reasons*," *Crawdaddy* no. 21, February 1973, p. 72.

6. Speaking of Toni Stern's writing, her lyrics for the *Tapestry* track "It's Too Late" feature a slightly less subtle use of internal rhymes. They don't get in the way as much as King's internal rhymes on *Rhymes & Reasons*, as there is so little obvious use of this kind of rhyme scheme on *Tapestry*.

7. "Albums: *Rhymes & Reasons*," *Melody Maker* 47, November 18, 1972, p. 25.

8. Although the term *agape love* often carries specifically Christian connotations, I use the term in its more general meaning of a general all-embracing brotherhood-and-sisterhood-of-humankind love.

9. Aaron Fuchs, "*Fantasy*," *Crawdaddy* no. 29, October 1973, pp. 76ff.

10. Stephen Holden, "Records: *Fantasy*," *Rolling Stone* no. 140, August 2, 1973, p. 48.

11. John Borgmeyer, "Singer-Songwriters: Rock Grows Up," *The Greenwood Encyclopedia of Rock History*, vol. 4 (Westport, CT: Greenwood Press, 2006), p. 108.

12. Stephen Holden, "Records: *Fantasy*," *Rolling Stone* no. 140, August 2, 1973, p. 48.

13. Ibid.

14. The *canto* section is that which most closely resembles American pop song. Here, the lead vocalist sings a composed melody that sets the basic text of the song. The *montuno* section features improvisation, both lyrical and melodic, by the lead singer.

15. "Deputy Parks Commissioner T. Mastroianni Lauds King Cleanup," *New York Times*, June 14, 1973, p. 46.

16. Timothy White, "Sadly, The Times They Are A-Changin'," *Billboard* 111, August 14, 1999, p. 5.

CHAPTER 5

1. The compact disc reissue comes with a sticker on the jewel case with excerpted quotes such as "A kid's album even grown-ups can love. A." (*Entertainment Weekly*); "Best of 1999." (*Child Magazine*); and "One of the best children's albums ever made." (*Los Angeles Times*). *Really Rosie*, compact disc reissue, Ode EK 65742, 1999.

2. Leslie Tannenbaum, "Betrayed by Chicken Soup: Judaism, Gender and Performance in Maurice Sendak's *Really Rosie*," *Lion & the Unicorn* 27, September 2003, pp. 362–376.

3. Dave Marsh, "Records: *Simple Things*," *Rolling Stone* no. 247, September 8, 1977, pp. 113–114.

4. "Pop Albums: *Simple Things*," *Melody Maker* 52, July 30, 1977, p. 14.

5. Richard C. Walls, "*Simple Things*," *Creem* 9, November 1977, pp. 67–68.

6. Robert Stephen Spitz, "Too Pooped to Pop?," *Crawdaddy* no. 77, October 1977, p. 63.

7. Don Heckman, "Carole King: Optimistic Craftsmanship," *High Fidelity/Musical America* 27, October 1977, pp. 142ff.

8. Don Heckman, "Carole King: Optimistic Craftsmanship"; Robert Stephen Spitz, "Too Pooped to Pop?"

9. In representing musical form, letters are used to label the various sections, with contrasting letters representing contrasting musical material. In a conventional Tin Pan Alley pop song, the structure is often statement-repeat-new section-original statement, or A-A-B-A.

10. Carole King, Liner notes to *Welcome Home,* 33–1/3 rpm phonodisc, Capitol SW-11785, 1978.

11. Ibid.

12. Ibid.

13. Ibid.

14. Ibid.

15. Tom Smucker, "Riffs: Bring Back the Hack," *Village Voice* 24, October 29, 1979, p. 65.

16. Susan Hill, "Touch the Sky," *Melody Maker* 54, September 15, 1979, p. 28.

17. I deliberately refer to this as King's "newfound" vocal style because, although *Simple Things* and *Welcome Home* incorporated the country-rock genre, never was it so pervasive and never before did King sing as a fully committed country-blues-rock singer.

18. For example, *Rolling Stone* critic Don Shewey suggested as much in his review of the album. See Don Shewey, "Records: *Pearls: The Songs of Goffin and King,*" *Rolling Stone* no. 323, August 7, 1980, p. 50.

19. See, for example, Don Shewey, "Records: *Pearls: The Songs of Goffin and King,*" *Rolling Stone* no. 323, August 7, 1980, p. 50; and Paul Grein, "Closeup," *Billboard* 92, May 31, 1980, p. 60.

CHAPTER 6

1. One of the more telling reviews of *Pearls* came from *Creem*'s Jim Feldman, who wrote, "No doubt King never should have left the Brill Building for California. I wouldn't object to a few more albums like this one." Jim Feldman, "*Pearls: The Songs of Goffin and King,*" *Creem* 12, September 1980, pp. 58–59.

2. Stephen Holden, "Records: *One to One,*" *Rolling Stone* no. 370, May 27, 1982, p. 62.

3. Lonnie Williamson, "King Sings, But Is No Fan of Public," *Outdoor Life* 173, January 1984, pp. 64ff.

4. See, for example, "*Speeding Time,*" *People Weekly* 21, February 6, 1984, p. 17.

5. "*Speeding Time,*" *People Weekly* 21, February 6, 1984, p. 17.

6. Sam Sutherland, "*Speeding Time,*" *High Fidelity* 34, March 1984, p. 78.

7. Joel Vance, "*Speeding Time,*" *Stereo Review* 49, April 1984, p. 88.

8. Elfman, incidentally, started out as the drummer for the new wave rock band Oingo Boingo.

CHAPTER 7

1. In casual conversations in the late 1990s, when I was writing my reference book, *Carole King: A Bio-Bibliography,* with several female college-age students who mentioned that *A League of Their Own* was one of their favorite movies, the King song emerged as one of the more memorable parts of the film.

2. The CD's insert includes the words "a black king," but King sounds as if she sings the word "kid." The "king" in the printed lyrics could be a typographical error, or a reference to the Rodney King beatings. Carole King, *Colour of Your Dreams*, compact disc, King's X Records/Rhythm Safari Records P2–57197, 1993.

3. *Sprechstimme* (German for "speech-song") was a singing style associated with expressionistic/12-tone Austrian composers such as Arnold Schoenberg and Alban Berg in the early twentieth century. In this style, the singer would consciously slide between pitches. The reader who is unsure about the connection between this hallmark of German Expressionism and the vocal style of Bob Dylan's vocal style should listen to Dylan's 1965–1966 output.

4. Manning, Kara, "Recordings: *Colour of Your Dreams*," *Rolling Stone* no. 659, 24 June 1993, pp. 80ff.

5. Carole King, Liner notes to *Colour of Your Dreams*, compact disc, King's X Records/Rhythm Safari Records P2–57197, 1993.

6. This, again, even though King's liner notes seem to suggest that it is a collection of individual songs that were not necessarily intended to go together as a concept album.

7. Charles Donovan, Review of *In Concert, All Music Guide*, http://www.allmusic.com/cg/amg.dll?p=amg&sql=10:kr6ibkg9jakn, Accessed 28 February 2006.

8. See, for example, Ellen Futterman, "*Tapestry Revisited: A Tribute to Carole King*," *St. Louis Post-Dispatch* 16 November 1995, p. GO 9; and Geoffrey Himes, "Reprise Packages: Two New Tributes That Don't Measure Up," *Washington Post* 24 January 1996, p. B7.

9. Carole King, Liner notes to *Love Makes the World*, compact disc, Rockingale/Koch Records CD-8371, 2001.

10. Carole King, Liner notes for *The Living Room Tour*, two compact discs, Rockingale RDC2–6200–2, 2005.

Annotated Bibliography

"Albums of the Year." *Rolling Stone* no. 101, February 3, 1972, p. 39.
　　King's *Tapestry* is included as one of the top albums of 1971.
"Albums: *Rhymes & Reasons.*" *Melody Maker* 47, November 18, 1972, p. 25.
　　A generally negative review of King's *Rhymes & Reasons* album, which, accord-
ing to the reviewer, suffers from the "blandness of the songs."
Bane, Michael. *Who's Who in Rock. s.v.* "King, Carole." New York: Facts on File, 1981.
　　A biographical sketch of King.
Barnes, Ken. "It's Never Too Late, Baby." *USA Today* April 24, 2002, p. Life 1.
　　A report that the Songwriters Hall of Fame announced that it will present
King with the Johnny Mercer Award on June 13, 2002.
Bernard, Stephen. "Rock Giants from A-Z: Carole King, From Teen Love to
Superstar." *Melody Maker* 49, January 19, 1974, pp. 25–26.
　　A biographical profile of King.
Bessman, Jim. "The Who, King Among Acts on Legacy's New 'Vaults' Live Series."
Billboard 108, October 12, 1996, pp. 19–20.
　　Included in this article is mention of the release of Carole King's previously
unissued *Live At Carnegie Hall—June 18, 1971* album.
Bloch, Avital H. and Lauri Umansky, eds. *Impossible to Hold: Women and Culture in
the 1960s.* New York: New York University Press, 2005.
　　King's role as a successful composer is included.
Bloom, Ken. *American Song: The Complete Companion to Tin Pan Alley Song.* New
York: Schirmer Books, 2001.
　　This book contains helpful entries on King, the Brill Building, and King's Brill
Building colleagues.
Bodroghkozy, Aniko. *Groove Tube: Sixties Television and the Youth Rebellion.* Durham,
NC: Duke University Press, 2001.

Includes discussion of *The Monkees* as a mildly counterculture television program and discussion of some of the Goffin–King songs that the Monkees recorded.

Boehm, Mike. "King: '70s Soft-Rocker Gets Tough for the '90s." *Los Angeles Times* August 18, 1989, p. VI 6.
A favorable review of King's performance at the Pacific Amphitheatre.

Borgmeyer, John. "Singer-Songwriters: Rock Grows Up," *The Greenwood Encyclopedia of Rock History,* vol. 4, Westport, CT: Greenwood Press, 2006.
Carole King is mentioned in this chapter, and her contribution to the singer-songwriter movement is sketched in the A-Z listing in the volume.

Brandes, Philip. "*Tapestry* Weaves King's Themes." *Los Angeles Times* July 28, 1995, p. F26.
A somewhat mixed review of the revue "*Tapestry:* The Music of Carole King," which was playing at the International City Theatre, Long Beach, California.

Bronson, Fred. *The Billboard Book of Number 1 Hits,* 5th ed. New York: Billboard Books, 2003.
This book contains interesting facts about *Billboard* magazine's No. 1 pop hit singles from 1955–2003.

Bronson, Fred. "Bits of *Tapestry* Back on Display." *Billboard* 107, October 28, 1995, p. 118.
A description of the *Tapestry Revisited* album, as well as other recent recordings of Carole King's songs.

Bronson, Fred. "The Years in Music." *Billboard* 113, December 29, 2001, p. YE-28.
An article that describes the top albums of 40, 30, 20, and 10 years prior. Carole King's *Tapestry* is included as one of the most important albums of 1971.

Brown, Joe. "Long and Varied Lives the King." *Washington Post* June 11, 1993, p. WW15.
A lengthy profile of Carole King as a preview of her June 16, 1993 concert appearance at Wolf Trap, Washington, D.C.

Caro, Mark. "On the Blandstand." *Chicago Tribune* December 7, 1995, p. V7.
Tapestry Revisited pales in comparison to King's original, according to this review.

"Carole: Grammy Queen." *Melody Maker* 47, March 25, 1972, p. 3.
A report detailing King's four Grammy Awards for her work in 1971.

"Carole King Lures 65,000 to Freebie Central Park Date." *Variety* 271, May 30, 1973, pp. 55ff.
A feature report on King's free concert in New York's Central Park.

"Carole King, Ode Split After 8 Years." *Rolling Stone* no. 232, February 10, 1977, p. 24.
A report on King's change of record label from Ode/Epic/Columbia to Capitol/EMI.

"Carole King Sues Adler." *Variety* 327, April 29, 1987, p. 141.
A report on King's lawsuit against her former manager and producer Lou Adler.

Carr, Roy and Tony Tyler. *The Beatles: An Illustrated Record.* New York: Harmony Books, 1975.
This book (and its later revised editions) contains a reproduction of a full-page profile of the favorite foods, composers, singers, and so forth of each of the

Beatles that originally appeared in *New Musical Express* in 1963. Paul McCartney lists Goffin and King as his favorite songwriters. McCartney has been widely quoted elsewhere as having said that all he and John Lennon wanted to do as songwriters was to "be as good and Goffin and King."

Champlin, Charles. "Carole King: We've Still Got a Friend." *Los Angeles Times* December 25, 1983, p. C5.

A feature biography of King.

Chorush, Bob. "Carole King, with New LP, Arrives." *Rolling Stone* no. 98, December 23, 1971, p. 20.

A preview of King's *Music* album, this article contains information about the start of her solo career.

Christgau, Robert. "Carole King: Five Million Friends." *Newsday* November 1972. Reprinted in Christgau's *Any Old Way You Choose It.* A comparison of *Tapestry, Music,* and *Rhymes & Reasons.*

The author characterizes King's piano playing as "the first widely recognized instrumental signature ever developed by a woman" in the rock era.

Christgau, Robert. *Any Old Way You Choose It.* Baltimore, MD: Penguin Books, 1973.

Contains a reprint of Christgau's comparison of *Tapestry, Music,* and *Rhymes & Reasons,* that originally had appeared in *Newsday.*

"Chronicle." *New York Times* September 12, 1997, p. B16.

Among the upcoming events mentioned in this article is King's performance at a benefit for the Hole in the Wall Camp, an organization for children with cancer.

Cohen, Mitchell S. *Carole King: A Biography in Words & Pictures.* New York: Chappell Music Company, 1976.

A general chronicle of and commentary on Carole King. The book contains some factual errors, including incorrect composer credits and incorrect matrix numbers in the discography, and the occasional incorrect singer credit in the text.

Coppage, Noel. "Carole Kings' Vintage *Pearls:* Not Only a Classy Album, But a Timely One." *Stereo Review* 45, September 1980, p. 74.

A favorable review of the *Pearls: The Songs of Goffin and King* album.

Coppage, Noel. "Troubadettes, Troubadoras, and Troubadines." *Stereo Review* September 29, 1972, pp. 58–61.

This article deals with such prominent female pop musicians as King, Grace Slick, Joan Baez, Janis Ian, and Laura Nyro. King's melodies are characterized as "understated," and her lyrics are called "plain and rather mundane." Compared with male pop musicians of a similar style such as James Taylor, King tends to treat cosmic subjects with down-to-earth language, taken from "the neighborhood tavern or the laundromat."

Cooper, Mark. "Songs of Experience." *The Guardian* April 7, 1989, p. 30.

Cooper profiles Phoebe Snow, Bonnie Raitt, and Carole King, all of whom had recently reemerged as songwriters after periods of personal trauma.

Cooper, Mark. "Stepping Out of the Shadows." *The Guardian* July 14, 1989, p. 34.

A feature-length profile of King in light of the release of *City Streets.*

Cromelin, Richard. "I Have Everything I Want." *Los Angeles Times* July 17, 1993, p. F1.

A feature-length profile of King in advance of her July 18, 1993 concert the Universal Amphitheatre, Los Angeles.

Crouse, Tim. "Records: Carole King's *Music*." *Rolling Stone* no. 100, January 20, 1972, p. 50.

A generally favorable review of King's *Music*, although the reviewer feels that the album pales in comparison with *Tapestry*, particularly in its musical arrangements. "Carole now has to choose between simplicity and complexity—between piano-cum-combo and a full scale orchestra. The middle ground where she is now standing isn't good enough for her and the sooner she moves on the better." Crouse also highlights King's affinity for African American music, both in her compositions and performance style.

Crowe, Cameron. "Carole King and Navarro Mellow Out." *Rolling Stone* no. 248, September 22, 1977, p. 15.

This article deals with the use of meditation by King and members of the band Navarro. It also contains information on the King's *Simple Things*, on which Navarro performs.

Davidson, Paul. "Record Labels Put Releases on Web; Internet Opens Music Market Niche." *USA Today* June 17, 1997, p. B7.

The availability of King's album *King in Concert* is noted. Todd Rundgren's Global Music Outlet will begin delivering recordings from Rhythm Safari (King's label at the time) through the World Wide Web.

Denselow, Robin. "Emerging from the Underground." *The Guardian* April 14, 1989, p. 32.

This article includes a review of King's *City Streets*.

"Deputy Parks Commissioner T. Mastroianni Lauds King Cleanup." *New York Times* June 14, 1973, p. 46.

A report on King's request at her concert in New York's Central Park that the audience members clean up their trash, and the fact that they actually complied.

DiMartino, David. "Carole King Charges that Adler Is No Friend of Hers." *Billboard* 99, May 16, 1987, pp. 6ff.

A report on King's lawsuit against her former manager and producer Lou Adler.

Donovan, Charles. Review of *In Concert*. *All Music Guide*. http://allmusic.com/cg/amg.dll?p=amg&sql=10:kr6ibkg9jakn. Accessed February 28, 2006.

A review of King's live album.

Emerson, Ken. *Always Magic in the Air: The Bomp and Brilliance the Brill Building Era*. New York: Viking Adult, 2005.

A comprehensive study of the Brill Building songwriters and their legacy.

Endrst, James. "Celebs Lend Energy to Earth Fund." *USA Today* May 13, 2002, p. Life 2.

A report on a fundraiser held for the Natural Resources Defense Council at which Carole King performed.

Evans, Paul. "Rollin' & Tumblin'" *King in Concert*." *Rolling Stone* no. 680, April 21, 1994, p. 88.

This brief favorable review of King's *King in Concert* album states that her "best [work] remains vital."

Ewen, David. *American Songwriters: An H. W. Wilson Biographical Dictionary. s.v.* "King, Carole." New York: H. W. Wilson, 1987.

This volume provides a nice biographical sketch of King.

Feehan, Paul G. Review of *Carole King* by Mitchell S. Cohen. *Library Journal* 101, December 15, 1976, p. 2581.

A thoroughly unfavorable review of Cohen's biography of Carole King.

Feldman, Jim. "*Pearls: The Songs of Goffin and King.*" *Creem* 12, September 1980, pp. 58–59.

A favorable review of King's *Pearls* album.

Fell, Ron. "Carole King: Rewriting Her Legacy." *The Gavin Report* no. 1753, April 21, 1989, p. 2.

Fell includes quotes from King regarding her view of the work of Brill Building songwriters such as herself.

Firestone, Shulamith. *The Dialectic of Sex: The Case for Feminist Revolution.* New York: Morrow, 1970.

One of the great political documents of the women's movement of the 1970s.

Fitzgerald, Jon. "When the Brill Building Met Lennon-McCartney: Continuity and Change in the Early Evolution of the Mainstream Pop Song." *Popular Music and Society* 19, Spring 1995, pp. 59–77.

The basic premise of this article is that the shift in style from innocuous love songs to message songs and the shift in the type of performers for whom the Brill Building composers wrote was not as much a reaction to the Beatles and other British invasion groups as a "further manifestation of trends already in place."

Friedan, Betty. *The Feminine Mystique.* New York: Norton, 1963.

One of the significant early books that influenced the feminist movement of the 1960s and 1970s.

Fuchs, Aaron. "Fantasy." *Crawdaddy* no. 29, October 1973, pp. 76ff.

A scathing review of King's *Fantasy* album, which "reaffirms [her] position as one of the most aggressively contrived artists today."

Futterman, Ellen. "*Tapestry Revisited: A Tribute to Carole King.*" *St. Louis Post-Dispatch* November 16, 1995, p. GO 9.

A generally unfavorable review of the tribute album.

Gaar, Gillian G. *She's a Rebel: The History of Women in Rock & Roll.* New York: Seal Press, 2002.

Carole King is among the numerous female performers, writers, and publishers of the rock era profiled in this book.

Gari, Brian. Liner notes for *The Colpix-Dimension Story.* Two compact discs. Rhino R2–71650, 1994.

Gari provides detailed notes about Gerry Goffin and Carole King's compositions for and work with the Colpix and Dimension record labels early in their Brill Building career.

George-Warren, Holly. "High Notes." *Rolling Stone* no. 773, November 13, 1997, pp. 179ff.

Includes a brief description of Carole King's *Tapestry,* which is included as one of the most important albums ever recorded by a female performer.

Gillen, Marilyn A. "On Stage." *Billboard* 105, February 22, 1993, p. 46.

A review of the revue "*Tapestry:* The Music of Carole King," which was playing at the Union Square Theatre, New York City.

Goldman, Albert. "A Season Saved by the Belles: Pop's Debt to the Women." *Life* 71, December 31, 1971, p. R.

This article deals with the 1971 emergence of female pop artists such as King, Laura Nyro, and Carly Simon.

Graham, Jefferson. "Sound Familiar? New LPs by Dion, Carole King." *USA Today* March 6, 1989, p. D1.

This article deals in part with King's "comeback album," *City Streets*.

Grattan, Virginia L. *American Women Songwriters. s.v.* "King, Carole." Westport, Connecticut: Greenwood Press, 1993.

A brief biographical sketch of King and an overview of her career up to the early 1990s.

Greene, Bob. "Carole King: She Reads Our Minds." *Chicago Tribune* August 1, 1989, p. V1.

The well-known columnist Greene provides commentary on King and her ability to "provide the right voice for a generation."

Greig, Charlotte. "As Good as Their Words." *The Guardian* April 19, 1993, p. 2.

Greig, a member of the band Crow Country, discussed the influence of female songwriters, including Carole King, on rock music.

Grein, Paul. "Carole King." *Los Angeles Times* May 14, 1989, p. C86.

A mixed review of King's *City Streets*.

Grein, Paul. "Carole King Reaches Silver Screen in *Murphy's Romance*." *Billboard* 98, February 1, 1986, p. 44.

A report on King's score for the film *Murphy's Romance*, as well as her walk-on role as an actor in the film.

Grein, Paul. "Closeup." *Billboard* 92, May 31, 1980, p. 60.

A favorable review of *Pearls: The Songs of Goffin and King*. "Dancing with Tears in My Eyes" and "Chains" receive the highest praise.

Grein, Paul. "Never Say Die: *Tapestry* LP Climbing." *Billboard* 87, June 14, 1974, p. 10.

A report that King's *Tapestry* remains on the *Billboard* top 100 album charts for the fifth straight year.

Harrington, Richard. Obituary of Laura Nyro. *Washington Post* April 13, 1997, p. G1.

This obituary of the late singer-songwriter mentions that the only time Nyro broke into the *Billboard* top 100 singles charts was not with one of her own songs, but when she recorded Gerry Goffin and Carole King's "Up on the Roof" in 1970.

"Hayes and King Win Top Awards at NARM Meet." *Variety* 266, March 15, 1972, p. 61.

This report includes a run-down of King's 1971 Grammy Awards: Record of Year for "It's Too Late," Album of the Year for *Tapestry*, Song of the Year for "You've Got a Friend," and Best Pop Vocal Performance by a Female for the *Tapestry* album.

Heckman, Don. "Carole King at Her Best with Tapestry." *Los Angeles Times* July 20, 1993, p. F6.

A favorable review of King's July 18, 1993 concert at the Universal Amphitheatre, Los Angeles.

Heckman, Don. "Carole King: Optimistic Craftsmanship." *High Fidelity/Musical America*, October 1977, pp. 142ff.

A generally favorable review of King's *Simple Things* album.

Hill, Susan. "Pop Albums: *Touch the Sky*." *Melody Maker* 54, September 15, 1979, p. 28.

Although Hill feels that King has taken on worthy environmental causes on *Touch the Sky*, "these laments from Tin Pan Alley hipsters are not instantly affecting." The author does comment favorably, however, on King's vocal, instrumental, and arranging work.

Himes, Geoffrey. "Carole King." *Washington Post* June 21, 993, p. C7.

A favorable review of King's June 16, 1993 concert at Wolf Trap, Washington, D.C.

Himes, Geoffrey. "Reprise Packages: Two New Tributes That Don't Measure Up." *Washington Post* January 24, 1996, p. B7.

According to this review, the *Tapestry Revisited* album is a disappointment and fails to measure up to King's original.

Hirshey, Gerri. "The Backstage History of Women Who Rocked the World: The Seventies." *Rolling Stone* no. 773, November 13, 1997, pp. 64ff.

Carole King's work from the early 1970s is featured as part of the discussion. According to Hirshey, King did what other singers of her generation failed to do in the early 1970s: deal with the reality of domestic life in popular song.

Hoerburger, Robert. "Carole King on the Road Again: First Tour in Six Years." *Billboard* 96, March 3, 1984, p. 37.

Includes information on King's 1984 concert tour.

Hoerburger, Robert. "*City Streets.*" *Rolling Stone* no. 552, May 18, 1989, p. 171.

While the reviewer finds King's music on *City Streets* to be fine, Gerry "Goffin hasn't written an outstanding lyric for her since 'Smackwater Jack.'"

Hoerburger, Robert. "Closeup." *Billboard* 94, May 8, 1982, p. 72.

A report on King's *One to One* album and accompanying video project.

Holden, Stephen. "Little Boxes, All Decked Out and Ready to Play." *New York Times* December 11, 1994, p. H34.

This article/favorable review includes information about *A Natural Woman: The Ode Collection (1968–1976)*.

Holden, Stephen. *The New Grove Dictionary of American Music.* s.v. "King, Carole." London: Macmillan Press, Ltd., 1986.

According to Holden, "King's tunes, with their gospel-music inflections, simple chord progression, and pronounced bass lines, defined a rock-and-roll songwriting style that, in its precision and craft, was an extension of Irving Berlin's less sophisticated Tin Pan Alley songs."

Holden, Stephen. "That New York Spirit." *New York Times* April 5, 1989, p. C22.

Holden discusses the impact of New York City on King's *City Streets.*

Holden, Stephen. "Recent Releases: Pop." *New York Times* April 16, 1989, p. H30.

Includes a brief, favorable review of King's *City Streets.*

Holden, Stephen. "Records: *Fantasy.*" *Rolling Stone* no. 140, August 2, 1973, p. 48.

A generally negative review of King's *Fantasy,* which "adds up to a formalized song cycle in which the Carole King Institution issues its summary social and philosophical expression to date."

Holden, Stephen. "Records: *One to One.*" *Rolling Stone* no. 370, May 27, 1982, p. 62.

A lukewarm review of King's *One to One* album, a recording that is described as being cut from "the same cookie cutter" as King's work going back to 1974.

Holden, Stephen. "Records: *Rhymes & Reasons.*" *Rolling Stone* no. 124, December 21, 1972, p. 61.

Although "musically less exciting than most of *Tapestry* and some of *Music,*" *Rhymes & Reasons* is described as King's "most unified, personal album."

Holden, Stephen. "Records: *Thoroughbred.*" *Rolling Stone* no. 209, March 25, 1976, pp. 58ff.

A favorable review of King's *Thoroughbred* album, which Holden calls "King's finest album since *Tapestry*."

Holden, Stephen. "The Tapestry of an Age of Message and Melody." *New York Times* February 19, 1993, p. C3.

A mixed review of the revue "*Tapestry:* The Music of Carole King," which was playing at the Union Square Theatre, New York City.

Horsburgh, Susan. "Harmonic Emergence: Swaddled from the Cradle in Song, Carole King's Daughters Find Their Own Music." *People Weekly* 56, October 15, 2001, p. 189ff.

A profile of Sherry Goffin Kondor and Louise Goffin, King's daughters who were working in the music industry.

Humphries, Patrick. "Pop Albums: *Pearls: The Songs of Goffin and King*." *Melody Maker* 55, August 9, 1980, p. 13.

A highly favorable review of King's *Pearls* album.

Inglis, Ian. "'Some Kind of Wonderful': The Creative Legacy of the Brill Building." *American Music* 21, summer 2003, pp. 214–235.

This article deals with the way in which Brill Building songwriters worked and the ways in which they separated themselves from their Tin Pan Alley predecessors.

Inness, Sherrie A., ed. *Disco Divas: Women, Gender, and Popular Culture in the 1970s.* Philadelphia: University of Pennsylvania Press, 2003.

Includes discussion of Carole King and her role within the women's movement in the 1970s.

"It's Good to Be King." *People* 52, November 1, 1999, pp. 181–182.

A report on a benefit concert at New York's Madison Square Garden that celebrated *People* magazine's 25th anniversary; King's songs were featured.

Jarvis, Jeff. "Carole King: *One to One*." *People Weekly* 28, August 3, 1987, p. 11.

A generally favorable review of King's *One to One* video, which was telecast on the A&E network on August 2, 1987.

Jewell, Thomas N. "*Pearls: The Songs of Goffin and King*." *Library Journal* 106, February 15, 1981, pp. 422ff.

A generally favorable review of the album *Pearls*.

Jones, Christopher. "*Tapestry: The Music of Carole King*." *Variety* 348, August 24, 1992, pp. 68–69.

A generally positive review of the revue *Tapestry: The Music of Carole King*, which was playing at the State Theater, Cleveland, Ohio.

Joyce, Mike. "Pop Recordings." *Washington Post* April 9, 1989, p. G5.

King's *City Streets* and David Crosby's *Oh Yes I Can* are reviewed in this article.

Karpel, Ari. "What a Gilmore Girl Wants." *TV Guide* 49, September 1, 2001, p. 6.

A discussion by creators of the television program *Gilmore Girls* of contracting with Carole King to re-record her song "Where You Lead" as the program's theme song.

Kasha, Al and Joel Hirschhorn. "Anatomy of a Hit: 'Up on the Roof.'" *Songwriter Magazine* 5, March 1980, pp. 14–15.

A detailed analysis of the words and music of the Gerry Goffin–Carole King composition "Up on the Roof."

Kehe, John. "Readers Disc-cover Desert Island Hideaway!" *Christian Science Monitor* 90, October 16, 1998, p. B4.

King's *Tapestry* is numbered among the top 20 albums *Christian Science Monitor* readers would want to have with them if they were stranded on a desert island.

"King as Queen?" *Time* 98, July 12, 1971, p. 52.

Medium-length profile of King. According to the article, when Gerry Goffin and King began writing for African American performers, "R&B lost some of its ethnic honesty," although the new "uptown" Rhythm and Blues "still had considerable emotional sweep, plus a new sophistication." King's voice is "far from a great natural voice, but it has the deceptive thin strength of a whip antenna."

King, Carole. Liner notes to *Colour of Your Dreams.* Compact disc.

King's X Records/Rhythm Safari Records P2–57197, 1993. King's notes include lyrics and information about the writing and/or recording of some of the songs.

King, Carole. Liner notes for *The Living Room Tour.* Two compact discs. Rockingale RDC2–6200–2, 2005.

King's notes include lyrics and information about the writing and/or recording of some of the songs.

King, Carole. Liner notes to *Love Makes the World.* Compact disc. Rockingale/Koch Records CD-8371, 2001.

King's notes include lyrics and information about the writing and/or recording of some of the songs.

King, Carole. Liner notes to *Welcome Home.* 33–1/3 rpm phonodisc. Capitol SW-11785, 1978.

King's notes include lyrics and information about the writing and/or recording of some of the songs.

King, Carole. "Wilderness Needs Strong Advocates." *Chicago Tribune* November 8, 1993, p. 116.

A response by King to an October 19, 1993 column in the *Chicago Tribune* about the Northern Rockies Ecosystem Protection Act.

King, Carole. *You've Got a Friend: Poetic Selections from the Songs of Carole King.* Edited by Susan Polis Schutz. Boulder, CO: Blue Mountain Press, 1978.

A presentation of King's lyrics as pieces of poetry. This volume is particularly intriguing, as King generally has been more highly regarded as a composer than as a lyricist.

"King, Goffin Win Award from NAS." *Variety* 333, November 23, 1988, p. 96.

An announcement that the National Academy of Songwriters has selected Gerry Goffin and Carole King for a Lifetime Achievement Award.

"King Sues Biz Manager Re: Video, Use of Funds." *Variety* 322, March 2, 1986 p. 95.

A report on King's lawsuit against Lou Adler.

Kipnis, Jill. "Carole King Invites Fans into Her Living Room." *Billboard* 117, May 28, 2005, p. 19.

An article previewing King's Living Room Tour 2005.

Landau, Jon. "All Things to All People." *Rolling Stone* no. 174, November 21, 1974, pp. 78ff.

A generally positive review of King's *Wrap Around Joy.* Landau's principal criticism is that King does not take enough musical and lyrical chances on the album, in an attempt to be all things to all people.

Landau, Jon. *It's Too Late to Stop Now.* San Francisco: Straight Arrow Books, 1972.

The chapter, "White Rock: Carole King: *Tapestry*," is based on the author's feature-length review of the album that appeared in *Rolling Stone.*

Landau, Jon. "Records: Carole King, *Writer, Tapestry.*" *Rolling Stone* no. 81, April 29, 1971, pp. 40–41.

A feature-length comparison of King's first two solo albums. Landau praises the improvements in production evident on *Tapestry.* He writes, "Carole King's second album, *Tapestry,* has fulfilled the promise of her first and confirmed the fact that she is one of the most creative figures in all of pop music."

Lanham, Tom. "Earth Still Moves to Carole King's Beat." *San Francisco Chronicle* August 13, 1989, p. DAT 24.

A lengthy profile of King in advance of her upcoming concert performance in San Francisco.

Lappen, John. "Carole King." *Hollywood Reporter* 385, August 23, 2004, p. 18.

A favorable review of King's "Living Room Tour" performance at the Greek Theatre.

Larkin, Colin, ed. *The Guiness Encyclopedia of Popular Music. s.v.* "King, Carole." London: Square One Books, Ltd., 1995.

In addition to standard biographical information about Carole King, this entry includes critical commentary on her work. Included is the assertion that King's recording of old material for *Pearls* was a tacit acknowledgment that her songwriting skills were waning, but that King's work on *Speeding Time* and *City Streets* proved that her compositional skills were still strong.

Lasswell, Mark. "Carole King—*A Natural Woman: The Ode Collection (1968–1976).*" *People Weekly* 42, December 19, 1994, p. 24.

A generally favorable review of the Carole King compilation album. According to the reviewer, however, "casual listeners might find the pleasures of nostalgia waning before they reach the end of all 36 tracks" due to the spare sound of Lou Adler's production and King's "limited singing style."

Lichtman, Irv. "Lava Weaves a New *Tapestry:* EMI Music Is Force Behind Carole King Tribute." *Billboard* 107, October 21, 1995, p. 45.

A feature article on the *Tapestry Revisited* album.

Longino, Miriam. Review of *A Natural Woman: The Ode Collection (1968–1976).* *Atlanta Journal Constitution* September 24, 1994, p. WL 22.

A brief mixed review of the King compilation two-compact disc package.

Lourie, F. "Record Reviews: *Tapestry.*" *Jazz & Pop* 10, July 1971, pp. 46–47.

A favorable review of *Tapestry.*

Manning, Kara. "Recordings: *Colour of Your Dreams.*" *Rolling Stone* no. 659, June 24, 1993, pp. 80ff.

Manning gives King's *Colour of Your Dreams* 3–1/2 stars in this generally favorable review and wonders if sexism is possibly behind the fact that this deserving album has received little FM radio airplay.

Marsh, Dave. "Records: *Simple Things.*" *Rolling Stone* no. 247, September 8, 1977, pp. 113–114.

A mixed review of King's *Simple Things* album. Because of its lyrics, *Simple Things* "completely lacks the halting dark misery and the striking imagery and metaphor of [King's] best work."

Mayer, Ira. "*One to One.*" *High Fidelity* 34, January 1984, p. 67.

A review of King's video recording *One to One.*

McCrary, Jim. "Carole King." *Presenting … Samples from a Half-Century of Works by Jim McCrary, Photographer.* http://www.jimmccrary.com/pages/page3/index.htm. Accessed February 15, 2006.

McGee, David, et al. "The *Rolling Stone* 200: *Tapestry*." *Rolling Stone* no. 760, May 15, 1997, pp. 73–74.

    More than 25 years after it was first issued, King's *Tapestry* remains on *Rolling Stone*'s list of the 200 most important albums of the rock era.

Miller, Edwin. "The Singer Is the Song." *Seventeen* 32, November 1973, p. 72.

    A profile of King's life and career with emphasis on the importance of New York City on her early musical development.

Mills, Melissa. "*Writer.*" *Rolling Stone* no. 69, October 29, 1970, pp. 46ff.

    A review of King's *Writer,* on which the arrangements are "excellent." The entire album, "though flawed, is still a listenable, indeed nice, record." The author's main criticism is that King's voice "is just not very strong."

Mirkin, Steven. "Carole King." *Variety* 396, August 30, 2004, p. 31.

    A favorable review of King's Living Room Tour performance at the Greek Theater, Hollywood, California.

Morris, Chris. "NAS Salutes Goffin & King: Songwriters Win Achievement Award." *Billboard* 100, December 17, 1988, p. 6.

    An announcement that the National Academy of Songwriters presented Gerry Goffin and Carole King with a Lifetime Achievement Award.

Morse, Steve. "Carole King." *Boston Globe* April 8, 1993, p. CAL7.

    A brief favorable review of King's *Colour of Your Dreams.*

Morse, Steve. "Carole King Still Reigns as Queen of Pop History." *Boston Globe* June 9, 1993, p. 69.

    A favorable review of King's June 8, 1993 concert at the Gosman Center, Waltham, Massachusetts.

Morse, Steve. "Carole King Weaves a New Tapestry." *Boston Globe* April 25, 1993, p. B25.

    A profile of Carole King and discussion of her album *Colour of Your Dreams.*

Morse, Steve. "Laura Nyro, 1947–1997." *Boston Globe* April 10, 1997, p. E1.

    In this obituary of Nyro, Carole King is mentioned, along with Nyro and Joni Mitchell, as being among the first pop singers to "write in an authentic women's voice."

Morse, Steve. "The Songs Retain the Names…" *Boston Globe* October 20, 1995.

    This article includes a generally unfavorable review of the *Tapestry Revisited* album.

"*Music* Fit for a King." *Melody Maker* 46, December 18, 1971, p. 14.

    A generally favorable review of *Music.* "Back to California" and "It's Going to Take Some Time" are described as highlights, but the reviewer expresses concern that King's current, more personal style of songs will probably not have the same degree of near-universal appeal as her 1960s collaborations with Gerry Goffin.

"*A Natural Woman: The Ode Collection (1968–1976).*" *Q Magazine* January 1995, p. 269.

    The King compilation receives a rating of "excellent" in this review.

"New Shows in Stock." *Variety* 304, September 9, 1981, p. 98.

    A report on the revue "King's *Tapestry.*"

Newman, Melinda. "The Beat: Atlantic, EMI Pub Weave New Tapestry." *Billboard* 106, July 30, 1994, p. 14.

    A report on the *Tapestry Revisited* album, a tribute to King's 1971 *Tapestry.*

"Nine Selected for Induction into Songwriters Hall of Fame." *Billboard* 98, December 27, 1986, p. 8.

A report on King's selection for the Songwriters Hall of Fame along with her frequent collaborator Gerry Goffin.

Novak, Ralph. "*City Streets*." *People Weekly* 31, April 3, 1989, p. 30.

A mixed review of King's *City Streets* album. Novak praises some of the album's music and arrangements, but finds fault with the lyrics, which are said to "sound like the romantic notions of a teenage girl—and a very naïve teenage girl at that."

"Now EMI Has All of Carole King." *Billboard* 88, December 18, 1976, p. 6.

A report on King's change of record label from Ode/Epic/Columbia to Capitol/EMI.

O'Brien, Ellen. "Neighbors Pan Clinton Soiree." *Boston Globe* August 29, 1997, p. B1.

King performed "The Reason" at a Martha's Vineyard party given by President and Mrs. Clinton. Neighbors complained to the police about the volume levels of the event.

"*One to One*." *People Weekly* 17, April 26, 1982, p. 26.

A lukewarm review of King's *One to One* album.

"*One to One*." *Stereo Review* 48, December 1983, pp. 103–104.

A generally negative review of King's *One to One* album.

Paoletta, Michael. "Albums: Love Makes the World." *Billboard* 113, October 13, 2001, p. 22.

A favorable review of King's *Love Makes the World* album.

Peeples, Stephen K. Liner notes for *A Natural Woman: The Ode Collection (1968–1976)*. Two compact discs. Sony Music 48833, 1994.

Peeples's extensive liner notes contain information on King's work from her days with the City (1969) through her *Thoroughbred* album of the mid-1970s.

Perone, James E. *Carole King: A Bio-Bibliography*. Westport, CT: Greenwood Press, 1999.

A comprehensive reference book on Carole King.

"Pop Albums: *Simple Things*." *Melody Maker* 52, July 30, 1977, p. 14.

A mixed review of King's *Simple Things* album. The reviewer finds some of the material too formulaic and that some of the lyrics cannot be taken seriously.

"Pop Albums: *Tapestry*." *Melody Maker* 46, May 22, 1971, p. 22.

A highly favorable review of *Tapestry*. This influential British pop music magazine describes the album as "difficult to turn off once you've started," and as "an essential album that transcends all the barriers."

"Pop Albums: *Thoroughbred*." *Melody Maker* 51, February 7, 1976, p. 25.

A mixed review of King's *Thoroughbred* album.

"Pop Albums: *Wrap Around Joy*." *Melody Maker* 49, September 28, 1974, p. 51.

According to this positive review of King's *Wrap Around Joy* album, *Music* and *Fantasy* were widely misinterpreted by critics as grandiose, overblown statements; *Wrap Around Joy* signals a return to good pop song writing and performing by King.

Powers, Ann. "Celebrating Carole King, Longtime Queen of Pop." *New York Times* October 16, 1999, p. B14.

A report on the October 14, 1999 concert at New York's Madison Square Garden that celebrated *People* magazine's 25th anniversary. Carole King's songs were featured and the benefit event raised substantial funds for charity.

Powers, Bill. *Behind the Scenes of a Broadway Musical*. New York: Crown Publishers, 1982.

This book, aimed at a juvenile audience, describes the Broadway production of *Really Rosie* from rehearsals to previews to opening night.

Rayl, A. J. "Carole King: Out in Front." *ASCAP in Action* Winter 1987, pp. 26–27.
An article profiling King as a songwriter and performer.

"Really Rosie." *Variety* 300, October 22, 1980, p. 112.
A review of the Chelsea Westside Theatre off-Broadway production of the stage version of *Really Rosie*. According to the reviewer, although the show "would make a terrific Eighth Grade class show," it is not entirely appropriate for this venue, due in part to song ideas that "are generally mundane."

"Recordings of Special Merit: Writer." *Stereo Review* 26, February 1971, pp. 119–120.
A review of King's *Writer* album. The performance is described as "Beautiful" and the recording as "Good." The reviewer writers that "Up on the Roof" "is performed better by the composer than by any of the pop groups who have recorded it." "Eventually" is described as a "mini-concerto."

"Records: *Pearls: The Songs of Goffin and King*." *Creem* 12, September 1980, pp. 58–59.
A review of King's album.

"Records: *Welcome Home*." *Rolling Stone* no. 275, October 5, 1978, p. 72.
A review of King's album.

Reich, Howard. "Manilow Rules." *Chicago Tribune* April 20, 1997, p. VII 1.
A reassessment of the pop music of the 1970s. Carole King is included among the people who were "writing songs where the words really mattered."

Ressner, Jeffrey. "Rock & Roll Hall of Fame: Nonperformers." *Rolling Stone* no. 571, February 8, 1990, p. 82.
Gerry Goffin and Carole King are listed as two of the year's inductees into the Rock and Roll Hall of Fame.

"Reviews: *One to One*." *High Fidelity/Musical America* 34, January 1984, p. 67.
A review of King's *One to One* album.

"Reviews: *Speeding Time*." *High Fidelity/Musical America* 34, March 1984, p. 78.
A review of King's *Speeding Time* album.

Rimler, Walter. *Not Fade Away: A Comparison of Jazz Age with Rock Era Pop Song Composers*. Ann Arbor, MI: Pierian, 1984.
This book contrasts the relatively long careers of Jerome Kern, Irving Berlin, and other Tin Pan Alley songwriters, with the sudden declines in popularity of rock era writers like King, Paul Simon, Lennon and McCartney, and Jagger and Richards.

Robbins, Ira. "*Tapestry Revisited: A Tribute to Carole King*." *Entertainment Weekly* 305, December 15, 1995, p. 83.
A generally unfavorable review of the *Tapestry Revisited* video documentary.

Rochlin, Margy. "*Gilmore Girls* Got a Friend." *TV Guide* 50, May 4, 2002, pp. 63–64.
A report on King's re-recording of "Where You Lead" for the television program *Gilmore Girls*. Also included is a report that King will make a guest appearance on the show as Sophie, a music-store owner.

"Rock & Roll Hall of Fame." *Rolling Stone* no. 571, February 8, 1990, p. 71–77ff.
Gerry Goffin and Carole King's contribution to rock music is detailed in this feature article on the year's inductees into the Rock and Roll Hall of Fame.

"Rock of Aging." *People Weekly* 58, July 22, 2002, pp. 46ff.

Carole King is among the musicians of the 1960s who are turning 60. She is quoted as saying that by the time she recorded *Tapestry* at the start of the 1970s, she knew "what she wanted out of life and success."

Russell, Deborah. "Former Hit Acts Find New Life on Independent Labels." *Billboard* 107, March 4, 1995, pp. 8ff.

King is among the musicians who have reemerged on independent record labels.

Sandoval, Andrew. Liner notes for *More of the Monkees*. Compact disc. Rhino Records R2–71791, 1994.

These liner notes deal in part with Gerry Goffin and Carole King's exacting approach to making demo records in the mid-1960s.

Sandoval, Andrew. Liner notes for *Pisces, Aquarius, Capricorn & Jones Ltd.* Compact disc. Rhino R2–71793, 1995.

Includes information on the Monkees' recording of "Pleasant Valley Sunday," including King's reputed dislike of the opening electric guitar figure.

Schaeffer, Martin. "*Tapestry:* The Music of Carole King." *Back Stage* 34, February 26, 1993, p. 44.

A generally positive review of the revue *Tapestry:* The Music of Carole King, which was playing at the Union Square Theatre, New York City.

Shaw, Arnold. "Carole King." *BMI: The Many Worlds of Music* Summer 1971, p. 20.

A profile of King in light of her success with *Tapestry.*

Shaw, Greg. "Brill Building Pop." *Rolling Stone* no. 226, November 18, 1976, pp. 64–69.

Reprinted from *The Rolling Stone Illustrated History of Rock & Roll,* this feature article details Carole King's early compositional work, particularly that done in collaboration with Gerry Goffin.

Shewey, Don. "Records: *Pearls: The Songs of Goffin and King.*" *Rolling Stone* no. 323, August 7, 1980, p. 50.

According to this generally favorable review, King's released of an album of old material is her tacit admission that "her songwriting talents have failed in recent years." Shewey describes "Dancin' with Tears in My Eyes" and "Snow Queen" as highlights, but the reviewer complains that some of the best-known Goffin and King hits receive "indifferent" treatment.

Shirley, Don. "A Slightly Rough *Tapestry* Makes Move to a Larger Stage." *Los Angeles Times* March 7, 1996, p. F6.

A generally favorable review and report on the revue "*Tapestry:* The Music of Carole King," which was playing at the Center Theater, Long Beach, California.

Simels, Steve. "Carole King: *City Streets.*" *Stereo Review* 54, July 1989, p. 78.

An unfavorable review of King's *City Streets* album.

Slevin, Joel. "*Tapestry* Recalls Mammoth King Success." *San Francisco Chronicle* November 25, 1994, p. C3.

A brief unfavorable review of *A Natural Woman: The Ode Collection (1968–1976).*

Slonim, Jeffrey. ". . .To the Woman Who Wrote What to Do When You're Down and Troubled." *Interview* 25, February 1995, pp. 58–59.

Smith, Danyel. "Laying Bare the Heart, One Hit Song at a Time." *New York Times* September 14, 1993, p. C12.

A favorable review of King's September 10, 1993 concert at the Beacon Theater, New York City.

Smith, M.B. "25 Essential Rock 'n' Roll Albums of the '70s." *Goldmine* 25, March 12, 1999, p. 104.

King's *Tapestry* is among the author's top 25 albums of the decade.

Smucker, Tom. "Riffs: Bring Back the Hack." *Village Voice* 24, October 29, 1979, p. 65.

A generally favorable review of King's *Touch the Sky* album. The author complains, however, that after the success of *Tapestry*, King started writing songs that were overly personal and "spacey." *Touch the Sky* represents a return to better, more accessible material. Smucker further suggests that King would do even better to return to the type of "hack," assembly line work she did in New York City in the late 1950s and early 1960s.

"So Far Away." *New Yorker* 69, March 8, 1993, p. 36.

A report on the off-Broadway production of the revue *Tapestry: The Music of Carole King*.

Solnik, Claude. "Spinning Gold." *Long Island Business News* 49, April 19, 2002, pp. 1Aff.

A report on Carole King's decision to form her own record label, Rockingale Records, for the release of *Love Makes the World*, so that she would have total control of her product. Much of the article concerns the business practices of Koch International (which distributes Rockingale Records' releases); Koch allows independent labels considerable freedom.

"Song Hall of Fame Names 9 Inductees." *Variety* 325, December 31, 1986, p. 62.

A report on Gerry Goffin and Carole King's selection to the Songwriters Hall of Famve.

"*Speeding Time*." *People Weekly* 21, February 6, 1984, p. 17.

A mixed review of King's *Speeding Time* album.

Spitz, Robert Stephen. "Too Pooped to Pop?" *Crawdaddy* no. 77, October 1977, p. 63.

A negative review of King's *Simple Things* album, which ponders the question, "How is it possible for such a gifted writer to release an album with not one—NOT ONE—hummable tune on it?"

Stark, John. "*Coast to Coast*." *People Weekly* 31, June 19, 1989, p. 9.

A favorable review of the June 17, 1989 television variety program *Coast to Coast*, on which King performed.

Strang, Patti and Julie Stacey. "*USA* Snapshots: Longest Stays in the Top 200." *USA Today* August 18, 1995, p. D1.

This article mentions that King's *Tapestry*, which had recently been certified for sales of over 10 million units, was on the *Billboard* Top 200 album list for 302 consecutive weeks.

Sutherland, Sam. "*Speeding Time*." *High Fidelity* 34, March 1984, p. 78.

A review of the King album.

Tabor, Lisa. "Rock On: Spotlight on Four Women Artists." *International Musician* 82, March 1984, pp. 7ff.

This article in the official organ of the American Federation of Musicians includes biographical information about Carole King.

Tannenbaum, Leslie. "Betrayed by Chicken Soup: Judaism, Gender and Performance in Maurice Sendak's *Really Rosie*." *Lion & the Unicorn* 27, September 2003, pp. 362–376.

A study of Sendak and King's musical version of *Really Rosie* and how it brings the dialogue about defining gender and Jewish-American identities to children.

Taylor, Chuck. "Songwriting, Recording, Performing: Carole King Makes It All Seem Natural." *Billboard* 111, January 30, 1999, p. 88.

This report on the television program *Divas Live* includes younger performers' reactions to King and King's reactions to younger performers.

Taylor, Chuck. "Year-End Trophies: Clint Black's Love, Beth Hart's Soul, Carole King's Thrills." *Billboard* 111–112, December 25, 1999–January 1, 2000, p. 72.

Among the end-of-the-year observations in this article is King's admission that she still gets "a big inner smile" when she hears one of her songs on the radio.

Taylor, Paula. *Carole King*. Mankato, MN: Creative Education, 1976.

A brief biography of King aimed primarily at a juvenile audience. A teacher's guide was also available.

Tiegel, Eliot. "Closeup." *Billboard* 89, August 27, 1977, p. 75.

A favorable review of King's *Simple Things* album.

Toepfer, Susan. "*The Maurice Sendak Library*." *People Weekly* 33, January 8, 1990, p. 29.

A favorable review of the video recording *The Maurice Sendak Library*, on which King performed "Alligators All Around."

Trakin, R. "The Sound of Music: Ten Albums That Changed the Art of Rock Record Production; Carole King: *Tapestry*." *Musician* no. 224, July 1997, p. 31.

A study of Lou Adler's production style on King's *Tapestry* and how it influenced other record producers.

Vance, Joel. "From Rock's Argentina, *Music* by Carole King." *Stereo Review* 28, March 1972, pp. 73–74.

A favorable review of King's *Music* album.

Vance, Joel. "*Speeding Time*." *Stereo Review* 49, April 1984, p. 88.

A generally negative review of King's *Speeding Time* album.

Vest, Randy. "*Tapestry Revisited: A Tribute to Carole King*." *People* 45, January 8, 1996, p. 26.

A brief description of the *Tapestry Revisited* album.

"Video Reviews: One to One." *Billboard* 95, August 20, 1983, p. 35.

A review of King's *One to One* video.

Walls, Richard C. "*Simple Things*." *Creem* 9, November 1977, pp. 67–68.

A mixed review of King's *Simple Things* album. According to this review, the lyrics are not as good as the music, but King's music makes them sound better than they are.

Walters, Laurel Shaper. "*Rosie* Springs from Page to Stage." *Christian Science Monitor* March 8, 1994, p. 10.

A chronicle of *Really Rosie,* from Maurice Sendak's children's book of the 1960s to Carole King's musical setting of the 1970s for television, to the new live stage show.

Werbin, Stuart. "Carole King's Day: A 'Little Something' in Central Park." *Rolling Stone* no. 138, July 5, 1973, pp. 13ff.

A feature report on King's concert in New York's Central Park.

Werbin, Stuart. "Taylor and King up in Boston." *Rolling Stone* no. 79, April 1, 1971, p. 14.

A report on the famous 1971 James Taylor concert tour on which Carole King made a guest appearance. By the close of the tour, King had become the headliner on the strength of *Tapestry*.

White, Timothy. "Sadly, The Times They Are A-Changin'." *Billboard* 111, August 14, 1999, p. 5.

White contrasts the 1969 Woodstock Music and Art Fair and Carole King's 1973 Central Park concert with Woodstock 1999 and the Lilith Fair concerts. Woodstock and the King concert were events of great humanity and peace, especially when compared with Woodstock 1999.

Williamson, Lonnie. "King Sings, But Is No Fan of Public." *Outdoor Life* 173, January 1984, pp. 64ff.

A feature-length article dealing with King's controversial decision to close an undocumented public access road to the Sawtooth National Recreation Area; the undocumented road ran through the Robinson Bar Ranch in Idaho, which King owned.

Wilson, Susan. "Carole King Comes Back with Punch and Passion." *Boston Globe* April 5, 1989, p. 36.

A lengthy, favorable preview of King's *City Streets* album.

Windeler, Robert. "Carole King: 'You Can Get to Know Me through My Music.'" *Stereo Review* 30, May 1973, pp. 76–77.

A profile of King's life and career.

Wise, Stuart M. "Pop Star's Legal Tapestry." *The National Law Journal* 4, July 19, 1982, p. 47.

A report on King's lawsuit against Custer County, Idaho, in an eminent domain case.

Wolff, C. "Seasons, Tops, Kinks, Who, Darin Among 13 Giants Set for Jan. Rock Hall Induction." *Billboard* 101, November 4, 1989, p. 92.

Gerry Goffin and Carole King are listed among those to be inducted into the Rock and Roll Hall of Fame as nonperformers.

Wolff, Ellen. "*Rhymes & Reasons.*" *Crawdaddy* no. 21, February 1973, p. 72.

Although Wolff finds that the lyrics of King's *Rhymes & Reasons* "do not bear up particularly well under scrutiny, [King] more than makes up for this with impeccable production, fine instrumentation, and possible her best vocal work yet."

Yandel, Gerry. "Carole King Trades Keyboard for Clipboard to Be Reporter." *Atlanta Journal Constitution* November 18, 1989, p. D12.

A report that King will be a guest journalist on the television news program *The Reporters* on November 18, 1989. She will be among the celebrities discussion wilderness preservation.

Zibart, Eve. "Carole King Too Soft for *Streets* Smarts." *Washington Post* July 28, 1989, p. WW20.

An unfavorable review of King's *City Streets*.

Zimmerman, Kevin. "Rock Hall of Fame Salutes Inductees As It Warns Industry to Keep Up Censorship Fight." *Variety* 338, January 24, 1990, p. 171.

Among the inductees to the Rock and Roll Hall of Fame who are mentioned are Gerry Goffin and Carole King, who were selected as nonperformers.

Index

About the Author

JAMES E. PERONE is Chair of the Music Department and Professor of Music at Mount Union College in Alliance, Ohio. He is the author of over a dozen books, including *Woodstock: An Encyclopedia of the Music and Art Fair* (2005), *Music of the Counterculture Era* (2004), and *The Sound of Stevie Wonder: His Words and Music* (2006). He is also the series editor of *The Praeger Singer-Songwriter Collection*.